THE EFFECTS OF EARLY EDUCATION

The Effects of Early Education

A report from the Child Health and Education Study

A. F. OSBORN AND J. E. MILBANK

CLARENDON PRESS · OXFORD

1987

Oxford University Press, Walton Street, Oxford OX2 6DP

Oxford New York Toronto
Delhi Bombay Calcutta Madras Karachi
Petaling Jaya Singapore Hong Kong Tokyo
Nairobi Dar es Salaam Cape Town
Melbourne Auckland

and associated companies in
Beirut Berlin Ibadan Nicosia

Oxford is a trade mark of Oxford University Press

Published in the United States
by Oxford University Press, New York

British Library Cataloguing in Publication Data
Osborn, A. F.
The effects of early education: a report
from the Child Health and Education Study
1. Education, Preschool—Great Britain
I. Title II. Milbank, J. E.
372.21′0941   LB1140.25.G7
ISBN 0–19–827801–2
ISBN 0–19–827800–4 Pbk

Library of Congress Cataloging in Publication Data
Osborn, A. F. (Albert F.), 1939–
The effects of early education.
Bibliography: p.
Includes index.
1. Education, Preschool—Great Britain—Longitudinal
studies. 2. Education, Preschool—Great Britain—
Evaluation—Longitudinal studies. I. Milbank, J. E.
(Janet E.) II. Title.
LB1140.25.G7073 1987   372′.21′0941   86–31186
ISBN 0–19–827801–2
ISBN 0–19–827800–4 (pbk.)

Set by Katerprint Typesetting Services, Cowley, Oxford
Printed and bound in
Great Britain by Biddles Ltd,
Guildford and King's Lynn

Acknowledgements

Our first thanks go to all the children and their parents who gave their time to take part in the two surveys on which this study is based. Without their willing co-operation our research would not be possible.

Secondly, we are most grateful for the help of the health visitors, teachers and administrators in the Health and Education Authorities throughout Britain for undertaking the task of carrying out the survey field-work, administering the tests and providing information about the children's primary school experience.

We would also like to thank the members of the DES Steering Committee, especially Rosemary Peacocke our Chairman, for their support and helpful advice throughout the duration of the project.

Special thanks are due to friends and colleagues for their critical appraisal of earlier drafts of this work or who helped in other ways. In particular we wish to mention Margaret Adams, Viv Calderbank, Willem van der Eyken, Kathy Sylva, Mike Wadsworth, Martin Woodhead and Professor Barbara Tizard who arranged a meeting of distinguished scientists in December 1985 to debate our findings. Their contributions are deeply appreciated but the interpretations of the findings reported in this book are those of the authors and are not necessarily shared by the organisations or individuals who have been associated with the study.

Finally, we acknowledge the financial support of the Department of Education and Science, the Department of Health and Social Security, the Medical Research Council, the Economic and Social Research Council, the Joseph Rowntree Memorial Trust, Action Research for the Crippled Child, the Leverhulme Trust, the Manpower Services Commission, The National Institute of Child Health and Human Development, USA (Grant No. 5 R01 HD 13347), the William T. Grant Foundation and many other independent Trusts.

Contents

List of Figures

List of Tables

Members of the Department of Education and Science Steering Committee

Chairman
Staff Inspector Mrs R. Peacocke

DES representatives

Miss A. Barlow	DES Schools Branch I (to Jan. 1984)
Mr C. Bellis	DES Statistics Branch
Mrs G. Dishart	DES Schools Branch I
Mrs. P. Heaslip	Bluebell Valley Nursery School, Avon
Mrs C. James	London Borough of Haringey Primary School Adviser
Mrs I. Magill	DES Statistics Branch
Mr J. Sheridan	DES Schools Branch I (from Jan. 1984)

University of Bristol representatives

Professor N. R. Butler	Professor of Child Health and Director, CHES
Dr A. F. Osborn	CHES Principal Research Officer

Child Health and Education Study Research Team responsible for design and conduct of five- and ten-year follow-up surveys

Director
Professor Neville Butler, MD, FRCP, FRCOG, DCH

Principal Research Officers
Sue Dowling, MFCM, M.Sc. (Soc.Med.), MB, BS
Mary Haslum, B.Sc., Ph.D.
Brian Howlett, B.Sc., BA
Albert Osborn, BA, Ph.D.

Research Associates
Walter Barker, B.Sc., MA (Ed.), Ph.D.
Richard Brewer, B.Sc., M.Sc., Dip.Soc.Admin.
Tony Morris, BA, M.Sc.
Sarah Stewart-Brown, MA, BM, B.Ch., MRCP

Administrative and Secretarial
Pam Lyons
Christine Porter, SRN, Dip.Ed.

Introduction

This book describes a study of preschool education in Britain and seeks an answer to the much debated question of whether there are long-term educational benefits for children who attend preschool facilities. The aim of this study was to carry out an evaluation of ordinary nursery schools and playgroups, rather than experimental or innovative schemes, and to investigate the significance for children's behaviour and development of key factors such as frequency and duration of attendance, parental involvement in preschool institutions and early entry to infant reception classes.

The study draws on data from a national, longitudinal survey in England, Wales and Scotland of all the children born during one week in 1970, and makes use of information obtained when the children were 5—the age of statutory school entry in Britain—and 10 years old. In addition, a census of all preschool institutions was carried out in 1975 from which were identified the particular institutions attended by the children in the cohort study. These two large data sets present a very comprehensive picture of preschool educational provision as it was in 1975, and provide a powerful statistical base for the evaluation of that provision.

The findings from the study showed that children who attended preschool institutions achieved higher test scores at 5 and 10 years than others who had no preschool experience. Much of the analysis following from this was a systematic attempt to explain away these differences by using statistical techniques which took account of the considerable variation in social and family background between children with different types of preschool experience. The final models presented in Chapter 10 were developed stage by stage in the analyses described in earlier chapters which were designed to identify factors having the most damaging effect on the association between children's preschool experience and their subsequent test performance; the object being, as we have said, to attempt to eliminate the preschool effect on child development.

Chapter 1 reviews the historical and research background against which our own study was set, and shows how most evaluation research on both sides of the Atlantic has focused on experimental preschool programmes, with very little attention given to the possible benefits of ordinary nursery education as practised in the average nursery school or playgroup.

Chapter 2 uses data from the survey of preschool institutions to show the main points of similarity and difference between seven types of British educational and day care facility for under-fives.

Chapter 3 contrasts rates of utilisation of preschool services in the maintained or independent/voluntary sectors and reveals large inequalities in such utilisation between children according to their social and family circumstances. Such inequalities indicated factors in the children's home backgrounds that were likely to be important intervening variables in the associations between their preschool experience and their subsequent educational progress as described in later chapters.

Chapter 4 examines the effect of the intervening variables, identified in the previous chapter, on the association between children's preschool experience and their cognitive and educational test performances at ages 5 and 10 years. The intervening variables found to reduce the preschool effect significantly were ultimately selected for inclusion in the final models presented in Chapter 10.

Chapter 5 repeats the processes described in Chapter 4 but with respect to children's behaviour in the home at age 5 and in school at age 10.

Chapter 6 investigates how changes in children's home circumstances between the five- and ten-year stages of the study might have influenced the long-term effects of their preschool experience.

Chapter 7 considers the implications of full-time as against part-time attendance at preschool institutions, the children's age when they first started attending their preschool groups, and their age at infant school entry.

Chapter 8 explores the way the characteristics of the preschool institution the child attended affected her subsequent school performance. This includes analyses of staffing, curriculum and the social composition of the institution.

Chapter 9 describes the extent of parental involvement in different types of preschool institution, and compares the educational progress of children whose own mothers were involved with that of children of non-involved mothers.

Chapter 10 brings together the essential findings of all the previous chapters, presents results of the final analyses which evolved from them and on the basis of these analyses draws the main conclusions of the study.

The Appendix provides an account of how the study was carried out, response rates, procedures used when matching the child-based and institution-based surveys, a discussion of bias and other methodological information.

A few conventional abbreviations have been used in this book. They are defined below for the benefit of readers who may be unfamiliar with them.

DES   Department of Education and Science
DHSS   Department of Health and Social Security
LA   Local Authority
LEA   Local Education Authority
EPA   Educational Priority Area
CHES   Child Health and Education Study

The lack of a gender-free personal pronoun in the English language obliges us to use the male and female forms randomly in this book in order to avoid partiality through the exclusive use of one or the other.

1

The research background

"In so far, then, as the expansion of early schooling is seen as a way of avoiding later school failure or of closing the social class gap in achievement, we already know it to be doomed to failure. (Tizard, 1975, p. 4)"

This well-known quotation from Barbara Tizard's research review of early childhood education in Britain accurately catches the mood of the research atmosphere surrounding preschool education in the mid-1970s. The recommendations of the Plowden Report (1967), the setting up of the Educational Priority Areas Programme (Halsey, 1972) and a Government White Paper (DES, 1972) all saw the expansion of preschool education as a priority. What happened in the next few years to quench the enthusiastic belief in the value of early intervention through preschool education for reducing the ill-effects of social inequality on children's development?

This chapter describes the social and political background against which the system of maintained and independent provision for under-fives developed in Britain and contrasts this with the American experience. In particular we draw attention to the different ideologies that underlie the British and American educational systems and consider how these factors may have influenced attitudes towards, and expectations of, the potential educational value of children's experience in preschool settings. Inevitably we have not attempted the formidable task of reviewing the whole of the literature on the preschool debate, but have endeavoured to draw out the main themes, issues and problems which have beset the question of the long-term effects of preschool experience.

A brief history

Children have attended school in Britain from the age of 2 and 3 years since the middle of the nineteenth century, though clearly not in great numbers until more recent times. However, nursery education, implying education intended specifically for very young children, was not officially introduced until 1908 (Blackstone, 1971). This was closely linked to a Board of Education Report in 1905 which pressed for nursery schooling for the most underprivileged children to be separated off, having its own particular features of high staff ratio and less regimented curriculum with ' . . . plenty of opportunities for free expression' (Board of Education, 1905, p. ii). From 1918 education authorities were empowered to provide nursery education but it was not until the 1944 Education Act that it became a requirement to make such provision according to local need. This requirement was subsequently downgraded in Ministry of Education Circular 8/60 which merely recommended the provision of preschool education but with no statutory obligation to do so (Blackstone, 1971, pp. 60–9). This policy effectively froze the number of places in nursery schools and nursery classes at 1957 levels until a further amendment to Circular 8/60 in 1965 allowed LEAs to set up nursery classes where it would thereby release teachers into the profession (DES Circular 6/65). However, there were no major initiatives aimed at substantially increasing the level of educational provision for under-fives until the publication of the Plowden Report in 1967. Even so, a further five years elapsed before a Government White Paper (DES, 1972) declared the Government's intention to finally withdraw the notorious Circular 8/60 and expand nursery education in line with Plowden's recommendations.

The 1972 White Paper appeared to mark the beginning of a new era in the provision of preschool education in Britain, but the economic resources required for the necessary expansion were still not forthcoming. Most Local Education Authorities declined the offer of loans for capital expenditure on nursery schools and classes as there were no extra resources made available to operate them once they were built. Central government recognised the need for more under-fives provision but was unable, or unwilling, to fund it:

"We face a daunting period of restraint in social expenditure as both the education and personal social service budgets over the next few years will be less than all of us would wish. Dr David Owen, Minister of State for Health (DHSS/DES, 1976)

The Departments recognise that resources available for the under-fives are still far short of what is needed to make adequate provision for the group.

DHSS/DES Joint Circular: *Coordination of Services for Children Under Five*, 1978"

Thus the formulation of a definite preschool policy was undermined by official ambivalence that was torn between the belief on the one hand that nursery education was desirable, and on the other that it was an expensive service. The result has been patchy and inconsistent levels of nursery provision, determined by the attitude of individual local education authorities towards the value of nursery education.

The arguments—particularly whether increased public expenditure on nursery education was warranted—have been complicated by the many conflicting views that the field of developmental psychology has propounded on the educational needs of young children (Pilling and Pringle, 1978). Social and political needs, plus the increasingly stringent economic constraints of the day, have further compounded the dilemma.

The concept of maternal deprivation, promulgated in particular by John Bowlby (1951), suggested that early separation could adversely affect mother–child bonding with serious and lasting consequences for the child's emotional well-being. Although Bowlby's early work was based almost entirely on babies and young children in long-term institutional care, the principle of maternal deprivation became an article of professional and popular faith that encompassed even relatively brief separations of a child from his mother, such as daily attendance at a day nursery (Hughes *et al.*, 1980, pp. 46–9). The wholesale and uncritical acceptance of this concept had such an impact because it lent substantial support to a fairly urgent current political problem. This was the necessity for encouraging mothers who had been in full employment during wartime years to return to full-time mothering in the home in order to vacate jobs needed for demobilised service personnel.

This political ploy also led to a closure of many day nurseries which had been set up during the war expressly to care for young children whose mothers were needed for war work (Tizard *et al.*, 1976, pp. 69–73). Furthermore the emphasis on the maternal deprivation paradigm was responsible for research into day care during this era being focused on the postulated negative effects of day nursery care because of the inferred harmful effects of separation from mothers (e.g. Douglas and Blomfield, 1958, pp. 123–6).

This view was still being debated in the 1970s, even though the consensus view then was that day care had little or no long-term adverse effect on the emotional development of the child (Clarke and Clarke (eds.), 1976; Rutter, 1972; Tizard, 1976; Tizard, 1986).

Despite the pioneering early work of Rachel and Margaret Macmillan, Susan Isaacs, Friedrich Froebel, Arnold Gesell and Maria Montessori, the further consequence that attendance at a preschool nursery could, under certain circumstances, be beneficial to the developing child did not fully grip the popular imagination until the 1960s. We suggest that the wider promulgation of the developmental psychology of Jean Piaget was a contributory factor in this change.

Recognition of Piaget's cognitive psychology, which emphasised the importance of environmental stimulation for mental and social development in children, threw a new light on the reasons for the inequalities in intellectual functioning and school attainment between children coming from different social backgrounds. Following Piaget's premise, it was realised that socially disadvantaged children were poor achievers because of their deprived and restricted home environment, whilst their counterparts from middle-class backgrounds were successful because they grew up in a culture-rich and stimulating environment.

This change of paradigm gave rise to a flood of new theories on the cultural aspects of the social explanation for school failure (Douglas, 1964), linguistic deprivation (Bernstein, 1961), transmitted deprivation or the cycle of disadvantage (Brown and Madge, 1982), and, most important in the context of the present study, compensatory education (Chazan *et al.*, 1971; Halsey, 1972). The latter concept of compensatory education emerged as a valid reality only after the environmental explanation of developmental delay became generally accepted. If a poor home environment was responsible for a child of a given innate ability progressing mentally at a less than optimal rate, then the obvious practical solution to compensate for this was to provide a cognitively stimulating nursery experience. The American Head Start schemes of the 1960s (Zigler and Anderson, 1979) were based precisely on this thinking, together with earlier research findings, and their impetus derived from the painful realisation that in the post-war American economic boom, substantial poverty still persisted in the midst of plenty.

It was also observed that children growing up in poor families tended to become the impoverished parents of the next generation. Moreover it was obvious that the majority of the most seriously disadvantaged families was black, and Head Start came into being as one of the vehicles for redressing this racial economic discrimination, and as part of the Civil Rights Movement.

The Great American Dream which derives from the belief that every US citizen has an equal chance of success in life because everyone has access to the same public school educational system, was very much undermined by this revelation of conspicuous, prevalent poverty. This discrepancy could only be explained by the widely contrasting social experiences of children entering school from different social backgrounds. The fact that the preschool period covered the years of most rapid development when environmental factors could be expected to exert the strongest influence on personal and cognitive development meant that children from poor homes entered school predestined to fall behind because of their understimulated previous phase. One psychologist calculated that 50% of the variance in adult intelligence was predictable at age five (Bloom, 1964). Moved by this revelation of gross social inequality and the rapidly growing Civil Rights Movement, the US Federal administration invested thousands of millions of dollars in Head Start schemes for poor children throughout North America, including substantial amounts for research and evaluation of such schemes. The results of this research were initially exciting as small gains were discovered; then disappointing as these gains washed out; and finally exciting again as long-term gains were rediscovered. This research is discussed in more detail later in this chapter.

In Britain trends in social change took a different turn. The wartime destruction of homes through air raids compelled a massive housing programme which improved the living conditions of millions of families who had hitherto occupied slum homes. Likewise, compared with the pre-war economic depression, unemployment after the war was low and the majority of the population was relatively well-off. These two factors were responsible for an improvement in the quality of life of many families and their children. From the educational angle the 1944 Education Act raised the school-leaving age to 15 and set about introducing a new system of universal secondary education geared to optimising the potential of the school population, thus creating greater scope for equality across the entire social spectrum. This trend, subsequently reinforced by the introduction of comprehensive schools to replace selection at age 11, and a further increase in the school-leaving age, clearly demonstrates the British policy of promoting equality of opportunity at the secondary school phase rather than in the pre-school period, and goes some way towards explaining the relative neglect of preschool provision (DES, 1972, para. 14).

The lack of LEA provision of nursery places for under-fives together with a strong demand for preschool education created a unique community response in Britain in the form of playgroups, which, as a low-cost alternative to LEA nursery schools, attracted considerable official support (DHSS/DES, 1976). It is curious that so little attention has been given to exploring the reasons why the playgroup movement, as it has been called, came into existence. Belle Tutaev's historic letter to the *Guardian* in 1960 describing the playgroup which she and other mothers had set up (van der Eyken, 1977) was not so much an inspiration to others, as a demonstration of the widely felt need for preschool provision and a method for meeting this need. The demand for preschool provision already existed, only the means of meeting that demand were lacking. It is interesting to speculate on why there was a demand for preschool education at all. Why did the middle-class mothers of the 1960s form the opinion that their 3- and 4-year-old children needed experiences that could not be provided within the setting of their own family?

This question demands historical research which is beyond the scope of the present book but a number of possibilities can be suggested. The withdrawal of day nursery services after the war may have left an unacceptable gap in provision for under-fives. The decline in family size and extended family may have reduced the opportunity for children to play with others of similar age and mothers might have felt that their children should be able to play with others. Similarly, opportunity to play with neighbours' children in the street might have been restricted by the increase in volume of traffic making street play hazardous. Finally, awareness of the educational value of play may have become more widespread in the 1960s through wider dissemination of the ideas of modern developmental psychologists, such as Piaget, in popular magazines and journals. Also, mothers who themselves had trained as teachers before marriage and were aware of these ideas, would wish to ensure that their own children had full opportunity to enjoy the benefits of play, and would spread this viewpoint among their middle-class counterparts. By contrast, working-class mothers who were preoccupied with more pressing and immediate problems of raising their families, were less affected by this new philosophy—the need of their children for play and its relevance to education.

By whatever means the advent of preschool playgroups is explained, the fact remains that they formed a major part of British preschool provision in 1975 and continued to expand into the 1980s. In 1985 there was a total of 465,000 playgroup places in England, Scotland and Wales which accommodated one third of the 3- to 4-year age-group. LEA nursery schools and nursery classes were taking 330,000 full-time and half-time pupils—equivalent to a quarter of 3- to 4-year-olds—and a further 282,000 children (20% of 3- to 4-year-olds) were attending infant reception classes. (Chapter 2 provides further details of the levels of educational and day care provision).

This evolution of voluntary sector playgroups was instrumental in reducing pressure on local authorites to expand their nursery education services and led to a system of mixed voluntary and maintained provision having profound implications for the utilisation of preschool services by children from different social backgrounds. These implications are elaborated in Chapters 2 and 3, but in summary, relatively more socially advantaged children attended playgroups, whereas LEA nursery schools and classes accommodated greater proportions of socially disadvantaged children. As the educational needs of these disparate social groups differed, so the staffing, general organisation and objectives of playgroups and LEA nurseries will have been adapted to meet these different needs.

Teachers and nursery nurses who work in maintained nursery schools and classes are trained to be sensitive to the increased risk of developmental delay and behaviour problems in children in their charge who come from disadvantaged homes. In contrast to this, playgroup teachers and their parent helpers, being less likely to encounter many children with special problems, offer a curriculum from which those from more advantaged homes can benefit. It is essential, therefore, when reading the findings of this study, to recall that the fundamental differences between institutions in the maintained and independent sectors may have had different implications for the educational and emotional development of the children who attended them.

The preschool services debate in Britain has been further complicated by the merging of the two concepts—preschool education and day care (Bone, 1977). Up till now we have been discussing preschool education, which is a child-centred concept. The demand for day care of under-fives, however, derives from pressure for equality of opportunity between women and men in the labour market and therefore focuses more on the needs of mothers. If women who are mothers are to pursue their chosen career, a comprehensive preschool day care service is required, together with out-of-school and holiday care for school-age children (Centre for Educational Research and Innovation, 1977; David, 1982; Equal Opportunities Commission, 1986; Hughes *et al.*, 1980; Organisation for Economic Cooperation and Development, 1979; Tizard, 1986). From the child's angle, the essential difference between the concepts of preschool education and day care is the length of time they spend in the educational or care setting. Day care usually entails the child being looked after for more hours per day and for more weeks per year than is customary in nursery schools or playgroups. The main providers of day care in Britain, other than members of the child's own family, are day nurseries and childminders, but as the focus of the present study is institution-based preschool education, children who attended childminders were not treated as a separate group for analysis. Even though their primary function is day care rather than education, day nurseries were included in our analyses because they were a form of institutional preschool facility, and provided an interesting comparison with nursery schools and classes through the differences in their organisation and staffing. Moreover, local authority day nurseries, as we shall show, were attended by the most severely disadvantaged children, and one of the objectives of the research was to ascertain the various ways in which the needs of children in vulnerable groups were being met.

This brief history suggests that the particular system of preschool provision in Britain has evolved against a background of social and economic change and educational policies which have focused more on secondary education reform than on primary education. The recommendations of the Plowden Report (1967) and the Government White Paper (DES, 1972) had only a small impact on primary and nursery education in comparison with the two massive restructurings of secondary education, and indeed the expansion of the universities, following the Robbins Report (DES, 1963).

Thus although there has been official concern in the past over the failure of the education system to create equality of opportunity for children from all social backgrounds, as expressed, for example, in the setting up of Educational Priority Areas in 1968 (Halsey, 1972), preschool education has not, in general, been seriously considered as a means of increasing the educational potential of socially disadvantaged children. We have contrasted this with the major Head Start programme initiated in the 1960s in America, where substantial Federal investment underwrote the concept of compensatory preschool intervention. In the following sections we review some of the American and British research which has investigated the effectiveness of preschool education in improving school attainment and behavioural adjustment.

Preschool evaluation research in America

In 1945 Beth Wellman published a review of some fifty American studies, the earliest of which was dated 1918, which compared the average IQ of children who had attended preschool centres with that of children who had no preschool education (Wellman, 1945). The results showed conclusively that children with preschool experience had an increased mean IQ compared with those who had not attended preschool programmes. These studies were carried out within the context of the nature–nurture debate and were not attempting to establish the value of preschool education. However, the fact that such studies were done at all demonstrates that at that time preschool education was expected to weigh significantly on the nurture side of the balance. It is a sobering thought that half a century later we are still trying to prove what many already accept—that preschool education is worthwhile.

Since that time a vast American literature has accumulated which describes the origins, history, progress and effects of the many Head Start groups and various experimental schemes that have been initiated since the 1960s. A very comprehensive account and evaluation of Head Start can be found in the book edited by Zigler and Valentine (1979), *Project Head Start: A Legacy of the War on Poverty*. Of all the projects reported, however, two have achieved outstanding significance and wide publicity in recent years. One is the Perry Preschool Project which began in Ypsilanti, Michigan in 1962, and is still continuing under the auspices of the High/Scope

Education Research Foundation (Clement *et al.*, 1984; Schweinhart and Weikart, 1980; Weber *et al.*, 1978; Weikart *et al.*, 1978). The other is the Consortium for Longitudinal Studies coordinated by Irving Lazar and Richard Darlington at Cornell University, which followed up children who had participated in eleven experimental projects starting in the 1960s, and included the Perry Preschool Project (Lazar, 1985; Lazar and Darlington, 1982; Royce *et al.*, 1983).

The Perry Preschool Project began with a sample of 123 educationally high-risk preschool-age children which was divided into 5 groups of approximately equal numbers entering the project at one year intervals. 58 of the children took part in the preschool programme and 65 served as controls. One reason for the imbalance in the numbers of experimental and control children in this sample was that 5 children who had been randomly assigned to the experimental group were subsequently transferred to the control group because their mothers were unable to transport them to and from the preschool centre. Although this contravened the statistical principle of randomisation, we believe it was insufficient to seriously undermine the main long-term findings reported from the study. The experimental group attended a preschool programme for $12\frac{1}{2}$ hours per week for a total of 2 years when they were 3 and 4 years old, and in addition teachers paid weekly $1\frac{1}{2}$ hour home visits to the mother and child. All the children selected were black, of very low IQ (70–85) and from poor socio-economic backgrounds. Both the experimental and control groups entered kindergarten (the first state school) at age 5, and grade school at age 6. In the American system children progress from grade to grade when they achieve the required educational standard and not according to chronological age as in Britain. Thus retention in a grade is frequently used as a criterion of educational delay in American children. Measures of IQ and school achievement were obtained almost every year up to the age of 11 and at age 14. Details of school career, behaviour, self-concept, delinquency, criminal activity and employment were also recorded in successive follow-ups to the age of 19 years. The main findings to emerge during the school years were these:

1. Cognitive ability

Compared with the control group the experimental group had substantially increased Stanford-Binet IQ scores between 4 and 7 years of age, but by age 10 this difference had disappeared and thereafter remained equal.

2. School commitment

There was some evidence that members of the study group at age 15 were slightly more committed to educational goals than were controls.

3. Educational achievement

The experimental group achieved better results in reading, arithmetic and language skills at all ages from 7 to 14 years but differences did not achieve a high degree of statistical significance ($p<.001$) until the children were 14 years of age.

4. Special education

39% of the control group had received special education compared with only 19% of the experimental group.

5. Behaviour

Teacher- and self-ratings of behaviour and school conduct suggested that the experimental group at various ages up to 15 years were better adjusted than were the controls. The differences, however, were not large and statistical significance was poor ($p<.10$) compared with that for educational outcomes.

Delinquency

57% of the experimental group had committed two or more offences compared with 75% of the control group. Chronic offenders (five or more offences) totalled 36% of the experimental group and 52% of the controls ($p<.05$).

7. Teenage employment

29% of the experimental group had had a part-time job in a two-months period compared with 16% of controls but this difference was not statistically significant ($p>.10$).

8. Self-esteem

No significant differences were found between the experimental group and controls in measures of self-esteem and locus of control.

The findings reported at age 19 revealed even more remarkable differences between the experimental group and the controls which for simplicity are summarised in the following table:

	Experimental group (%)	Controls (%)
Classified as mentally retarded	15	35
Completed high school	67	49
Went on to college or job training	38	21
Had a job	50	32
Had been arrested	31	51
Charged with serious crime	24	38
On public assistance	18	32

The results from this study are surprising because they were found despite the small sample size which required substantial differences to achieve statistically significant results; in the later stages there were fewer than fifty cases in the experimental and control groups for some longitudinal analyses and the authors were prepared to accept a lower level of statistical significance ($p<.10$) than is customary. The importance of the study, however, lies in the general pattern of results across all the different measures. The experimental group consistently did better than controls in almost every respect even though in many instances statistical reliability was low.

Of special interest, in our view, were the findings related to educational outcomes where substantial and highly significant ($p<.001$) gains in achievement at age 14 were found even though at earlier grades differences for these outcomes were much smaller, and there were no differences in IQ at 14 years between experimental and control groups. Schweinhart and Weikart (1980, p. 44) explain this apparent anomaly by showing that the experimental group at 14 showed more persistence in their school work, and that this led to differences in scores from achievement tests which were administered on a group basis. IQ tests, in contrast, were carried out in a one-to-one situation with a tester, where the child's lack of persistence interfered less with the conduct of the test. This argument suggests that the differences in attainment in test scores were in part a result of the test situation, but that the greater degree of task persistence in the experimental group might itself be of more significance than the increased test scores *per se*.

The marked reductions in mental retardation and criminal behaviour and the increases in educational achievement and employment success in the experimental group compared with the controls at age 19 were the most remarkable findings from the study. It is difficult to see how a limited intervention in the pre-school years could achieve such extensive long-term effects, and whilst the integrity of the researchers is certainly not questioned, one feels there must be other explanations.

Schweinhart and Weikart use a transactional model to explain why preschool intervention is effective (1980, pp. 5–7). Early success from preschool experience tends to evoke positive responses from parents and teachers, which in turn encourage the child to apply himself even more to school tasks; a process which is seen as of major importance in producing the association between early intervention and subsequent attainment. Comparisons between different types of preschool curriculum did not suggest that any particular type was more effective than others in increasing cognitive development (Weikart *et al.*, 1978(b)); however, the authors naturally insist that the preschool programme should be of high quality, and use the results of the Perry Preschool Project to promote High/Scope's own 'Cognitively-Oriented Curriculum' (Hohman *et al.*, 1979).

One of the great difficulties of the Perry Preschool Project evaluation research was the small sample size which rendered its statistical viability very shaky. This problem also afflicted many other American preschool intervention evaluations (Palmer and Anderson, 1979). The large number of children involved in the Consortium studies coordinated by Lazar and Darlington was a major advantage which broadened the base for generalisation and permitted analyses that were not possible with smaller numbers. However, as the authors point out, the method adopted was not without its difficulties (Lazar and Darlington, 1982, p. xi). These were, (a) the research-oriented preschool programmes were experimental in nature and possibly not typical of the average Head Start programme, (b) the data were specific to a particular time in history and social change might mean that the conclusions would not apply to a subsequent situation, (c) the method adopted provided a broad indication of the effectiveness of preschool intervention in general but could make little detailed observation of the value of one or other type of programme.

The Consortium research was the result of a collaboration between twelve investigators who individually initiated important preschool intervention projects in the late 1950s and early 1960s; the Perry Preschool Project was included among them. Although all these schemes differed in various ways, they had sufficient elements in common to enable the researchers to pool the data on a total of 3,593 children born between 1958 and 1968; of these, 2,008 children were traced and followed up in 1976. Over 90% of the subjects in these studies were black and from low-income families, and about 70% of those followed up had taken part in intervention programmes and 30% were controls.

Methodological constraints precluded the possibility of combining all the data from the eleven separate projects into one data set and the authors used instead a procedure which they called 'multi-sample secondary analysis' (Lazar and Darlington, 1982, pp. 21–4). This entailed analysing the data from each project separately and then statistically 'pooling' the results afterwards. The pooled p value provided an estimate of the combined statistical significance and was obtained from a statistical manipulation of the p values from each individual project using procedures suggested by Mosteller and Bush (1954). The Consortium also followed up as many as 74% of all the original subjects in 1976 and 1980 to find out about their progress at school and their success in the labour market after leaving school.

The research set out to answer two general questions, namely (a) did programme participation enhance children's progress relative to that of control children (the main effects of early education)? and (b) did programme participation affect one type of child more than another (the differential effects of preschool education)? The main results were as follows:

1. School competence

On average across six of the projects with relevant information, 14% of experimental group children had been placed in special education classes compared with 29% of controls (N = 558, p<.001). Across eight projects with relevant data, 25% of programme children had been retained in grade compared with 31% of controls (N = 858, p<.05). This latter effect disappeared, however, when the project with the most significant individual result was excluded as a test of robustness of the pooled result. The association between school competence and preschool experience did not differ after adjustment for the child's gender, ethnic background, pre-test IQ, family size, family structure (presence or absence of father) or maternal education.

2. School achievement

Methodological problems, particularly bias due to attrition and differences between projects in testing procedure, meant that differences in mathematics and reading scores between experimental and control groups could not be established with certainty. The analysis suggested, however, that reading and mathematics scores were somewhat higher in the experimental group especially in grade three (age 8). Lazar and Darlington opined that the Perry Preschool Project evaluation (reported above) had the best design for the evaluation of preschool effects on later school achievement.

3. Cognitive development

Average differences of 4–5 IQ points between experimental and control groups were found up to two years after their leaving the preschool programme (pooled p<.001). However, these IQ differences became non-significant at later ages when home background factors were taken into account. Differential effects of preschool experience on IQ were not found for children from different social/family circumstances.

4. School commitment and self-concept

The experimental group children were more likely than controls to express views that were achievement-orientated, but they were no more realistic in their occupational and educational aspirations than were the control group. In general the programme group were no more likely than the controls to rate their own school performance as being better than that of their peers.

5. Post-school experience

Young people who had participated in early intervention programmes were more likely than their controls to have jobs and to have attended a post-secondary educational programme.

These results from the Consortium studies demonstrated positive effects of preschool intervention with respect to some outcomes but not others. The reduced need for special education, non-retention in grade and increased employment prospects were major effects but there was no indication of long-term increase in IQ, reading or mathematics scores, or improved self-concept.

Much of the American research into the effectiveness of preschool intervention has been carried out by workers who were strongly committed to the concept of early intervention and the Head Start programme. The attitude has been that preschool programmes must have a beneficial effect but empirical research methods have been insufficiently sensitive to measure them reliably, or else subsequent school provision has been unable to build on or take advantage of the gains achieved in the preschool (Bissell, 1973; Garber, 1979; Moore, 1979). Research such as the Westinghouse study (Westinghouse Learning Corp., 1969), which was conducted by researchers who were frankly sceptical of the possible effectiveness of early intervention, and found no long-term associations between attendance at preschool programmes and school achievement, has been subject to intense methodological criticism from others (Palmer and Anderson, 1979, p. 456) who, in contrast with the Westinghouse team, were fully convinced of the benefits of such programmes. Results from the Westinghouse study were nevertheless used selectively by the Nixon administration to freeze public spending on Head Start (Harmon and Hanley, 1979, pp. 391–2). The saga of the Head Start programme and its evaluation provides a salutary warning of the way in which research findings and public policy can interact, so that objectivity in research is constantly in danger of being undermined by pressing political and economic considerations.

The question of how to interpret research results is a difficult one. Studies as complex as those described above do not provide unequivocal answers to questions as general as 'Does preschool intervention work?' If the perspective is broadened to cover many different evaluations of preschool education it is always possible to find evidence to support a particular view (see for example Palmer and Anderson, 1979), whilst others using the same sources draw opposite conclusions (e.g. Jencks, 1972; Jensen, 1969). When the question is more specific, 'Does preschool education improve IQ?', answers still require qualification of the type 'Yes, in the short-term but not in the long-term', or 'Yes, according to some studies but not according to others'. The question of degree also enters into it as when statistically significant differences are found but their size is insubstantial, amounting only to a few points on a test scale.

Assuming that the effects of the experimental programmes can be generalised to ordinary preschool programmes, investment in preschool education may result in considerable financial savings in the long run (Weber *et al.*, 1978), and there is at least one British study suggesting that early educational intervention can benefit handicapped children (Reader, 1984); this may increase confidence in the possibility that such provision may reduce the need for expensive special education at a later stage.

The importance of the American intervention studies for preschool education in Britain is that they provide fairly conclusive evidence that quality preschool programmes can increase children's educational potential and that it is very probable that they can have lasting effects. That these conclusions are not directly transferable to the UK setting is cogently argued by Martin Woodhead (1985), who points out that the majority of children in the Consortium projects came from families in the lowest social class, were of very low IQ and were black. Also ' . . . the social and educational circumstances affecting the urban black poor in the USA at a time of still widespread segregation but rapid change may have affected the impact of intervention at the time, and the changes since may alter its impact now' (op. cit., p. 142). To what extent, therefore, is the potential suggested by the American research also being realised in Britain?

Preschool evaluation research in the UK

We have argued that the preschool education debate in Britain has been discussed from the angle of social policy rather than that of developmental psychology, as in the USA. The value of nursery schools and playgroups is generally seen less in terms of the cognitive and educational advantages they provide for the children attending them than in terms of meeting the public demand for preschool places (e.g. DHSS/DES, 1976). There has been much concern about the need for coordination between available services so as to maximise the use of existing resources (Bradley, 1982; DHSS/DES, 1978) and particularly to make more provision for day care to meet the needs of employed mothers (David, 1982; Hughes *et al.*, 1980; Moss, 1978; Mottershead, 1978).

This primary focus on day care and levels of provision rather than the educational value of preschool services has given rise to many excellent reviews of the various types, quantity and quality of preschool provision in Europe (notably—van der Eyken, 1977; van der Eyken, 1981; Hughes *et al.*, 1980; Mayall and Petrie, 1983; Parry and Archer, 1974; Preschool Playgroups Association, 1985; Tizard *et al.*, 1976; Woodhead, 1979), but very little attention has been paid to evaluating their effects on the later development and behaviour of the children who attended them.

In her review of research in early childhood education being carried out in the early 1970s Barbara Tizard found only three major projects that were concerned with the effects of attendance at a preschool institution on children's achievement (Tizard, 1975, p. 1). Her conclusion drawn from these three studies was that early schooling was not an effective way of improving the educational potential of socially disadvantaged children. In response to this pessimistic view of preschool education, Smith and James (1977) drew attention to the evidence of the Educational Priority Area project in the West Riding of Yorkshire and also the American research findings available at that time and concluded ' . . . the evidence we have reviewed suggests that preschool intervention can make an impact, and with the right support this can be maintained for considerable periods' (Smith and James, 1977, pp. 310–11).

By 'right support' Smith and James meant that disadvantaged children should be given special attention throughout the school years (cp. Follow-Through programmes in the USA, e.g. Bronfenbrenner, 1974, p. 19) and, in particular, that teachers should involve parents in their children's education. More recently, however, informed opinion is leaning more towards the idea of the long-term effects of preschool intervention being mediated by a 'transactional' process involving the positive expectations and responses of significant others, such as parents and teachers, towards the child as a result of his initial cognitive gains from preschool experience, which in turn lead to increased achievement in school and hence to further consolidation of parental and teacher expectations in a cumulative iterative process (Clarke, 1984(b); Schweinhart and Weikart, 1980, pp. 5–7; Woodhead, 1985). Such a model, however, has yet to be tested.

With regard to the type of preschool provision that is likely to have the strongest impact on children's educational development, the conventional nursery or playgroup environment is not considered to be optimal:

"The need (in the Educational Priority Area project) was for a preschool curriculum that concentrated more on cognitive skills, and for this reason the traditional approach with its emphasis on social skills and free play methods was felt not to be adequate. (Smith and James, 1977, p. 299)

The general conclusion appears to be that structured programmes which emphasise adult–child verbal interaction best fulfil the goals of compensatory education at least in the short-term. (Woodhead, 1979, p. 32)"

And again:

"Ordinary nursery education, with its emphasis on free play, does not in general produce (educational) gains. (Hughes *et al.*, 1980, p. 41)"

In one study it was estimated that 80% of infant school teachers believed that preschool education had no lasting effect, and one in four thought that children who had been to nurseries or playgroups were less cooperative and more boisterous (Morsbach *et al.*, 1981). The same research also reported that parents had 'unrealistic hopes' that nursery experience would increase their child's IQ.

It is difficult to see why there has been such a lack of confidence in the traditional preschool curricula of nursery schools and playgroups since very little research has been carried out in normal nurseries or playgroups to warrant such judgements. A notable exception to this was the National Foundation for Educational Research (NFER) study of 241 children who attended five nursery schools in Slough, Berkshire in 1973 (Woodhead, 1976).

This study showed that children who had experienced a special preschool language programme had improved linguistic skills compared with those who had experienced the normal nursery curriculum. There was no difference, however, in perceptual skills between children who had attended the special programme and those who had not. Of three measures of social adjustment only one showed a difference between the programme and non-programme children. These findings suggested that the children who attended nursery schools without the special language programme enjoyed somewhat better social adjustment at the end of their nursery experience. The number of terms spent in the nursery school was not found to affect any of the test scores.

After two years in infant school the two groups of children showed no differences in tests of reading or mathematics, and a comparison with infant children having no preschool experience showed no differences in reading attainment. However, children who had attended normal nursery schools had slightly better mathematics scores than those with no preschool experience.

Our interpretation of these NFER findings is that special language programmes appear to improve linguistic ability in the short term, but these skills do not necessarily give the child a special across-the-board learning advantage in the infant school. The traditional preschool curriculum, however, might stimulate all-round development and increase general cognitive skills that enable the child to more readily assimilate and adapt to new ideas, concepts and knowledge across all subjects. It is unlikely that only one skill, such as language, holds the key to early learning; children must develop all skills together in order to achieve optimal scope for learning. The traditional nursery environment might achieve this as successfully as might specially devised curricula.

There is in fact some further evidence that 'ordinary nursery education' *can* be effective. A study of 365 children aged 3 years who attended nursery schools/classes, day nurseries or playgroups in a London borough achieved significantly higher scores in three language tests than did 745 non-attenders (Stevenson and Ellis, 1975). A survey of 120 4-year-old children who attended 12 Belfast playgroups and 120 non-attending controls used a test–re-test design to evaluate the effect of playgroup experience on cognitive and social development (Turner, 1977). Children who attended playgroups achieved higher mean scores than the controls on measures of vocabulary and mental maturity, and their social development was also enhanced. A comparison between 12 children who had attended nursery classes in Educational Priority Area primary schools and 12 children in the same schools who had not attended nursery classes, suggested that the ex-nursery children were superior in certain tests of psycholinguistic ability (Lewis and Garvey, 1980).

Data from the National Survey of Health and Development (Atkins *et al.*, 1980) were used to compare the verbal skills of 1,373

8-year-olds who had attended any form of preschool institution between 1969 and 1975, with 303 others who had no preschool education (Wadsworth, 1986). After statistical adjustment for maternal education, parenting methods and stimulation at home at the age of four years, children with preschool experience attained higher scores on tests of vocabulary, reading and sentence completion at eight than those without preschool education. The preschool effect achieved a high degree of statistical significance (p<.001) in all three tests and was a stronger and more consistent explanatory factor than indicators of home discipline and stimulation which were included in the analyses. Wadsworth points out, however, that the effects of all the factors examined, including preschool experience, were small when compared with the major influence of maternal education on children's verbal ability.

The children on which this study was based were the first-born of parents who themselves were members of a cohort which has been studied from birth in 1946 to the present day. Many interesting comparisons have been made between the childhood experiences of the original cohort and those of their own children in the second generation (Wadsworth, 1981, 1985). One such comparison concerns the preschool experience of the first generation of whom only 7% had attended preschool institutions between 1949 and 1951. Those who had attended nursery schools or classes did not achieve significantly better test results at 8, 11 or 15 years than non-attenders from similar social backgrounds (Douglas and Ross, 1965). The contrast between the results for those two generations could be attributable to ecological change resulting in the second generation being more able to benefit from preschool education; changes in the preschool system itself with newer teaching methods being more effective; or to the greater sophistication of more recent research methodology and analysis due to the advent of powerful computing and data processing technology.

These were by no means definitive studies, but they provided evidence that normal nursery education or playgroup experience can have a measurable effect on a child's cognitive development, even though his subsequent social and school experience might obfuscate any initial gains. These studies suggested that some of the pessimism of the research reviewers quoted above was misplaced.

It is important to note, however, that there are also many instances of research findings which show no educational advantage accruing from attendance at preschool institutions. In the studies cited above the typical pattern of results was for children with preschool experience to gain in some respects but not in others. It should also be recognised that studies not producing positive or 'interesting' results frequently remain unpublished. Against this, however, we have not encountered a single research project which demonstrated that attendance at preschool institutions actually hindered a child's development, although it is possible in some circumstances that children's behaviour is adversely affected (Osborn *et al.*, 1984, pp. 142–5).

Enthusiasm for the cognitive curriculum (e.g. Bereiter and Engelmann, 1966) and the perceived need for linguistic stimulation (e.g. Bernstein, 1961) persuaded preschool theorists that compensatory education for children from socially disadvantaged homes could only be achieved through programmes with a strong emphasis on language. This thinking has been carried through to the more recent research of Tizard and Hughes (1984) which compares verbal interaction between adults and 4-year-old girls at home and in nursery settings and concludes that the amount and complexity of conversation in the children's own homes were greater than in the nursery school. Whilst this research makes an important contribution to the debate on linguistic styles and development following the work of Labov (1969) and Wells (1984), there is a danger that its focus on linguistic interaction may lead to the many other types of cognitive stimulation in the nursery setting being ignored. A contrasting study by Jowett and Sylva (1986), which compared the activities of working-class children in maintained nursery schools with those in voluntary playgroups from similar home backgrounds, found that playgroup children spent more time in adult-led activities and less on 'school readiness' activities such as matching and sorting games and using templates. The children who had attended nursery schools subsequently engaged in more challenging, creative and imaginative play and showed more persistence in their work in the infant school than did the playgroup graduates. After six months the differences between the two groups narrowed but the nursery school children were still slightly ahead.

Whilst the Tizard and Hughes study was critical of the standard of linguistic interaction in nursery schools, Jowett and Sylva's research implied that the nursery school regime as a whole was of greater benefit to working-class children than was that of the playgroups they studied. The point we are making here is that the success or otherwise of a child's preschool experience does not rest on one single aspect of the curriculum—even one as important as language. One of the notable findings of the American research in this respect was that no single aspect of the programme could be picked out as a major determinant of the subsequent success of the children who attended (Lazar, 1985, p. 30; Weikart *et al.*, 1978). The need for a 'rounded' programme for preschool-age children is frequently emphasised by curriculum specialists (Curtis, 1985; Parry and Archer, 1974).

Although it is the child's total experience that is significant there is widespread agreement in Britain and America that involving the child's parents in the educational process is an important contributory factor to the success of a preschool programme (Tizard *et al.*, 1981). In Britain, a study of primary school children carried out by Hewison and Tizard (1980) showed how poor readers increased their reading skill after their parents had spent some time listening to them read at home; the advantage was greater than that achieved through remedial education. This study is interesting because it suggests that even when parental attention to the child's education has to be elicited by the school, rather than being a spontaneous attitude having implications for many aspects of parent–child interaction, actual educational gains can be achieved. In the preschool education world the concept of parental involvement is frequently referred to, but unfortunately the degree and manner of involvement varies from being merely nominal to a total commitment, and we suspect that much lip-service is given to the idea of parental involvement in preschool education while in fact the majority of children enjoy very limited active participation of this type from their own mothers or fathers. Some attention is given to this issue in Chapter 9.

Conclusions

Britain has a long tradition of nursery education but successive governments, despite acknowledging its value, have been reluctant to make a major investment in the expansion of nursery schools and classes and have focused instead on the reform of secondary and tertiary education. The recommendations of Plowden (1967) for nursery expansion were heeded (DES, 1972; Halsey, 1972) but radical change did not ensue. Instead, the emergence and rapid development of voluntary playgroups served to meet parental demand for group experience for thousands of under-fives. This, we suggest, substantially reduced pressure on local authorities and central government to provide a more comprehensive pre-school education service and to meet, in particular, the needs of employed mothers for whom existing services are still woefully inadequate.

Preschool services in Britain have evolved spontaneously and haphazardly in response to parental demand rather than as a consequence of a properly formulated and sustained educational and day care policy. This has resulted in inequalities in utilisation of facilities between different social groups, which is described in detail in Chapters 2 and 3, and is possibly of some consequence for the effectiveness of preschool facilities in achieving educational goals. The American Head Start Programme, in contrast, was a deliberate attempt by the Federal government to provide a compen-satory educational experience for children from circumstances of severe socio-economic disadvantage, in an attempt to increase their ability to be more effective in the grade school system. Substantial funds were also made available to carry out research into the most effective forms of preschool intervention. Only recently has this research begun to show the educational advantages of preschool intervention in which the Head Start pioneers believed.

Whilst the American experience raises hopes that British pre-school education may be just as effective, Martin Woodhead (1985) wisely cautions that findings based on the American experimental studies may not be generally applicable to the British situation. What these studies seem to show, however, is that early education can have demonstrable long-term effects.

Most of the British research has also been carried out with small-scale experimental studies and reviewers have tended to differ in their interpretation of the results. However, a small number of studies addressed to traditional preschool settings have shown educational advantages for children who attended normal nursery schools and classes or playgroups as compared with non-attenders. The general impression is that preschool education can be effective in some respects but not all. Very often the sheer complexity of the research problems defeats the analytical methods that are available, because children are affected by such a myriad of factors in their day-to-day lives, in the preschool years and after, that to tease out the independent effect of a single factor is far from easy.

It was against this historical and research background that this first major evaluation of British preschool education was under-taken. It is unique not only in terms of the large number of children involved, but also because it is an evaluation of the whole gamut of preschool provision throughout the country, rather than being based exclusively on facilities with specially devised nursery curricula.

2

The provision of preschool education and care

There is no integrated policy for the provision of educational and day care services for children under 5 in Britain, and the need for greater coordination of preschool services is manifest (Bradley, 1982). One of the reasons why this lack of coordination has come about is that whilst responsibility for the education of the under-fives rests with the education authorities, day care comes under the aegis of social services departments. This, together with the differences in terms of employment and career structure between teachers and nursery nurses, and between the educational and day care functions of preschool facilities, has created a variety of types of provision, none of which completely satisfies the need for a comprehensive day care and educational service (Hughes *et al.*, 1980; pp. 114–37). One solution to this problem is combined nursery centres which offer the extended hours of opening necessary for day care purposes but also provide an educational input (Ferri *et al.*, 1981). Such nursery centres, however, are expensive to set up and run and cost is a major constraint on achieving any significant reorganisation or expansion of local authority provision for the under-fives.

Apart from the problem of how a comprehensive preschool service can be financed, there are conflicting opinions about whether a day care policy designed to meet the needs of families in which both parents go out to work is in the best interests of the children. The feminist argument is that the official view of preschool provision focuses on the social and educational needs of the child and ignores the fundamental changes that are taking place affecting the role of women in the economy and in family life (David, 1982; Penn, 1984). This argument demands full day care for all children under the age of 5 where both parents wish to pursue full-time occupations, and tends not to consider the possible implications for the behavioural and educational development of the children, or else to suggest that the mother–child relationship is enhanced as a result of the mother having a satisfying occupation in addition to pursuing her maternal role (Hughes *et al.*, 1980, p. 36).

The opposite view is best represented in the writings of Mia Kellmer Pringle (1976, 1980) who held that young children need the care and attention of one person during their early years, that short periods spent in a nursery school or playgroup are beneficial but not prolonged day care in a group setting, that parenting can be a fulfilling experience and is of such value to the future economy that mothers should be paid a wage for doing it. Hughes *et al.*, (1980, pp. 69–73) oppose the idea of a mother's wage because it undermines the fundamental principle of equality of opportunity in the workplace, and it is this difference in ideology between proponents of equality of opportunity for women and men, mothers and fathers, and those who believe in the traditional pattern of family life with one partner being predominantly responsible for child care and home-making whilst the other occupies the role of breadwinner, that lies at the root of the education/day care dichotomy in the provision of preschool facilities.

In time of financial exigency it is not surprising that local authorities have turned a blind eye to demands for the provision of all-day care for under-fives whose parents have full-time occupations, and have instead favoured Kellmer Pringle's ideas on home-based care and the provision of part-time nursery classes and playgroups. The lack of a comprehensive policy for the provision of preschool services, however, has resulted in a variety of types of facility which differ in many ways. The purpose of this chapter, therefore, is to describe the main points of similarity and difference between these preschool facilities.

Types of preschool provision

Provision for the education and day care of preschool-age children in Britain falls into a number of fairly well-defined categories according to the providers of the facilities, their main function and their organisation. A convenient typology is given in Figure 2.1 which separates providers between maintained (or Local Authority) and independent sources, with education and day care as their main functions. Within these, institutions are classified according to their organisation, depending chiefly on their type of accommodation, staffing and hours of opening. This defines the six main types of preschool institution with which this study is concerned. There are other types of institution, for example special institutions for handicapped children, nurseries run specifically for the children of service families and mother-and-toddler groups. Childminding, a major source of day care for children of employed mothers, is also excluded from this typology as the focus of our research is institutional group experience rather than individual substitute care. The six types of provision we have defined, however, represent the mainstream of preschool institutional facilities for under-fives in Britain.

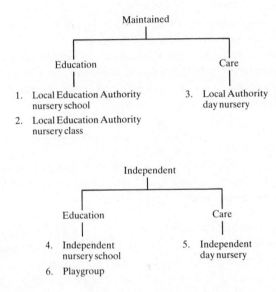

FIG. 2.1. Typology of preschool institutional provision in Britain

The following descriptions summarise the main characteristics of preschool institutions which provided the basis for the typology in Figure 2.1.

1. *LEA nursery schools*

Run by Local Education Authorities in self-contained nursery premises and not part of a primary school attended by older children. Staffed by teachers with nursery/primary teacher's qualifications and assisted by Nursery Nursing Examination Board (NNEB) trained nursery nurses. The head teacher is concerned only with preschool-age children. Opens five days a week from 9.00 a.m. to 3.30 p.m. approximately. Closes during normal school holidays.

2. LEA nursery classes

The same as LEA nursery schools in all respects except that classes are part of a primary school attended by children aged 5 and over. The head teacher has responsibility for school-age as well as pre-school-age children.

3. LA day nurseries

Run by Local Authority Social Services Departments with a strong emphasis on the care of children from families where there are known problems that might affect the child's health or well-being. Staffed mainly by NNEB trained nursery nurses in self-contained nursery premises. Provides all-day care with extended hours— nominally from 7.30 a.m. to 6.00 p.m.—and open all the year round.

4. Independent nursery schools

Privately run on a fee-paying basis with teacher-trained staff. Hours and period of opening similar to LEA schools. Usually accommodated in nursery premises.

5. Independent day nurseries

Privately run on a fee-paying basis with State Registered Nurse (SRN) or NNEB trained staff offering extended, all-day care all year round. Usually accommodated in nursery premises.

6. Playgroups

Voluntary groups run by residents in the community, often the mothers of the children who attend. They operate on a non-profit-making basis, with fees being charged to cover the costs of hiring a hall, heating, refreshments and other expenses. Playgroup helpers may have teaching, nursing or NNEB qualifications, but many are without relevant qualifications. Some, however, attend special courses arranged by voluntary organisations such as the Preschool Playgroups Association (PPA). Playgroups normally operate on a sessional basis—so many mornings or afternoons a week—that is determined by the availability of helpers or accommodation and the level of demand for places. They rarely open for as many as 10 sessions a week and normally close during the school holidays. Playgroups operate in community or church halls, in private houses or anywhere that has sufficient space and can provide storage facilities for equipment.

Independent day nurseries and playgroups are registered with their local Social Services Department. Staff from the Social Service Department ensure that premises and persons offering services for under-fives comply with health and safety regulations and standards, but no assessment is made of the adequacy of the educational experience offered. Local Authority day nurseries also have no special obligation to provide an educational experience. Independent nursery schools are registered with the Department of Education and Science (DES) and they must meet the same educational requirements and standards of health and safety as the LEA's own schools.

These descriptions indicate the broad parameters which define the different types of preschool provision in Britain. There is of course likely to be substantial variation between institutions of any one type so that although they have certain characteristics in common they may also differ in other respects. The purpose of the present chapter is to highlight some of the differences between and within the various types of preschool institution that are likely to have implications for the later cognitive and behavioural development of the children who attend them.

Before proceeding with this descriptive account of British preschool facilities, however, it is appropriate to present estimates of the actual extent of the various types of preschool provision in Britain and how this has changed in the ten years since the time of our 1975 survey.

The extent of preschool provision in Britain

Margaret Thatcher as Secretary of State for Education issued a Government White Paper in 1972 in which it was declared that,

"(the Government's) aim is that within the next ten years nursery education should become available without charge, within the limits of demand estimated by Plowden, to those children of three and four whose parents wish them to benefit from it. (DES, 1972, para. 17)"

The Plowden Report (1967) estimated that places were needed for up to 90% of 4-year-olds and 50% of 3-year-olds. An OPCS survey carried out in 1974 (Bone, 1977), concluded that 89% of mothers of 3- to 4-year-olds and 65% of mothers of 0- to 4-year-olds desired day provision, which was a substantially larger percentage than the Plowden estimate. It is reasonable to assume that in the 1980s the demand for preschool places is even greater than that found in Margaret Bone's survey and the expectation is that close to 100% of parents of 3- to 4-year-olds would like their child to attend a preschool group of some kind.

In 1975 official statistics showed that the total number of places in preschool institutions of all kinds was considerably below the level of demand suggested by either Plowden or Bone. If all the full-time and part-time places in nursery schools, nursery classes, playgroups and day nurseries were allocated only to the 3- to 4-year age group, there would have been sufficient for no more than 40% of these children. A further 18%, however, were occupying places in infant classes. This interpretation of the statistics ignores demand for preschool places from parents of children under 3 years old. Considerable expansion of preschool provision would have been required, therefore, for Mrs Thatcher's promise to be fulfilled.

In Table 2.1 we show the numbers of pupils in schools and the numbers of places in day nurseries, playgroups and with child minders in England, Wales and Scotland at three points in time; 1975, 1980 and 1985. Differences in methods of collecting and presenting these published statistics between Authorities and between countries, and variation in the ages of children who attend different types of provision created difficulties of interpretation and comparison between groups. Nevertheless, certain major trends were prominent.

The most important development between 1975 and 1985 was the very considerable increase in the number of part-time pupils in LEA nursery classes which more than doubled over the ten-year period. This was made possible by the falling infant rolls during this period due to the decline in birth rate during the 1970s, and which made places in infant reception classes available for more under-fives. In England, some of the full-time places in reception classes occupied by under-fives were evidently transformed into nursery class places during this decade. Despite this large increase in part-time pupils in nursery classes by 1985, there were still almost as many under-fives in infant reception classes as in nursery schools or classes. It is likely, however, that many of those in infant classes were rising fives, i.e. would reach 5 years of age in the term in which the count was taken, whereas nursery schools and classes would have accommodated a larger proportion of younger children.

The number of places in registered playgroups continued to expand in England and Wales but declined in Scotland where there was a relatively large number of playgroup places achieved partly by the judicious use of playbuses (see note 12 to Table 2.1). LA day nursery places also increased in all three countries, in response, perhaps, to changes in the perception of local authorities of the day care needs of children from priority groups. Finally, there was a substantial increase in the number of places with registered child-minders over the decade. However, we suspect that much of this increase was due to 'unofficial' childminders becoming registered rather than to an actual increase in childminding services.

The growth in the 0- to 4-year-old population between 1980 and 1985 indicates that the size of the infant population will increase in the second half of the 1980s and in all probability will result in fewer under-fives gaining access to LEA school places than in 1985. Thus fluctuations in the size of the under-five population will significantly affect what proportion of that population will obtain preschool places. However, in 1985, the number of pupils in LEA and independent nursery schools and classes, plus the number of places in LA and registered day nurseries and playgroups amounted to 64% of the population of 3- and 4-year-olds. A further 20% of this population was attending LEA infant reception classes. These figures provide only an approximate estimate of the total level of provision because many children in day nurseries and playgroups were under 3 years old, therefore fewer 3- to 4-year-olds were accommodated, and an unknown number of this age group were with childminders. Counter to this, however, is the fact that many playgroup places are shared between two or more children, thereby increasing the numbers attending but for fewer sessions. These figures demonstrate that the promise of free nursery education for 70% of 3- to 4-year-olds pledged in the 1972 DES White Paper has not been fulfilled. Whilst there has been a creditable increase in

Table 2.1 Trends in preschool education and day care in England, Wales and Scotland 1975–1985

		England			Wales			Scotland		
		1974/75	1979/80	1984/85	1974/75	1979/80	1984/85	1974/75	1979/80	1984/85
Pupils in:										
LEA nursery schools	FT	13,740	14,079	11,890	1,477	1,702	1,387	2,833	3,732	2,908
	PT	29,777	34,377	37,723	2,975	2,624	2,737	17,629	28,038	34,959
LEA nursery classes	FT	23,925	32,464	30,473	10,430	6,615	6,202	} (combined)		
	PT	70,476	134,531	186,850	4,488	10,223	13,913	} (combined)		
LEA infant classes	FT	246,717	197,878	226,936	24,309	22,437	24,612	6,609	10,087	10,583
	PT	19,251	15,591	18,695	184	1,041	1,440	—	—	—
Independent schools	FT	17,463	17,790	17,987	with England	470	623	1,009	672	811
	PT	12,603	10,659	14,094		75	116	—	—	—
Places in:										
LA day nurseries		25,992	28,437	28,884	30	109	230	3,499	3,645	3,829
Registered day nurseries		25,893	22,017	24,400	1,183	817	1,013	418	350	246
LA playgroups		2,696	2,865	2,794	284	292	309	1,371	967	2,077
Registered play-groups		328,086	365,003	398,559	14,383	17,753	19,406	44,847	40,783	41,784
Registered child-minders		85,616	n/a	126,613	1,336	2,280	4,506	1,012	2,875	7,465
Population aged 0–4 (000s)		3,227.9	2,786.0	2,973.4	194.7	169.4	177.2	375.5	320.7	324.9

FT = Full-time. PT = Part-time. n/a = not available.

Table 2.1 *Notes*

1. *Sources*: Statistical Bulletins and personal communications from DES, London; DHSS, London; Welsh Office, Cardiff; Scottish Education Department, Edinburgh; Scottish Social Work Services Group, Edinburgh; Office of Population Censuses and Surveys, Population Estimates Unit, London.

2. Education statistics are as at 31 December or 1 January in the period given for England and Wales, and at 1 September with age at 31 December for Scotland.

3. Social Services/Social Work Dept. statistics are as at 31 March 1975, 1980 and 1985.

4. Population figures are revised mid-year estimates as at 30 June 1975 and 1980, and mid-year projections for 30 June 1985.

5. Pupils in LEA nursery schools and nursery classes include some children aged 5 on 1 January.

6. Figures for under-fives in infant classes in Wales are minimal estimates because they are calculated by subtracting the number of children in nursery classes from all under-fives in primary schools and some children in nursery classes are 5 years old.

7. The 1974/75 figure for pupils under age 5 in independent schools in England includes those for Wales also.

8. Numbers of pupils in Scottish nursery schools and nursery classes are merged—a breakdown between these two types of provision is not available.

9. There were no recorded part-time pupils under five in Scottish LEA primary or independent primary schools. No information is collected from independent nursery schools.

10. The number of places in day nurseries and playgroups and with childminders in England for 31 March 1985 are provisional estimates. Four authorities had not submitted returns and their latest available data were substituted to estimate the totals for England as follows: Kirklees, 1982; Camden, 1983; Kingston-upon-Thames, 1979; Kent, 1981.

11. Childminders are persons registered with Social Services Departments who provide in their homes day-care for children for reward, though a small number may be running home playgroups rather than offering what would be generally understood to be a childminding service.

12. The increase in numbers of places in Scottish LA playgroups in 1985 is largely accounted for by an increase in the use of playbuses in two regions. A single playbus may service ten or more different groups at different locations each week, and these are counted by the Authority as ten separate playgroups.

part-time places in LEA nursery classes during this decade, there has also been a heavy dependence on the playgroup movement in meeting demand for preschool places—particularly in the younger age group, as we shall show. Finally the provision of part-time, as against full-time, places in LEA nursery schools and classes and the low level of day nursery provision, has drawn severe criticism from those campaigning for more comprehensive day care services for the children of employed mothers (Tizard, 1986). This is particularly a problem for mothers with children under 3 years old for whom day care facilities are very scarce.

Having described the trends in levels of provision of the various types of preschool services in Britain, we turn now to a national survey of preschool institutions carried out in 1975 which provides a valuable source of information on the preschool institutions attended by the children in our study.

The Nursery/Playgroup survey

In 1975 contact was made with almost every preschool institution in Britain attended by more than 5 children to invite them to complete a questionnaire about the service they offered and the children who attended. The purpose of this survey was twofold; firstly, we needed to know more about staffing, activities and the mode of operation of the various types of preschool institutions, and secondly, we planned to identify the particular institutions that had been attended by children in the Child Health and Education Study in order to discover whether particular types of preschool environment had differential effects on children's cognitive and behavioural development. Further details of the methodology of the Nursery/Playgroup survey are given in the Appendix and in van der Eyken *et al.* (1984).

A total of 18,209 institutions took part in the study but in this chapter we describe the results for 16,948 institutions which exclude special schools for handicapped children, crèches, groups run for the children of parents in the armed forces and infant reception classes with under-fives. Table 2.2 shows the numbers of institutions in each of the main types specified above, and the total numbers of children attending them. Playgroups were subdivided into two categories in this study; hall-based and home-based playgroups. The home-based playgroups were simply a

Table 2.2 *Preschool institutions and children in the Nursery/Playgroup survey*

Type of institution	Institution		Children	
	N	%	N	%
Maintained				
LEA nursery school	713	4.2	57,163	8.1
LEA nursery class	1,932	11.4	95,503	13.5
LA day nursery	544	3.2	26,253	3.7
Independent				
Nursery school	195	1.2	8,005	1.1
Day nursery	712	4.2	26,673	3.8
Hall playgroup	11,620	68.6	466,123	65.7
Home playgroup	1,232	7.3	29,329	4.1
All	16,948	100.0	709,049	100.0

subset of all playgroups, as defined in the Appendix, but were run in private houses rather than in community or church halls. Although we had not realised the full implications of this classification when it was first created, the children who attended home-based playgroups were subsequently found to have achieved the highest test scores of all the preschool groups. Comparisons of this group with other types of preschool institution in this chapter are, therefore, of special interest.

Numerically hall playgroups predominated in the study but, overall, institutions in the maintained sector were larger in size than those in the private sector and therefore accommodated a higher proportion of children as shown in Table 2.2. Thus while LEA nursery schools comprised only 4% of all institutions studied, they accounted for 8% of all the children in the sample who attended a preschool facility. However, the number of children who attended a particular type of institution was also affected by the degree to which places were shared between children who attended part-time. Thus an institution could double its attendance rate simply by having the children attend only half the sessions the institution operated. For the sake of simplicity, some of the descriptive statistics in this chapter are based on the numbers of children attending rather than the numbers of institutions. This provides a useful way of making comparisons between types of institution, but it obscures any variation between institutions of a given type.

The results presented here describe the pattern of preschool provision in 1975 and although there will have been some changes in the characteristics of the different types of institution between then and the present day, such changes tend to be slow and the extent to which the essential differences in practice between, say, LEA nursery schools and playgroups have changed in the past decade is an open question. Regardless of such changes, for the purposes of the present study, it was the nature of preschool institutions in 1975 which was important for the children in the birth cohort who were attending them at that time and whose preschool experience we shall be relating to their subsequent ability and attainment.

Type of premises

The type of premises in which preschool institutions were accommodated determined to some degree how they were defined. Thus the majority of all playgroups operated in community or church halls whilst home playgroups were run in private houses, LEA nursery classes were always attached to a school taking infant children, but 14% of them had their own separate premises and a further 49% had self-contained accommodation within the main school. In more than a third, however, the classrooms for the under-fives were not separate from the main infant school and it is possible that some of these nursery classes were not unlike infant reception classes in the way they were run.

Periods of opening

The institutions in the study mainly conformed to the expected pattern with LEA nursery schools and classes open 40 weeks a year, day nurseries all year round and independent nursery schools and playgroups for 38 weeks a year on average. There was little deviation from these norms. It is worth noting that there was virtually no institutional provision for mothers who worked full-time and, as we showed above, there had been very little increase in the amount of all day care by 1985 with expansion in educational provision being confined almost entirely to part-time places. In the maintained sector nearly all types of institutions opened for 10 sessions per week; in contrast to this only private day nurseries in the independent sector were likely to operate on a full-time basis (85%) and whilst 40% of independent nursery schools were open for 10 sessions a week, an equal number (43%) operated only 5 sessions a week. Few playgroups could offer more than 5 sessions a week; one third of hall playgroups opened for 5 sessions but over half functioned for only 1–4 sessions, and the majority of home playgroups opened 5 sessions per week (49%) or less often (37%).

The only types of institution which were open all day (more than seven hours) were day nurseries, both maintained and independent. 83% of playgroups were open for no more than three hours per day.

Patterns of attendance

The frequency with which children attended preschool institutions varied considerably with some children attending full-time and others for fewer sessions. The lower attendances may be explained by several factors. Firstly, staff and parents may have decided that younger children should attend fewer sessions when they were first enrolled in a nursery or playgroup. Secondly, some parents could only afford to pay for a limited number of sessions per week, and thirdly, there may have been a deliberate policy of limiting the number of children attending full-time in order to accommodate a larger number on a part-time basis. The fact that institutions operated for different numbers of sessions per week, had different numbers of places available and took some children for more sessions per week than others created difficulties for analysis and presentation of the data. The method we adopted was to calculate for each type of institution the total number of children on the attendance register who attended for 1 session, 2 sessions, 3 sessions a week and so on up to 10 sessions a week. The resulting distributions showed that certain frequencies of attendance occurred more often than others; these were 1–4, 5, and 10 sessions per week. Within each type of institution there was some variation in the balance between the numbers of children attending different numbers of sessions, but to give an indication of the contrast between types of institutions we calculated the proportion of all the children on the registers who attended 1–4, 5, 6–9 or 10 sessions per week (Table 2.3). This showed that 90% of children in LA day nurseries attended 10 sessions per week which was a much greater

Table 2.3 *Frequency of attendance of children attending preschool institutions*

Type of institution		Number of sessions attended per week					N = 100%
		1–4	5	6–9	10		
Maintained							
LEA nursery school	%	1.3	64.9	0.1	33.7		56,797
LEA nursery class	%	1.2	65.7	0.3	32.7		94,379
LA day nursery	%	3.3	4.8	2.8	89.1		24,722
Independent							
Nursery school	%	33.1	39.2	4.7	23.0		7,564
Day nursery	%	31.2	21.7	5.3	41.8		25,297
Hall playgroup	%	90.4	8.5	0.3	0.8		454,398
Home playgroup	%	83.4	15.2	0.4	1.0		28,326

proportion than any other type of institution. In contrast, 90% of playgroup children attended 1–4 sessions per week; for the most part this was because the playgroups only operated for this number of sessions.

In LEA nursery schools and classes about two-thirds of all the children attended 5, and one-third 10 sessions a week. More variation was found in the pattern of attendance in independent nursery schools and day nurseries; whereas about a third of the children attended 1–4 sessions in both types of institution, two-fifths of those in independent nursery schools were half-time attenders, and two-fifths in independent day nurseries attended full-time.

The size of institutions

It is customary to express the size of the institution in terms of the number of children who attend. However, because it was common practice to share some places between part-time attenders, the total number of children on the attendance register was usually greater than the number of children present at any one session as shown in Table 2.4. Maintained institutions were larger than those in the independent sector and the two extremes were LEA nursery schools which accommodated an average 50.6 pupils per session and home playgroups with 12.7 per session. Part-time attendance in many LEA nursery schools resulted in the mean number of pupils on the

Table 2.4 *Number of children by type of institution*

Type of institution	Number of children present per session		Number of children on attendance register	
	Mean	Standard deviation	Mean	Standard deviation
Maintained				
LEA nursery school	50.6	18.9	80.2	31.5
LEA nursery class	30.2	11.7	49.4	23.3
LA day nursery	44.9	12.7	48.3	14.2
Independent				
Nursery school	28.0	11.4	41.1	27.9
Day nursery	24.0	12.3	37.5	26.6
Hall playgroup	22.7	6.9	40.1	23.8
Home playgroup	12.7	5.5	23.8	16.7

attendance register rising to 80.2, whereas the smaller proportion of part-time attenders in LA day nurseries meant that the total attendance (48.3) was not much greater than the number present at any one session (44.9). The standard deviations indicate that there was quite considerable variation in the size of institutions particularly among LEA nursery schools (SD = 18.9).

Staffing

The analysis of staffing was complicated by the fact that whilst most maintained institutions opened for 10 sessions a week, the majority of independent/voluntary institutions operated for no more than 5 sessions. Thus the distinction between full-time and part-time staff based on a 10-session week would not be appropriate for institutions which only opened for part of the week. Furthermore, many playgroups do not have staff as such but are run by helpers who work on a rota basis. Thus in some playgroups a very large number of helpers can be involved on a regular basis but any individual helper might be present only once or twice a term. For the purposes of comparison, therefore, we will consider all the staff and helpers who were present in the institution for at least one session per week. These, we suggest, would have been more influential in the day-to-day running of the nursery or playgroup than those who were present less frequently.

Table 2.5 *Number of staff by type of institution*

Type of institution	Number of staff present per session		Number of staff present ≥ 1 session per week	
	Mean	Standard deviation	Mean	Standard deviation
Maintained				
LEA nursery school	7.0	3.0	6.5	4.8
LEA nursery class	3.4	1.6	3.9	2.4
LA day nursery	11.0	3.6	10.4	3.9
Independent				
Nursery school	3.5	2.2	4.7	3.5
Day nursery	4.3	2.7	5.5	3.3
Hall playgroup	3.8	1.4	5.6	4.0
Home playgroup	2.1	1.0	3.0	2.4

The mean number of staff present for at least one session a week varied from a maximum of 10.4 in LA day nurseries to a minimum of 3 in home playgroups (Table 2.5). The number of staff present per session, however, was slightly less on average than this figure (except for LEA nursery schools and LA day nurseries), but still showed LA day nurseries to have had the largest, and home play-groups the smallest, numbers of staff. Differences between the average number of staff present at a session and the average number present at least once a week gave some indication of the degree to which institutions had part-time staff. On this criterion, hall playgroups were shown to be the most likely to have had different helpers present throughout the week. If staff continuity is an important factor in helping young children to settle in a play-group then the succession of different helpers might be a source of anxiety for some children who attend playgroup.

Staff qualifications

In describing the formal qualifications of the staff in preschool institutions we are conscious of the fact that there is more to working with under-fives than can necessarily be acquired in a teacher training or nursery nurses' college or from a playgroup course. The experience of a mother who has successfully brought up her own children can be a very important asset and some women have an intuitive skill in dealing with young children that enables them to achieve far more than others with more qualifications. Such factors, however, are immeasurable in surveys such as ours and we must leave such evaluation to smaller-scale observation studies. Nevertheless, we cannot ignore the importance of training as a source of information and ideas about child development and pedagogic techniques appropriate for children aged under five. It is within this context that we compare and contrast the qualifications of the staff who were present for at least one session per week in the different types of institutions.

The number of staff varied considerably between institutions, thus the comparison of staff qualifications between types of institution was simplified by basing percentages on the total staff within each particular type of institution. Furthermore, many staff had more than one qualification but each person is recorded only once in Table 2.6 by giving priority to the left-hand qualifications in the table.

Table 2.6 *Percentage of all staff with the given qualification by type of institution*

Type of institution		Qualification							N = 100%
		Nursery/Infant teaching	Other teaching	Nursery nursing	Playgroup qualification	SRN	Other	None	
Maintained									
LEA nursery school	%	32.9	3.2	44.0	0.5	1.3	3.8	14.2	4,607
LEA nursery class	%	32.9	5.9	39.0	0.9	1.1	1.8	18.5	7,513
LA day nursery	%	0.8	0.6	70.9	1.0	5.7	3.0	17.9	4,718
Independent									
Nursery school	%	21.8	12.8	13.1	11.5	3.3	4.6	33.0	766
Day nursery	%	5.8	3.7	19.8	19.5	5.2	3.9	42.0	3,414
Hall playgroup	%	4.5	4.8	5.0	35.4	3.2	1.8	45.2	54,148
Home playgroup	%	11.4	9.4	6.5	27.7	4.6	3.3	37.2	3,162

Note: Only main qualifications counted, with hierarchy in given order. Sample is all staff and helpers present in the institution for at least one session per week.

Teaching qualifications were held by more than a third of all the staff in LEA nursery schools and classes and a further 40–45% were trained nursery nurses. In LA day nurseries there were almost no qualified teachers, whereas over 70% had NNEB certificates. Thus the majority of staff in maintained institutions had formal qualifications either in teaching or nursery nursing. In sharp contrast to this, the majority of staff in the independent sector were without these qualifications. The highest proportion of staff with teaching or nursery nursing qualifications was found in independent nursery schools (48%) but only 14% of staff in hall playgroups were teachers or nursery nurses. More than a third of hall playgroup staff had attended playgroup courses as had small proportions of staff in other types of independent institutions. However, the proportion of staff with no relevant qualifications was higher in the independent sector (between 33% and 45%) than in the maintained sector (between 14% and 19%).

Ratio of children to adult

The recommended ratio of children to adults varies according to the age of the children who attend the institution. Nurseries accommodating significant numbers of babies and toddlers need more staff than do institutions taking older children. In 1975 the recommended ratio of children to staff in LA day nurseries was 5 : 1 (reduced to 4 : 1 as from 1985), in LEA nursery schools and classes

Table 2.7   *Child–adult ratio by type of institution*

Type of institution		Children per adult			N = 100%
		≤5	>5 ≤10	>10	
Maintained					
LEA nursery school	%	4.6	92.2	3.2	694
LEA nursery class	%	4.4	59.2	36.4	1,861
LA day nursery	%	84.2	15.4	0.4	493
Independent					
Nursery school	%	6.1	66.1	27.9	165
Day nursery	%	32.1	65.2	2.5	647
Hall playgroup	%	25.8	73.2	0.9	11,287
Home playgroup	%	26.3	72.2	1.5	1,135

it was 10 : 1, and many infant school children were in classes of 30 or more with one teacher, whereas playgroups aimed to keep a ratio of 6 children for every adult. These ratios were clearly reflected in the results of our study in which 92% of LEA nursery schools had child–adult ratios between 6 : 1 and 10 : 1 and 84% of LA day nurseries had ratios not exceeding 5 : 1 (Table 2.7). In LEA nursery classes, however, more than a third exceeded the recommended 10 : 1 ratio which suggests that although these classes were designated nursery classes some of them may have differed little from infant reception classes. A substantial proportion of independent nursery schools (28%) also had child–adult ratios which exceeded 10, although in keeping with other independent institutions, the most frequently occurring ratio was between 6 : 1 and 10 : 1.

Age of children

The only preschool institutions equipped and staffed to accommodate significant numbers of very young children were day nurseries and our figures show that two in five children in LA day nurseries and one in five of those in independent day nurseries were under 3 years old. The majority of children in maintained nursery schools and classes (60% and 66% respectively) were 4 years old. In independent nursery schools and classes there was a more even spread over the 3- to 4-year age range. Thus the average age of children was lowest in LA day nurseries and highest in LEA nursery classes which, again, suggests that some of the latter resembled infant reception classes.

Location of preschool institution

Generally speaking, preschool institutions serve children in the immediate locality. Few mothers want to travel great distances to playgroups or nurseries, particularly if the child is only going to stay for a three-hour session before having to be collected again. Thus the type of neighbourhood in which the institution is located is an important determinant of its social composition.

A special classification of types of neighbourhood was devised for this study which assigned neighbourhoods to the following four broad groups (see also Appendix Table A.11):

1. Poor neighbourhoods

Are characterised by high population density, ill-maintained and multi-occupied housing and low-income families, typical of many inner urban areas.

2. Average neighbourhoods

Are characterised by low-cost, privately-owned areas of housing or council estates.

3. Well-to-do neighbourhoods

Are areas of well-spaced, well-maintained housing where families have above-average incomes.

4. Rural neighbourhoods

Are small country towns and villages.

There was a marked contrast between the geographical locations of maintained and independent institutions. The majority of the former were in poor or average urban neighbourhoods whereas the latter were more often in well-to-do or rural areas (Table 2.8). More than a third of the LA day nurseries were in poor or inner urban neighbourhoods. More than half the independent nursery schools and home playgroups were in well-to-do neighbourhoods, whereas over a third of hall playgroups were in rural areas. This distribution was clearly the outcome of two factors—local authority response to the needs of urban families, and the entrepreneurial initiative of the middle-class parents in response to their own demand for such facilities. Playgroup provision in rural areas was especially important in view of their relative lack of LEA nursery schools and classes.

In most preschool institutions more than three-quarters of the children who attended came from the immediate neighbourhood. The main exception to this was independent day nurseries in 23% of which most children came from outside the local area. This may have been due to employed mothers travelling to the day nursery to leave their children before going on to work. Even so, in 55% of independent day nurseries more than three-quarters of the children lived nearby.

The location of the different types of institution in areas which differed in terms of the social characteristics and needs of the

Table 2.8 *Type of neighbourhood in which institution is located by type of institution*

Type of institution		Poor	Average	Well-to-do	Rural	N = 100%
Maintained						
LEA nursery school	%	17.6	65.1	6.2	11.0	708
LEA nursery class	%	18.6	62.3	7.4	11.7	1,915
LA day nursery	%	34.1	56.0	4.9	5.1	534
Independent						
Nursery school	%	8.3	20.3	51.0	20.3	192
Day nursery	%	11.3	45.6	30.7	12.3	706
Hall playgroup	%	5.7	38.1	20.3	35.9	11,539
Home playgroup	%	2.1	17.0	52.3	28.6	1,222

families living there, inevitably meant that the typical child in a maintained nursery was more likely to come from a poor or working-class background, whereas institutions in the independent or voluntary sector attracted the children of well-to-do or middle-class families. Differences in cognitive development and behavioural adjustment that are associated with social inequality may have meant that the children in maintained institutions were more difficult to manage and to teach than those who attended private nurseries and playgroups located in well-to-do neighbourhoods. This was hypothesised as a potentially significant factor when considering differences in test scores between children who attended different types of preschool institutions (Chapter 8).

Criteria for admission

In addition to the type of neighbourhood in which a preschool institution was located, a policy of giving priority to certain groups of children may have resulted in further social differentiation between types of institution. In institutions where demand for places necessitated the use of a waiting list, which occurred more frequently in the maintained than in the independent sector, a child's position on the list was often influenced by his or her family circumstances. Nearly all LA day nurseries and more than half the LEA nursery schools reported that allocation of places was based on the child's needs, whereas no more than 15% of the independent nursery schools and playgroups used this criterion (Table 2.9). Entry to independent nursery schools and playgroups was, in the majority of cases, determined by the child's position on the waiting list on a first-come-first-served basis. Interestingly, the need to maintain a good 'social balance' in the nursery school, which is often expressed by nursery head teachers as being of some importance, hardly featured as a criterion for admission. Factors most likely to influence an institution's decision to offer a child a place were the child's having been seen as 'socially at risk' or referred by a social worker, health visitor or other professional; 45% of LA day nurseries cited these grounds for admitting a child. Single-parent families were also likely to be given priority in LA day nurseries and LEA nursery schools. Relatively few institutions took account of other types of home circumstances such as poor housing.

Table 2.9 Criteria used for allocation of places by type of institution

Type of institution		Special needs	Waiting list	To maintain balance	Religion or ethnic	Other	Places available	N = 100%
Maintained								
LEA nursery school	%	56.9	38.5	0.3	0.1	1.0	3.3	707
LEA nursery class	%	38.7	50.4	0.2	0.2	0.4	10.2	1,912
LA day nursery	%	95.9	2.8	0	0.2	0.4	0.7	539
Independent								
Nursery school	%	15.3	62.4	0	0.5	1.1	20.6	189
Day nursery	%	27.2	42.6	0.1	0.1	1.1	28.8	698
Hall playgroup	%	12.5	63.8	0.1	0.2	0.1	23.3	11,552
Home playgroup	%	9.8	76.3	0.1	0	0.2	13.6	1,217

Note: Hierarchy of criteria in given order.

Children who are physically or mentally handicapped or present definite behaviour problems may have a special claim to a place in a preschool institution—if only to provide the mother with a respite from the stress of caring for such children. However, such children can create problems in a facility where the staff are not trained to cope with their special needs, therefore it is perhaps not surprising that fewer than 2% of independent institutions mentioned handicap as a factor that influenced the decision whether or not to offer a child a place. In the maintained sector, however, 30% of LA day nurseries and 19% of LEA nursery schools mentioned handicap as an influencing factor. About one in four playgroups and independent nurseries said that they could not always offer a place to a child with behaviour problems; this compared with only 6% of LEA nursery schools and 2% of LA day nurseries.

Thus a very consistent pattern emerged in which children with a wide range of difficulties were likely to be given priority by LA day nurseries and to a slightly lesser extent by LEA nursery schools. Institutions in the independent sector, however, were far less likely to make special provision for children with problems, and an interesting finding was that LEA nursery classes did not closely follow the pattern of LEA nursery schools as might be expected. Far fewer LEA nursery classes gave priority to children with special needs, handicapped children or children with behaviour problems. Thus the admissions policy in LEA nursery classes appeared less orientated to meeting the needs of specific social groups than in maintained nursery schools or day nurseries. In the next section we consider how the effects of these policies were reflected in the characteristics of the children who attended the institutions.

Social composition of preschool institutions

The institutions were asked to estimate the proportion of children on the attendance register who were from homes presenting some difficulty; this included overcrowding, presence of only one parent, marital difficulties, family ill-health, poor standard of child care, or similar problems. There was a marked contrast between the maintained and independent sectors in the proportion of children living in situations of these kinds (Table 2.10). More than half of the independent day nurseries, and over three-quarters of all other

Table 2.10 *Proportion of children from difficult homes by type of institution*

Type of institution		Proportion of children from difficult homes					
		None	<¼	¼ to ½	½ to ¾	>¾	N = 100%
Maintained							
LEA nursery school	%	23.8	40.4	20.8	8.1	4.2	694
LEA nursery class	%	32.6	33.8	18.1	9.1	3.0	1,865
LA day nursery	%	2.2	1.3	2.6	13.4	79.6	539
Independent							
Nursery school	%	75.4	11.8	2.6	0.5	0.5	177
Day nursery	%	52.1	26.4	7.7	3.4	3.5	663
Hall playgroup	%	75.4	11.5	1.8	0.6	0.8	10,488
Home playgroup	%	86.8	7.3	0.8	0.3	0.2	1,176

Note: This included homes with some difficulty such as overcrowding, only one parent, marital difficulties, family ill-health, poor standard of child care, etc.

types of independent institutions reported that they had no children from homes experiencing such difficulties. In contrast, few LEA schools and practically no LA day nurseries could say that none of their children was from a difficult home; in a third of all LEA nursery schools and classes at least one child in four was from a home experiencing social or family problems, and in 80% of LA day nurseries at least three-quarters of the children were subject to such problems.

A similar picture emerged from the statistics describing the proportion of children who had been referred to the institution by a social worker, health visitor or other professional. In the majority of independent institutions no children had been referred, but 85% of LEA nursery schools had at least one referred child, as did more than half the LEA nursery classes; in the majority of LA day nurseries more than 30% of the children were referred. Children who were mentally or physically handicapped or who had other health or developmental problems were also more likely to be found in LA day nurseries or LEA nursery schools than in independent nurseries or playgroups.

The importance of all-day and all-year-round care for children of employed mothers was demonstrated by the high proportion of such children in most LA and independent day nurseries. However, despite their shorter hours of opening, the majority of LEA nursery schools and classes also had significant numbers of children whose mothers went out to work, whereas the majority of playgroups and independent nursery schools had relatively few children of employed mothers. These differences can be attributed mainly to the fact that most playgroups did not open for more than four or five sessions a week, and no more than three hours a day, which is inadequate for the needs of most employed mothers.

It is evident from these results that preschool institutions in the maintained sector were more likely than independent institutions to take children who were socially disadvantaged or handicapped. To summarise and to provide an indication of the extent to which some institutions needed to cope with multiple problems, an index was compiled based on the six items given in Table 2.11. A Problem Index score was obtained by totalling the weights for individual items. Since the individual items in this index identified groups with a high degree of disadvantage, only institutions serving substantial numbers of children with problems achieved a score of 3 or more;

Table 2.11   *Problem index*

Item	Weight
Institution sited in poor neighbourhood and more than half of the children attending come from this neighbourhood	1
More than 10% of children attending the institution referred by social worker, health visitor, etc.	1
More than 10% of children attending the institution have a handicap	1
More than 10% of children attending the institution speak little or no English	1
More than 10% of children attending the institution have health, behaviour, speech, or other developmental problems	1
More than half the children attending the institution come from homes where there are difficulties	1

Note: Problem Index score = sum of scores for each item. Range = 0 to 6.

indeed only 3.8% of the whole sample scored at this level, whereas 75% scored zero.

Very large differences were found between types of institutions in terms of their Problem Index score (Table 2.12). As our previous discussion might lead us to expect, maintained institutions were more likely to accommodate children with problems than were independent institutions and the findings for LA day nurseries were suggestive of the extreme difficulties many of them were facing. As many as 43% of LA day nurseries had scores of 3 or more on the Index, the next highest percentage was 11% of LEA nursery schools and only 1% of hall playgroups. One LA day nursery actually scored the maximum of 6 which meant that every one of the descriptions given in Table 2.11 applied to that institution. At the other end of the scale only 4% of LA day nurseries scored zero on the Problem Index compared with as many as 83% of hall playgroups.

The general picture drawn from these findings is that LA day nurseries had large proportions of children who were referred by a professional worker, or who had a troubled home background, or suffered some form of handicap or developmental delay, or a multiplicity of such problems. LEA nursery schools also had numbers of such children, whereas they were slightly less frequent

Table 2.12 *Problem index by type of institution*

Type of institution		Problem index score				N = 100%
		0	1	2	≥3	
Maintained						
LEA nursery school	%	44.2	28.8	15.8	11.2	713
LEA nursery class	%	55.7	24.4	12.6	7.2	1,932
LA day nursery	%	3.5	12.9	41.0	42.6	544
Independent						
Nursery school	%	79.5	15.9	3.1	1.5	195
Day nursery	%	63.2	23.2	10.3	3.4	712
Hall playgroup	%	83.4	12.1	3.2	1.4	11,620
Home playgroup	%	81.3	15.2	3.0	0.5	1,232

in LEA nursery classes. The independent sector in contrast was less likely to take socially disadvantaged or handicapped children in all its facilities. We have argued that this variation was partly a consequence of where institutions were located and of admissions policies. Also the necessity for independent institutions to charge fees would have been a further deterrent to families facing financial hardship, whereas LEA and LA maintained institutions would clearly give priority to those who could not afford to pay fees. All these factors resulted in each type of institution having a different social composition, and this was likely to have an important effect on the way a child's experience in the nursery or playgroup influenced her behaviour and cognitive development.

Ethnic minorities

The two main ethnic minority groups in Britain are those of Afro-Caribbean, and Indian or Pakistani origin. These groups differ from the European population in Britain in important social, cultural and religious ways and also suffer the effects of racial prejudice in its many guises (Osborn and Butler, 1985). During the early years, the use of different languages or dialects can be a further source of difficulty for the child in her transition from home to infant school. Therefore the preschool nursery or playgroup could provide the opportunity for children to make contact with and get to understand the culture of children from different social and ethnic origins.

Of all the preschool institutions, LA day nurseries had the greatest proportion of ethnic minority children (Table 2.13), with 11% of all children in this type of facility being Afro-Caribbean and 2.5% Indian/Pakistani. In LEA nursery schools and classes, Indian/Pakistani children made up 5% of all those attending and Afro-Caribbean 2%. Thus in the maintained sector, Afro-Caribbeans favoured day nurseries and Indian/Pakistanis nursery schools or classes.

Very few ethnic minority children attended independent nursery schools or playgroups. Only 3% of all the children in independent nursery schools and fewer than 2% of those in playgroups were of Indian/Pakistani or Afro-Caribbean origin. However, these minority groups comprised 7% of all the children in independent day nurseries. Our evidence suggested that the ethnic minority children

Table 2.13 *Ethnic origins of children attending preschool institutions*

Type of institution		European (UK)	European (not UK)	Indian/ Pakistani	Afro- Caribbean	Other or mixed	N = 100%
Maintained							
LEA nursery school	%	90.9	0.9	5.0	1.9	1.3	57,163
LEA nursery class	%	90.6	0.8	5.1	2.2	1.3	95,503
LA day nursery	%	81.0	1.1	2.5	11.2	4.2	26,253
Independent							
Nursery school	%	92.8	1.9	1.9	1.4	2.1	8,005
Day nursery	%	87.5	2.4	4.3	3.0	2.7	26,673
Hall playgroup	%	96.8	0.5	1.2	0.7	0.8	466,124
Home playgroup	%	97.2	0.7	0.7	0.2	1.1	29,329

were not evenly distributed throughout the institutions. As many as 68% of hall playgroups and 75% of home playgroups did not include a single child from an ethnic minority family. Only 5% and 2% respectively of these institutions included more than one Afro-Caribbean or Asian child in ten on their registers. In contrast, nearly a quarter of independent day nurseries and a third of LA day nurseries had over 10% from these ethnic groups, and as few as 36% and 28% respectively were attended only by Europeans. Nearly half the LEA nursery classes had no minority group children compared with 38% of LEA nursery schools; this again suggests that LEA nursery schools were more responsive than LEA nursery classes to groups that might be more in need of nursery education.

Closely allied to the question of ethnic minority children in preschool institutions is the proportion of children who speak little or no English. As many as 45% of LEA nursery schools had at least one child who spoke little or no English, although only 12% had more than one non-English-speaker in ten. Home playgroups were the least likely to have children who could not speak English.

Curriculum

Creating summary variables from the items in the Nursery/Playgroup questionnaire which describe the equipment and activities available in the preschool settings posed certain methodological and conceptual problems. Factor analysis, as one possibility, was inappropriate in this case as certain items tended to correlate because they were common features in particular types of institution rather than because they shared a common educational principle. We decided, therefore, to attempt to group items together on the basis of their hypothesised educational content.

To achieve this we consulted the literature on preschool curricula, and also spent some time with nursery school teachers, some of whom originally helped to design the questionnaire, trying to arrive at a consensus concerning the primary educational purposes of the various activities and items of equipment available. It became apparent that a consensus or ideal solution could never be achieved mainly because so much of what goes on in the nursery or playgroup is multi-purpose. Sand-play, for example, can be a medium for creative activity, cognitive development, pre-mathematics and, in conjunction with a member of staff, language skills. The same applies to most of the other activities and equipment in the pre-school setting.

Nevertheless, we felt that certain themes could usefully be explored by combining groups of items in scales. These are described in Tables 2.14 to 2.17. Scale scores were achieved by totalling the weights assigned to categories of the items comprising the scales. The ranges of the scales were thus determined by the number of items in the scale and the number of categories in the

Table 2.14   *Skills scale*

Items	Scoring—availability			
	Not available at all	Used some sessions	Used most sessions	Used every session
Equipment				
Clay and dough, etc.	0	1	2	3
Construction toys e.g. Lego	0	1	2	3
Workbench and tools	0	1	2	3
Musical instruments of any sort which children use themselves	0	1	2	3
Facilities for children to do real cooking	0	1	2	3

	Scoring—frequency			
	Never or hardly ever	Some sessions	Most sessions	Every session
Activities				
Painting, crayoning, etc.	0	1	2	3
Cutting and pasting	0	1	2	3
Junk modelling	0	1	2	3
Matching, sorting, ordering, grouping activities	0	1	2	3
Doing puzzles	0	1	2	3
Singing, i.e. children themselves singing	0	1	2	3

Note: Skills score = sum of scores for each item. Range = 0 to 33.

Table 2.15 *Language scale*

Items	Scoring—availability			
	Not available at all	Used some sessions	Used most sessions	Used every session
Equipment				
Book corner	0	1	2	3
Home corner, Wendy house	0	1	2	3
Dolls and accessories, e.g. clothes, prams, beds, etc.	0	1	2	3

	Scoring—frequency			
	Never or hardly ever	Some sessions	Most sessions	Every session
Activities				
Fantasy/dramatic play, e.g. dressing up and pretending	0	1	2	3
Finger plays	0	1	2	3
Stories read or told to whole group	0	1	2	3
Discussion with whole group	0	1	2	3
Talking about pictures	0	1	2	3
Problem-solving, e.g. where children are encouraged to describe or explain simple events	0	1	2	3

Treatment of language in the institution	Score
No special or conscious emphasis is given to language development, except through normal interaction with staff	0
Staff make special efforts to introduce new words and/or concepts to children	1
Special language schemes or equipment are used, e.g. Peabody Language Kit, Schools Council Booklets, etc., to develop language in some or all children	2

Note: Language score = sum of scores for each item. Range = 0 to 29.

Table 2.16 *Finding-out scale*

Items	Scoring—availability			
	Not available at all	Used some sessions	Used most sessions	Used every session
Equipment				
Sand and sand equipment	0	1	2	3
Water-tray and water equipment	0	1	2	3
	Not available	Available		
Pets, e.g. fish, rabbit, stick insects, etc.	0	1		
Interest/discovery table or display prepared mainly by staff	0	1		

Note: Finding-out score = sum of scores for each item. Range = 0 to 8.

Table 2.17 *Gross motor scale*

Items	Scoring—availability			
	Not available at all	Used some sessions	Used most sessions	Used every session
Equipment				
Climbing apparatus, slide, etc.	0	1	2	3
Tricycles, scooters, trucks, etc.	0	1	2	3
	Scoring—frequency			
	Never or hardly ever	Some sessions	Most sessions	Every session
Activities				
Dance or movement to music	0	1	2	3
Organised physical games	0	1	2	3
Going for walks	0	1	2	3

Note: Gross motor score = sum of scores for each item. Range = 0 to 15.

Table 2.18 *Median scores on curriculum scales for different preschool institutions*

Type of institution		Scale				N
		Skills	Language	Finding-out	Gross motor	
Maintained						
LEA nursery school	Median	26.1	24.1	7.3	8.0	713
	(Range)	(11–33)	(11–29)	(3–8)	(2–15)	
LEA nursery class	Median	23.2	23.7	7.1	7.2	1,932
	(Range)	(7–33)	(7–29)	(0–8)	(2–15)	
LA day nursery	Median	21.6	20.8	6.6	8.3	544
	(Range)	(6–33)	(5–28)	(0–8)	(2–15)	
Independent						
Nursery school	Median	20.3	19.9	4.4	6.8	195
	(Range)	(4–33)	(3–29)	(0–8)	(0–15)	
Day nursery	Median	18.4	19.5	4.0	7.8	712
	(Range)	(1–33)	(2–28)	(0–8)	(0–15)	
Hall playgroup	Median	20.2	20.1	3.8	7.1	11,620
	(Range)	(0–33)	(0–29)	(0–8)	(0–15)	
Home playgroup	Median	19.7	20.5	3.7	6.7	1,232
	(Range)	(0–33)	(0–29)	(0–8)	(0–15)	

items, which inevitably resulted in greater variation in some scales than in others.

The median scores and ranges were computed for the seven types of institution (Table 2.18). The main contrast was between LEA nursery schools and classes, and institutions in the independent sector. The scores suggest greater emphasis on 'skills', 'language' and 'finding out' in the former. Little difference was found between LEA nursery schools and classes on these curriculum dimensions. However, the ranges show that there was also substantial variation *within* the different types of institution in terms of these scales.

In presenting these results we recognise the limitations of a questionnaire approach to the assessment of practice in the pre-school institution compared with direct observational methods. The results are best interpreted as representing the general disposition of the nursery or playgroup towards these various types of activity, and the implications of this for the later ability of children who attended institutions with differing approaches to the curriculum are dis-cussed in Chapter 8.

Conclusions

Services for the education and day care of children under 5 years of age are provided in Britain by local authorities and by independent and voluntary agencies. In 1975, when our surveys were carried out, the total number of places occupied by under-fives in main-tained and independent preschool institutions was sufficient for no more than 40% of the population of children aged 3 to 4 years. The next ten years to 1985 saw a considerable increase in the number of children attending part-time LEA nursery classes and there was also a steady increase in the number of playgroup and LA day nursery places. These trends resulted in a rise in the level of provision to the equivalent of 64% of 3- to 4-year-olds. The proportion of children under 5 in infant reception classes also increased from 18% in 1975 to 20% in 1985.

A Nursery/Playgroup survey designed to reach every preschool institution in Britain was carried out in 1975. The object of this survey was, firstly, to provide descriptions of the main character-istics of the various types of preschool facility, and secondly, to obtain information about the particular institutions attended by children in the 1970 British birth cohort which may help to explain variations in their subsequent ability and behaviour (see Chapter 8).

Seven main types of preschool facility were identified and are described below. These descriptions are not comprehensive and only the features which especially distinguish one type of institution from another are mentioned.

1. LEA nursery schools

Open 10 sessions a week for 40 weeks a year in self-contained premises with children attending 5 or 10 sessions a week. They tended to be large, taking on average 51 children in a session. Staff had teaching or nursery nursing training. Fewer than 1% of the children were under 3 years of age and 60% were 4 years old. Three-quarters were attended by children from families experiencing difficulties and 85% contained at least one child who had been referred by a social worker, health visitor or other professional. More than half were attended by ethnic minority children.

2. LEA nursery classes

Hours of opening and patterns of attendance were the same as for LEA nursery schools but they were located in primary schools attended by school age children and were attended on average by 30 children per session. Although they accommodated fairly high proportions of disadvantaged children, these were less in evidence than in LEA nursery schools; for example, two-thirds were attended by children from difficult homes, and 55% contained children who had been referred.

3. LA day nurseries

Open 10 sessions a week for 52 weeks a year in self-contained premises with the majority of children attending 10 sessions a week. They tended to be large, taking on average 45 children, and were staffed by nursery nurses at a ratio of 5 children to each adult. 42% of all the children were under 3 years of age and only 25% were 4 years old. Priority was given to socially disadvantaged children as 96% of LA day nurseries used 'special needs' as their criterion for admission and 34% were located in poor, inner urban neighbourhoods. This resulted in a very high proportion of children coming from socially disadvantaged backgrounds; in 93% of LA day nurseries more than half the children were from difficult homes, in 84% at least one child had been referred, and 14% of all the children were from ethnic minorities.

4. Independent nursery schools

Open 5 or 10 sessions a week for 38 weeks a year, often in shared premises with children attending 5 or 10 sessions a week. They tended to be small, taking on average 28 children in a session. 48% of the staff had teaching or nursing qualifications but 33% had no relevant qualification. 7% of the children were under 3 and 45% were 4 years old. Over half these schools were located in well-to-do neighbourhoods, three-quarters had no children from difficult homes and only 3% of the children were from ethnic minorities.

5. Independent day nurseries

Open 10 sessions a week for 50 weeks a year, often in shared premises with children attending 5 or 10 sessions a week. They tended to be small, taking on average 24 children in a session. One in five of the staff was a trained nursery nurse but 42% had no formal qualifications. One in five of all the children was under 3 and 37% were 4 years old. 48% had at least one child from a difficult home background. As many as 47% contained children who had been referred, and 7% of all the children were from ethnic minority families.

6. Hall playgroups

Open 1 to 4 sessions a week for 39 weeks a year in church or community halls with children attending 1 to 4 sessions a week. They tended to be small, taking on average 23 children in a session. More than half the children were under 4 years old and as many as 7% were younger than three. 35% of the helpers had attended playgroup courses but 45% had no relevant qualifications. 36% of hall playgroups were located in rural areas and 38% in average urban areas. Three-quarters had no children from difficult homes and only 23% had one or more children from an ethnic minority family.

7. Home playgroups

Tended to open 5 sessions a week for 38 weeks a year in private houses with children attending 1 to 4 sessions a week. They were the smallest of all the types of institutions in the study, taking on average only 13 children in a session. Distribution of children's ages was the same as for hall playgroups and independent nursery schools. 27% of the staff had teaching or nursery nursing qualifications, 28% had attended playgroup courses and 37% had no qualifications. Only 2% were located in poor neighbourhoods and 52% were in well-to-do areas. They were the least likely of any type of institution to be attended by socially disadvantaged children. 87% had no children from difficult homes, 72% had no children who had been referred and only 1% of all the children who attended was from an ethnic minority family.

These profiles outline some of the main points of similarity and difference between the seven main types of preschool institutions we have defined. In Chapter 8 we discuss the extent to which such features contribute to the differences in children's test performances which, in Chapter 4, are attributed to their attendance at the various types of preschool institution.

Apart from the basic structural differences between preschool institutions—their hours of opening, patterns of attendance and staffing—the most fundamental contrasts shown in this chapter were in the social and family background of the children who attended. Broadly speaking, maintained institutions accommodated larger proportions of children from families experiencing difficulties such as poor housing, marital problems and other stressful situations, but in independent nurseries and playgroups such problems were far less frequent. The social composition of a preschool institution could have important implications for the way it functions and how successful it might be in enhancing children's cognitive development. Achieving educational goals in a group containing a high proportion of children with behaviour problems presents more of a challenge to those in charge than it does in a group consisting of bright children who are eager to cooperate with whatever activities are offered. We suggest that the demands placed on LEA nursery schools and classes and LA day nurseries, which accommodate relatively high proportions of children from socially disadvantaged families, require teaching and management skills only found in appropriately trained staff. Institutions in the independent sector also require capable staff who can stimulate and interest young children in a variety of ways, but since there are relatively few children with special problems in the average independent institution, there is less need for fully trained professional staff.

What we are suggesting is that the social background of the children who attend and the staffing of institutions in the maintained and independent sectors result in the educational processes within these two sectors being different in subtle ways that we are unable to show from our survey methodology. However, observational studies have highlighted differences in practice and child response between nursery schools and playgroups which could in part be due to the kind of factors to which we have drawn attention (Jowett and Sylva, 1986). Thus the point that we make from this is that the processes by which maintained institutions achieve their educational goals are likely to be quite different from those practised in independent institutions. This has important implications for the interpretation of the results described in subsequent chapters.

3

Social variation in utilisation of preschool education and day care services

In Chapter 2 we described the variety and extent of preschool provision in Britain and some of the defining characteristics of the most widely available types of institution. In doing so we adopted the conventional method of describing levels of provision as the number of places available expressed as a proportion of the population of 3- and 4-year-olds in Britain. When discussing *utilisation* of services in contrast with *provision* it is important to recognise that this use of the 3- and 4-year-old population as a base for percentaging is quite arbitrary, as it does not reflect the true age distribution of children in preschool institutions. In addition, children start their infant education at different ages and this also has implications for the age at which a child starts attending a preschool placement. The decision to offer part-time as against full-time preschool places also effectively increases the absolute numbers of children who can attend a facility and there is more scope for this type of variability in nursery schools and classes, which typically function for 10 sessions a week, than in playgroups which generally operate for no more than 5 sessions per week. Finally, demand for preschool services is affected by the costs to parents both directly through the charges made by independent and voluntary schools and playgroups, and indirectly because of the time and expense involved in transporting the child to and from the facility. Such costs are balanced against the parents' perception of the value of preschool education for their child and also for themselves if such attendance provides a brief respite from the demanding task of child care.

To summarise, utilisation of preschool services depends on the level of provision of full- or part-time places, the age-groups that can attend, age at infant school entry and the demand for such services on the part of the parents of under-fives. Obtaining estimates of rates of utilisation of preschool services is, therefore, a more complex procedure than is involved in estimating levels of provision. As the first follow-up survey of the children in the 1970 birth cohort took place at about the time of their fifth birthday, which is the age of statutory school entry in Britain, it provided an excellent opportunity for recording their preschool educational and day care experience and thereby obtaining a reliable indication of the level of utilisation of preschool services at that time.

The first important finding was that the age at which these children started attending infant school varied by more than a year even though they were all born in the same week and were, therefore, statutorily required to start school at the same time. The cumulative rate of entry to infant reception classes is shown in Figure 3.1 where it can be seen that 35% of the sample had started infant school by October 1974 which was the beginning of the school year following their fourth birthday in April 1974. A further 32% had started school by January 1975 (Spring term) and another 26% by April 1975 (Summer term). Thus a total of 93% of this sample had entered infant school by the time they were five. The balance started at the beginning of the next school year.

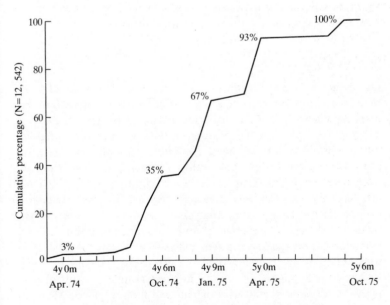

FIG. 3.1. Pattern of infant school entry—cumulative percentage

There was substantial regional variation in the age at school entry, with Wales and the North and North West regions of England having the highest proportion of early entrants, whereas in Scotland fewer than 4% had started school before their fifth birthday (Osborn *et al.*, 1984, p. 97).

It is important to note that the pattern of school entry would be different for children born at other times of the year. The majority of children born during the Summer or the Autumn term are likely to start school in October at the beginning of the school year. This tendency for Summer-born children to start school after their fifth birthday can result in their having as much as a year less primary education than Autumn-born children (Palmer, 1971).

This variation in age at infant school entry created complications when developing our classification of preschool experience in the cohort because at any one age point there were children who had not yet begun their preschool education whilst others had left preschool and were already in the infant reception class. Fortunately this situation had been anticipated and questions were designed that would provide a comprehensive record of the child's preschool experience up to the time of entry to infant school. The details of the child's preschool experience were provided by his mother in a home interview carried out by a health visitor.

The preschool classification

Our preschool classification was based on the last preschool placement the child had attended prior to entering infant school. The resulting classification did not refer to any particular age because, as we have explained, the children in the cohort started attending infant schools at different ages. The implication of these age variations for children's cognitive development and behaviour are, however, investigated in Chapter 7. A few children (under 1%) had attended two institutions concurrently and it was decided to exclude these cases from analyses examining the associations between preschool experience and subsequent attainment and behaviour. For the descriptive analyses in the present chapter, however, they were assigned to the preschool category that they had attended longest or for the greatest number of sessions per week. A substantial minority of children had attended other preschool institutions prior to the most recent one and the implications of this, also, are discussed in Chapter 7.

To verify the accuracy of the mother's report on the type of preschool institution the child had attended, a comparison was made between the designation according to the mother and that decided from the characteristics of the preschool institution itself for all those cases that were matched with an institution in the Nursery/Playgroup survey described in Chapter 2. (Complete details of the procedures and results of the matching exercise are given in the Appendix). This showed that although the distinction between the maintained and independent institutions from the mother's report was highly reliable, mothers were often inaccurate when distinguishing between nursery schools and classes and day nurseries, and also between private nurseries and playgroups. Thus estimates of the proportions of children who attended different

Table 3.1   *Main preschool placement (mother's report)*

	Estimated %	Actual %	N
No preschool education or care		28.6	3,715
Maintained			
LEA nursery school	7.1		
LEA nursery class	12.1		
LA day nursery	1.3		
All maintained		20.4	2,652
Independent			
Nursery school	0.6		
Day nursery	2.2		
Hall playgroup	45.2		
Home playgroup	2.6		
All independent		50.5	6,555
Special nursery or group for handicapped children		0.4	49
Other		0.1	12
ALL		100.0	12,983
No information			152
TOTAL SAMPLE			13,135

Note: The estimated percentages are based on the proportions obtained within the maintained and independent sectors for the matched subsample.

types of preschool institution were obtained by extrapolating from the proportions calculated from the matched subsample.

Table 3.1 shows that half the children had attended independent nurseries and playgroups, one in five had attended a LEA nursery school/class or LA day nursery and 29% had no preschool experience as such. It was estimated that 7% and 12% respectively had attended LEA nursery schools and nursery classes and only 1.3% LA day nurseries. For nearly half (45%) of this sample of 5-year-olds in 1975, hall playgroup was the main preschool experience and only small proportions of children had attended other types of independent institutions. Thus in the discussion presented below in which utilisation of maintained and independent types of provision is described, the main institutions involved are LEA nursery schools and classes and hall-based playgroups.

Of the 49 children said to be attending special institutions for handicapped children, only 5 were actually matched with such institutions. 'Other' types of institution attended by 12 children included Sunday schools and small informal groups. These 61 children were excluded from further analysis for lack of adequate information about the groups they attended.

Infant classes as a form of preschool provision

It is appropriate at this point to say something about under-fives in infant reception classes. The statistics of educational provision presented in Chapter 2 showed that in 1985 there were almost as many under-fives in infant classes as in designated nursery schools or classes. Thus early entry into infant school might be regarded as an alternative to the designated forms of preschool provision. It is certainly the case that some education authorities have adopted a policy of accommodating a high proportion of under-fives in infant classes rather than developing nursery education. This raises the question of whether infant reception classes can provide an educational experience comparable with that of nursery schools and classes in which staff are appropriately qualified and curricula are designed specifically for under-fives.

Lady Plowden in her speech as retiring president of the Preschool Playgroups Association in 1982, held strongly to the view that 4-year-olds should not be routinely admitted to infant reception classes;

"I deplore the present practice of beheading nursery schools and play-groups by sending the 4-year-olds into the reception class of the infant school, so as to fill empty spaces and no doubt keep the numbers up in the school. The criterion for sending a small child into school should be whether he or she is ready for it—the majority of 4-year-olds are simply 4-year-olds and are better off as leaders, gaining a feeling of responsibility from being the big ones, with the 3-year-olds, than in striving to achieve the same skills as children who have lived a year or more longer than they have. At that stage a year is a very long time."

One suspects that this is not a view that is shared by the majority of parents with 4-year-olds or by educational authorities who are attempting to meet the demand for educational places for under-fives with limited financial resources at their disposal. The question we are addressing, however, is whether early entry into infant classes is as effective in educational terms as attendance at nursery schools and nursery classes.

More than 40% of the children in the CHES (Child Health and Education Study) cohort with no designated preschool experience had started attending infant school before the age of $4\frac{1}{2}$ and it would be possible to provide a separate category for this group in the preschool classification; indeed, this approach has been adopted in previous CHES publications (Osborn *et al.*, 1984). Such a procedure in the present book, however, would not be appropriate because more than 30% of the children who *had* some form of preschool placement also started infant school before $4\frac{1}{2}$. Thus age at infant school entry is an equally important consideration for those who had attended preschool institutions as for those who had not.

It is for this reason, then, that infant classes cannot appear as a separate category in our preschool classification. In Chapter 7, however, the effect of early entry to infant school on children's ability and behaviour is analysed as an independent factor.

Sources of variation in utilisation of preschool education and day care facilities

In order to show important social differences underlying the pattern of utilisation of preschool education and day care services, a comparison was made between the three main groups of children who had attended maintained, independent or no preschool institutions. This analysis is restricted to these three broad categories because, as we have explained, the mother's report was not sufficiently reliable with respect to the particular type of institution her child had attended and, as will be seen, the percentages quoted must be based on the whole cohort rather than the sub-sample of cases whose preschool experience had been verified by matching with the Nursery/Playgroup survey.

The kinds of factors we hypothesised as potentially influencing the type of preschool experience a child has are grouped under four broad headings in Tables 3.2 to 3.5. These are social/geographical factors, family factors, personal factors and maternal factors.

Social/geographical factors

The conventional measure of the socio-economic position of a family is the father's occupation, classified according to a standard scheme such as that used for the census of population (OPCS, 1980). We have classified fathers' occupations using the OPCS social class classification which provides six occupational groups (Table 3.2a). This showed large social class differences in patterns of preschool utilisation with 76% of children from social class I homes (professional fathers) compared with only 29% of those from social class V homes (unskilled manual workers) attending independent (including voluntary) preschool institutions. A trend in the opposite direction was found between children who attended maintained institutions which partly counteracted the inequality in the independent sector. Nevertheless, as many as 44% of the children from social class V homes had no preschool experience compared with only 10% of those from social class I homes.

One of the disadvantages of occupational class as an index of social position is that families with no male head or where the father is unemployed have no occupational information on which their social class can validly be based. Prior occupations or mother's occupation cannot be regarded as equivalent to father's occupation for the purpose of social grading (Osborn and Morris, 1979) and this results in important social groups, such as single-parent families, being excluded from all analyses which include social class as a variable. To overcome these problems and also to provide a more sensitive index of socio-economic position, a composite Social Index has been developed which is a key variable in this study. The Social Index is comprised of 7 items hypothesised as being indicative of a single underlying socio-economic dimension. These items are: father's occupation; highest educational qualification of either (or the only) parent; housing tenure; type of accommodation; persons-per-room ratio; car ownership and telephone availability. The items are scored such that when totalled they give a distribution having a mean of 50 and standard deviation of 10. (Full details are given in the Appendix.) Families with higher than average Social Index scores are relatively advantaged whereas those with low scores are relatively disadvantaged in terms of the hypothesised socio-economic dimension. This method has been shown to provide a more sensitive measure of socio-economic position than the conventional social class based only on the father's occupation (Osborn and Morris, 1979; Osborn, 1987).

A further advantage of the Social Index is that it provides a normally distributed score having a range from 19 to 73 and can thus be used to advantage as a covariate in analyses of variance and regression which is its main function in the major part of this study. For our present purpose, however, the Social Index has been grouped into 5 categories as in Table 3.2b so that it can be cross-tabulated with the variable describing the child's preschool experience. This grouped version of the Social Index divides the children in the sample into 5 categories: most disadvantaged (9.1%), disadvantaged (20.4%), average (39.2%), advantaged (20.1%) and most advantaged (11.3%).

There was a marked trend in the proportion of children who attended independent nurseries and playgroups from one in five of the most disadvantaged to almost four in five of the most advantaged Social Index groups. There was a reverse trend amongst those who went to maintained nurseries from one third of the most disadvantaged children to little more than one in ten of the most advantaged children. Although the maintained sector accommodated relatively more socially disadvantaged children, it could not compensate for the considerable imbalance in the independent sector. Thus as many as 46% of the most disadvantaged and 43% of the disadvantaged Social Index group children had no preschool education or day care experience compared with only 10% of the most advantaged children. The Social Index showed a larger degree of inequality in utilisation of preschool services than did the social class classification based only on father's occupation despite the substantially larger numbers of cases in the most advantaged and

Table 3.2 Preschool experience by five-year social/geographical factors

Five-year social/ geographical factors		Preschool experience			
		None	Maintained	Independent	N = 100%
(a) Father's occupation					
Social Class I	%	9.8	14.6	75.6	837
II	%	19.7	14.4	66.0	2,380
III non-manual	%	19.5	17.0	63.5	1,057
III manual	%	32.5	21.3	46.2	5,611
IV	%	37.3	23.3	39.4	1,584
V	%	43.7	77.7	28.6	588
(b) Social Index group					
Most advantaged	%	10.1	11.3	78.6	1,448
Advantaged	%	16.3	13.7	70.0	2,579
Average	%	29.2	20.3	50.5	4,995
Disadvantaged	%	42.7	26.5	30.8	2,557
Most disadvantaged	%	46.1	33.4	20.4	1,140
(c) Type of neighbourhood					
Poor	%	39.8	35.8	24.4	1,005
Average	%	33.8	24.9	41.3	6,190
Well-to-do	%	15.3	15.1	69.6	2,928
Rural	%	27.3	8.9	63.8	2,364

(d) Region of the country				
North	%	41.9	22.4	35.7	793
Yorkshire & Humberside	%	33.5	25.8	40.7	1,256
North-West	%	33.5	21.9	44.6	1,703
East Midlands	%	30.5	17.7	51.8	876
East Anglia	%	31.5	20.1	48.4	1,395
South-East	%	19.6	18.7	61.7	3,546
South-West	%	23.2	8.0	68.9	967
Wales	%	38.8	27.0	34.2	732
Scotland	%	28.3	27.0	44.7	1,067
(e) Household moves					
None	%	28.3	19.6	52.1	5,497
One	%	27.8	20.7	51.5	4,464
Two	%	30.1	19.7	50.1	1,428
Three	%	30.7	21.6	47.7	742
Four or more	%	35.4	22.7	41.9	616

Note: All associations in this table are significant at the $p < .0005$ level.

most disadvantaged categories of the Social Index compared with social classes I and V.

We have shown in Chapter 2 that maintained institutions were more likely to be located in poor urban neighbourhoods than were independent institutions whereas the latter tended to be more frequent in well-to-do or rural areas. It was not surprising, therefore, to find large differences between children in the type of pre-school experience they had depending on the type of neighbourhood in which they lived (Table 3.2c). Less than a quarter of the children who lived in poor urban neighbourhoods attended independent institutions compared with 70% and 64% of those in well-to-do and rural neighbourhoods. The reverse trend occurred in the proportions of children who attended maintained institutions. The net result, however, was that 40% of those in poor neighbourhoods had no preschool experience compared with only 15% of the children in well-to-do neighbourhoods. The lack of maintained provision in rural areas resulted in as many as 27% of these children having no preschool experience notwithstanding the relatively high levels of independent, particularly playgroup, provision in these areas.

Variation in the social, demographic and economic profiles of different regions of England, Scotland and Wales can create different patterns of demand for preschool services. The provision of preschool facilities also varies between local authorities according to the availability of resources and the policies and priorities adopted by education and social services departments. Such factors lead to regional variation in the rates of attendance at preschool institutions (Table 3.2d).

The proportion of English children attending independent nurseries and playgroups was highest in the South West of England (69%) and declined to the lowest levels in the North region (36%). The proportion in maintained institutions followed an opposite trend from north to south in England with a maximum in Yorkshire and Humberside (26%) and a minimum in the South West (8%). In the North region, however, where there was, and still is, widespread poverty, as many as 42% of the children had no preschool experience. In this region, however, many Local Education Authorities had a policy of early admission to infant reception classes so that only 1 per cent of their children had no preschool education or care whatsoever (Osborn *et al.*, 1984, p. 324).

Children in the South East region were the least likely to have had no preschool experience (20%). A comparison between England, Scotland and Wales showed more children attending maintained institutions in Wales and Scotland than in England where relatively more children attended independent nurseries and playgroups.

Moving house frequently is disruptive and likely to result in a child's preschool education being interrupted or discontinued. Whatever the reasons for the household moves there was a tendency for a greater proportion of children who moved frequently to have had no preschool experience (Table 3.2e). This was due mainly to differences in utilisation rates in the independent sector as the proportion of children who attended maintained institutions differed little according to the frequency of moves.

Family factors

If a mother has other, especially younger, children to care for, it may be more necessary for a child of appropriate age to attend a preschool placement. However, in large families it is often difficult to arrange to take one child to a nursery or playgroup when others need to be delivered to school elsewhere or if a baby has to go along also. Our results show marked variation in utilisation of preschool services according to the number of children in the family (Table 3.3a). More than half the children with no more than one sibling attended independent nursery or playgroup compared with only 29% of those in families with four or more children but there was little variation in the maintained sector. Consequently, as many as 46% of children in large families had no preschool experience compared with about one child in five with no more than one sibling.

It is well established that large family size is associated with increased risk of behaviour problems in children and poorer cognitive development (Davie *et al.*, 1972; Osborn *et al.*, 1984). The fact that children in large families are less likely than others to attend preschool institutions might be a contributory factor in their poorer educational performance.

One-parent families are especially vulnerable to such problems and their need for day care as well as for social and emotional support is widely recognised. Social isolation and stress frequently lead to depression and helplessness in mothers of young children who then find it difficult to take advantage of any preschool

Table 3.3 *Preschool experience by five-year family factors*

Five-year family factors		Preschool experience			N = 100%
		None	Maintained	Independent	
(a) Number of children in the family					
One	%	24.0	21.0	55.0	1,319
Two	%	21.8	18.4	59.8	6,295
Three	%	33.1	21.2	45.7	3,173
Four or more	%	46.4	24.5	29.1	2,092
(b) Type of family					
Both natural parents	%	28.4	19.4	52.2	11,646
Adoptive parents	%	21.9	10.4	67.7	96
Step family	%	36.6	25.3	38.1	344
Supported single parent	%	31.5	32.8	35.7	241
Lone parent	%	34.2	33.0	32.8	491
Neither natural parent	%	34.4	29.5	36.1	61
(c) Ethnic origin of parents					
European (GB)	%	28.3	19.5	52.2	11,684
European (not GB)	%	31.7	21.2	47.1	605
Afro-Caribbean	%	35.1	46.5	18.4	185
Indian/Pakistani	%	45.5	30.9	23.6	233
Other and mixed	%	28.0	29.8	42.3	168

Note: All associations in this table are significant at the $p < .0005$ level.

services that might be available (Shinman, 1981). Our findings showed that children who were no longer living with both their natural or adoptive parents by the age of 5 were less likely than those with both natural or adoptive parents to attend preschool services (Table 3.3b). Maintained institutions enrolled relatively more children from atypical families than independent institutions. Whilst playgroup philosophy is to reach mothers as well as children, especially those experiencing stress and isolation, our results suggest that the most vulnerable mothers were the ones who were least likely to be in touch with the preschool services. (A full definition of the family classification used in this study is given in the Appendix.)

The preschool period is the ideal time to bring together children of different ethnic origins thereby providing the opportunity for them to increase mutual understanding and acceptance of other cultures. Many children brought up in Asian homes speak little or no English when they start school (CRC, 1976; Osborn and Butler, 1984, Chapter 8). This creates obvious difficulties in the classroom and suggests that the teaching of English to children whose first language is not English could be an important feature of the preschool curriculum. Our results show, however, that although 31% of Indian/Pakistani children and 47% of Afro-Caribbean children attended maintained nurseries, only 24% and 18% respectively went to independent nurseries or playgroups (Table 3.3c). Consequently as many as 46% of Indian/Pakistani children and 35% of Afro-Caribbean children had no preschool experience. This compared with 28% of the European (GB) children who were non-attenders.

Personal factors

There were small, though statistically significant, differences in preschool utilisation according to the child's gender (Table 3.4a). Girls were slightly more likely to have attended a preschool placement than were boys.

In Chapter 2 we saw that maintained institutions were more likely to accept handicapped children than were those in the independent sector. Such differences in admission policy appeared to result in small, but significant, variations in the rate of utilisation of preschool services between the maintained and independent sectors (Table 3.4b).

Table 3.4 *Preschool experience by personal factors*

Personal factors		Preschool experience			
		None	Maintained	Independent	N = 100%
(a) *Child's gender*					
Boy	%	30.1	19.7	50.2	6,687
Girl	%	27.5	21.0	51.5	6,204
(b) *Physically or mentally handicapped*					
No handicap	%	28.6	20.1	51.2	12,093
Handicap	%	32.0	23.4	44.6	798

Note: All associations in this table are significant at the p< .005 level.

Maternal factors

The age of the mother is associated with many social and family factors such as family size and socio-economic position, but many older mothers also have different attitudes towards children's needs compared with those held by younger mothers. Rates of utilisation of maintained nurseries were highest for children whose mothers were either under 25 or over 45, whereas attendance at independent institutions was highest for children whose mothers were aged 30 to 35 years (Table 3.5a). Children whose mothers came in the youngest or oldest age groups were also the ones most likely to have had no preschool experience.

Parental educational achievement is strongly associated with the parents' socio-economic position; indeed the parents' qualifications have been included as a contributory factor in the Social Index. However, parents with at least minimal qualifications are likely to value education for their children more highly than are parents without qualifications and, as expected, there were higher rates of utilisation of independent preschool services amongst children whose mothers had at least minimal qualifcations (Table 3.5b). As many as 39% of children whose mothers had no qualifications did not attend a preschool institution compared with only 11% of those whose mothers had professional or degree level qualifications. This was mainly due to differences in the proportion of children who attended independent institutions. Only 39% of children whose mothers had no qualifications attended independent nurseries or playgroups compared with 71% of those whose mothers had professional or higher educational qualifications.

Almost half of all the mothers in the CHES cohort had been employed full-time or part-time outside the home for a period during the five years since the birth of the study child. Care of the child whilst the mother was at work was more often the responsibility of the father or other relatives than day care institutions or childminders (Osborn *et al.*, 1984, Chapter 14). A full-time place in a nursery school or nursery class, however, could increase a mother's opportunity to go out to work despite the short school hours and long holidays. This is suggested by the higher proportion of children of employed mothers who attended maintained institutions (23%, Table 3.5c) compared with those whose mothers were full-time housewives for the whole period (18%). In contrast, the proportion of children attending independent institutions was

Table 3.5 *Preschool experience by five-year maternal factors*

Five-year maternal factors		Preschool experience			N = 100%
		None	Maintained	Independent	
(a) Mother's age					
<25	%	33.8	25.1	41.1	1,083
≥25 <30	%	28.3	20.7	51.0	4,549
≥30 <35	%	26.2	18.0	55.8	4,029
≥35 <40	%	29.1	19.4	51.5	1,976
≥40 <45	%	33.3	21.2	45.5	765
≥45	%	37.7	27.7	34.6	292
(b) Mother's education					
No qualifications	%	38.7	22.5	38.8	6,838
Vocational qualifications	%	20.2	18.2	61.6	1,898
GCE 'O' or 'A' level	%	15.6	16.8	67.6	2,655
State Registered Nurse, Certificate of Education, Degree or higher qualification	%	11.4	17.2	71.4	936
(c) Mother's employment					
Employed during child's preschool period	%	27.6	23.0	49.4	6,107
Not employed	%	30.0	17.7	52.3	6,693
(d) Maternal depression					
Mean score		.15	.12	−.14	.00
Standard deviation		1.06	1.06	.91	.99
N		3,644	2,566	6,476	12,686

Note: All associations in this table are significant at the $p < .0005$ level.

higher where the mother had not been out to work. This was partly due to the fact that many playgroups operated no more than 4 sessions a week which was insufficient for day care purposes. The situation is further complicated if the mother's hours and type of employment and her social background are also taken into account, but this is fully explored elsewhere (Osborn *et al.*, 1984, Chapter 8). For our present purposes, the importance of maternal employment depends on whether it proves to be a significant intervening factor in our analyses of children's ability and behaviour.

A final factor likely to be especially relevant to our analyses of behavioural deviance is the mother's level of depression. Social stress increases the risk of maternal depression (Brown and Harris, 1978) and to the extent that a child's attendance at a preschool institution reduces stress for the mother, this may help reduce depression and thus also indirectly reduce behavioural deviance in the child. We have used the Malaise Inventory (Brodman *et al.*, 1952) as our measure of depression. This is a 24-item scale completed by the mothers themselves and subjected to principal components analysis which provides a score with a mean of zero and a standard deviation of one. (Details are given in the Appendix.)

Table 3.5d shows that mothers of children who had no preschool experience had the highest mean depression score (.15 SD). However, those whose children attended maintained institutions had a mean score only marginally lower (.12 SD) whilst mothers whose children attended independent institutions had the lowest score (−.14 SD). These differences were more likely to be due to the social variation between the mothers of children in the three preschool groups than to the fact of the child's attendance *per se*. Nevertheless, maternal depression was included in subsequent analyses as a potentially important intervening factor.

Social differences between children attending different types of preschool institution

We have so far established that a child who was disadvantaged for social or other reasons was more likely to have had no preschool experience than the relatively advantaged child. Also, proportionally more disadvantaged children attended maintained than independent institutions. We now compare the social circumstances of children who attended particular types of institutions, although

Table 3.6 *Selected five-year social and family factors by main preschool placement*

Selected five-year social and family variables	Main preschool placement								All children
	None	Maintained			Independent		Playgroup		
		LEA NS	LEA NC	LA DN	PRV NS	PRV DN	Hall	Home	
	%	%	%	%	%	%	%	%	%
(a) Most advantaged Social Index group	4.0	8.1	5.4	2.6	30.8	14.5	15.6	28.7	9.3
(b) Most disadvantaged Social Index group	14.4	13.7	15.1	15.8	0.0	2.6	3.7	1.1	10.2
(c) Poor neighbourhood	11.2	12.0	14.2	17.1	10.0	10.0	3.4	0.6	8.7
(d) Well-to-do neighbourhood	12.5	19.9	15.2	14.5	50.0	32.7	30.8	52.6	21.0
(e) Rural neighbourhood	18.0	9.1	6.8	3.4	20.0	11.3	23.5	25.1	17.7
(f) England	84.1	79.5	84.0	85.7	87.8	89.5	89.0	88.9	85.7
(g) Wales	7.7	7.8	6.9	0.0	4.9	6.5	2.9	5.0	5.8

(h) Scotland	8.2	12.7	9.1	14.3	7.3	3.9	8.0	6.1	8.5
(i) Only child	8.5	13.0	7.0	26.9	12.5	17.6	10.4	13.3	9.8
(j) 4 or more children in family	26.1	15.8	22.7	17.6	7.5	9.2	9.1	9.4	18.3
(k) Not with both natural or adoptive parents	10.5	11.7	10.4	51.3	2.5	13.7	5.7	5.6	8.5
(l) Afro-Caribbean origin	1.8	2.0	3.0	9.2	2.5	0.7	0.4	0.0	1.5
(m) Indian/Pakistani origin	2.9	2.6	3.0	2.5	2.5	2.6	0.7	0.0	2.1
(n) Mother aged under 25	10.0	11.5	9.6	16.8	2.5	8.1	6.7	6.7	8.9
(o) Mother employed	45.6	55.1	53.9	78.9	35.0	60.7	46.1	39.4	48.0
(p) Maternal depression									
Mean	.15	.02	.13	.43	−.29	−.06	−.15	−.31	−.02
SD	1.06	.99	1.09	1.16	.90	.98	.89	.82	1.01
TOTAL N = 100%	3,719	646	1,105	119	41	153	3,169	180	9,132

Note: Actual totals on which percentages are based vary from the numbers given in the totals row depending on the numbers for whom information was available for each independent variable. All associations in this table are significant at the $p < .0005$ level.

this can only be done for the subsample of children for whom a corroborative match has been established between the institution described by the mother and an institution in the Nursery/Playgroup study. This analysis is necessary in order to appreciate the social and family differences between children who attended LEA nursery schools and classes and LA day nurseries, for example, or the contrasts between children who attended the different types of independent nursery or playgroup. Such social and family differences will indicate important intervening factors in our analyses relating children's preschool experience to their subsequent attainment and behaviour.

The LA day nursery was the type of institution which consistently had the highest proportion of disadvantaged children according to almost every criterion used (Table 3.6). These children were the most likely to be in the most disadvantaged Social Index group, to live in poor urban neighbourhoods and to come from an ethnic minority group—particularly Afro/Caribbean. Half the children in the sample who went to LA day nurseries were no longer living with both natural parents by 5 years of age, 79% of the mothers had jobs and many mothers were under 25 years old. The risk of depression among the mothers of these children was very high (mean score =.43 SD).

Interesting results were found with regard to family size. As many as 26.9% of LA day nursery children in this cohort had no siblings. This compares with 9.8% for the whole sample. The next highest proportion of only children was in independent day nurseries (17.6%). We have not investigated the possible explanations for this association but suggest that the feasibility of full-time employment is greatest for mothers with only one child if a day nursery place can be obtained for that child. Mothers with school-age children are often unable to work full-time because of the short school hours and long holidays and so a full-time day nursery place for an under-five would not necessarily help. Socially disadvantaged mothers often need full-time employment and are also more likely to be eligible for a LA day nursery place. Such a combination of circumstances might well result in the relatively high proportion of only children in LA, and also independent, day nurseries. Large families, with at least four children, were most often found amongst children with no preschool experience. This could be due to the logistic problems of taking older children to school and coping with toddlers as well as delivering the 3- or 4-year-old to nursery or playgroup. In many instances it is easier to forgo the opportunities offered by preschool services than to make the necessary effort to get a child ready and undertake the extra journey. Whatever the explanations for these differences in family size between children who attended different types of preschool institution, it is clear that the number of children in the family is an important intervening factor when examining the association between preschool experience and subsequent outcomes.

Whilst LA day nurseries undoubtedly took the highest proportions of seriously disadvantaged children, there were also more such children than average among those who went to LEA nursery schools and classes or who had no preschool experience. This especially applied to children who attended LEA nursery classes of whom 15.1% were in the most disadvantaged Social Index group, and 14.2% lived in poor urban areas.

It was surprising to find in our sample high proportions of seriously disadvantaged children who attended LEA nursery classes in view of the findings reported from the Nursery/Playgroup survey which suggested that LEA nursery classes were *less* likely to accommodate socially disadvantaged children than were LEA nursery schools (see Chapter 2). This raises the question of whether staff in LEA nursery classes were less aware of the needs of vulnerable children in their care than were their colleagues in LEA nursery schools, and, anticipating following chapters, whether this could be a contributory factor in the relatively poor achievement of children who attended nursery classes.

In contrast to the maintained sector, children who attended institutions in the independent sector were more likely to come from socially advantaged families. Home playgroup and independent nursery school attenders shared much in common in that they were very likely to come from the most socially advantaged homes and live in well-to-do neighbourhoods. No children of Afro-Caribbean or Asian origin in the CHES sample had attended a home playgroup although they were well represented in private nursery schools.

All these social and family differences between children with different types of preschool experience indicated the need for great care when evaluating the possible contribution of preschool education to a child's subsequent attainment.

Conclusions

In 1975, one in five of the CHES sample had attended a maintained nursery school/class or day nursery and half the sample had attended some form of independent preschool institution by the time they reached their fifth birthday. Most of this latter group had attended playgroups. As many as 28%, however, had no preschool educational or day care experience. Substantial variation was found between social groups in the rates of utilisation of the various types of preschool institution. In general, maintained institutions were attended by relatively high percentages of socially disadvantaged children and children living in poor neighbourhoods. In contrast, institutions in the independent sector were more likely to accommodate socially advantaged children and those living in well-to-do or rural areas. The overall result of the heavy dependence on independent or voluntary preschool provision, however, was that nearly half the most disadvantaged children in the sample had no preschool experience compared with fewer than one in ten of the most advantaged children. Thus the children most in need of preschool education were the ones who were most likely to have had none.

Other factors were also associated with different rates of utilisation of preschool services; these included in particular the number of children in the family, type of family (two-parent, step-family, one-parent, etc.), ethnic origin and region of the country in which the child lived. All these differences meant that the typical social and family characteristics of the children who attended maintained institutions differed in important ways from those who went to private nurseries and playgroups and the children with no preschool experience.

Such differences are not only important in themselves as evidence of inequality in utilisation of preschool services; they also have implications for our analyses of the association between children's preschool experience and their subsequent development. It is essential, therefore, that such differences are taken into account as intervening variables when assessing the possible effects of preschool education on the children's behaviour and test scores. This theme is developed fully in Chapter 4 for cognitive and educational tests and Chapter 5 for behavioural assessments.

4

Preschool experience, cognitive development, and educational achievement

The majority of preschool institutions do not claim to have specific educational goals, such as promoting the children's linguistic or reading skills. However, the opportunity they offer for interacting with peers, engaging in a wide variety of activities and having access to books and other educational materials will inevitably help to stimulate cognitive development. In addition, exposure in the preschool setting to a different and wider range of experience to that provided in the home is another source of mental stimulation.

Although preschool facilities do not have a didactic aim it is nevertheless important for a child to be cognitively ready for preschool education. The average age of children in playgroups is slightly lower than it is in LEA nursery schools and classes, therefore playgroup activities might need to differ from those in LEA nursery schools and classes in order to match the children's general level of ability. Chronological age, however, is not the only criterion for school readiness; differences in home and family background can profoundly affect the rate of cognitive development so that by a given age a child from a socially advantaged home is more able to take advantage of preschool education than his socially disadvantaged peer.

To add further to the complexity, the social composition of a group of children attending one type of preschool institution often differs substantially from that of a group attending another type of institution. This is most marked in the contrast between maintained and independent institutions as described in Chapters 2 and 3. These social differences have two separate implications. Firstly, a preschool institution with a large proportion of socially disadvantaged children might be less successful in stimulating cognitive development among the group as a whole than in another establishment where the majority of children come from relatively advantaged homes. This is because the former group, with the increased risk of cognitive delay and behavioural problems caused by family factors, places more demands on staff time and skills than does the latter group. Secondly, a valid evaluation of the possible effects of preschool education on a child's cognitive and educational skills must recognise that the child's own social background is a powerful determinant of these skills, which otherwise might be spuriously attributed to the preschool experience. Clearly, the social differences in utilisation of different types of preschool institution, described in Chapter 3, could easily result in attendance at independent institutions being associated with higher test scores than attendance at maintained institutions. Most of this chapter is devoted to an examination of this central issue; namely the effect of intervening variables on the association between children's test scores and their preschool experience.

Criteria for evaluation

A full evaluation of preschool facilities should take account of the aims and purposes of such facilities and, possibly, the expectations of the parents also. Consumer satisfaction might indeed be a sufficient criterion for deciding whether or not a playgroup or nursery school is providing an adequate service. Margaret Bone's day care study (1977) suggested that dissatisfaction was most often related to availability; for example sessions were too infrequent or too brief or that taking and collecting the child was difficult. The most common reason for actually having stopped attending a facility, however, was that the child had been unhappy (op. cit., pp. 17–18), although this applied to only about 2% of the total sample of 0- to 4-year-olds. For the majority of parents who make use of preschool facilities therefore, the possible cognitive benefits for the child are implicitly assumed and any criticism they have tends to centre on practical considerations.

When the mothers in the CHES sample were specifically asked if they had noticed any changes in their child which they attributed to their preschool experience, only half the mothers thought there had been any change at all. Of those who thought that there had been some kind of change the majority, about two thirds, expressed this in terms of the child's personality, temperament or social adaptation, whereas cognitive skills—speech, language, reading, knowledge—were mentioned by only a quarter of these mothers. Thus mothers of preschool age children do not appear to think of nurseries and playgroups as places where their children's intellectual abilities are being fostered and are more likely to express the influence of preschool experience in terms of the child's sociability or temperament.

In contrast to this, researchers concerned with early education and child development tend to favour tests of cognitive maturity, conceptual ability or linguistic competence rather than measures of social adaptation. The selection of such criteria for assessment depends on a number of factors such as the objectives of the preschool facility being evaluated, the availability of appropriate tests and the scale and methodology of the research project. In a study of a preschool intervention programme for 'socially handicapped children' particular tests were chosen, '... because they were the best teacher administered tests that could be located of basic conceptual understanding and social maturity.' (Curtis and Blatchford, 1981, p. 36). This was a large study, initially involving 684 children to be tested by teachers; and this determined to some extent the types of evaluation that were feasible. Smaller-scale studies can undertake other types of evaluation. In a two-stage longitudinal study of 90 working-class children in reception classes, of whom half had attended LEA nursery classes and half playgroups, observations of classroom behaviour, totalling 120 hours, were made by trained observers. This allowed an assessment of school readiness in terms of conduct within the classroom and relations with peers and teachers and provided the means of investigating more closely the processes and underlying variation in children's scores on the Boehm Test of Basic Concepts (Jowett and Sylva, 1986).

We suggest that the overall purpose of a research programme determines the type of methodology adopted. This in turn has implications for the type of evaluation criteria that can be implemented, and the advantages of one or other type of methodological approach are balanced against the need to obtain appropriate assessments of children's developmental progress. In the case of the Child Health and Education Study, which involved a maximum of 15,000 children spread throughout Britain, the choice of tests and assessments was limited by considerations of cost and the diversity of test situations. In the five-year follow-up all the field work was implemented by health visitors who interviewed the mothers and carried out the tests with the children. In the ten-year follow-up tests were administered by class teachers. It was necessary, therefore, to select tests that could reliably be administered in these diverse settings and would also be of relevance to the many research issues with which the study as a whole was concerned. The tests and assessments used, however, were highly appropriate as criteria for the evaluation of children's preschool experience, as they provided measures of verbal and non-verbal cognitive skills and assessments of behaviour in the home at 5 and 10 years, and behaviour at school at 10 years. The behavioural assessments are described in Chapter 5, and the cognitive tests are described below.

Five tests were carried out in the five-year follow-up (Osborn *et al.*, 1984) of which two were used in the present study.

Copying Designs test

The ability to copy designs or geometric shapes is included as one element of assessment in many standard tests of intelligence. Design copying requires a child to have reached a certain level of conceptual development in order to be able to recognise the principles governing the different geometric forms. In addition, however, the Copying Designs test also required the child to reproduce these geometric shapes. This raises the problem of whether failure to copy a design was due to a lack of conceptual ability or to poor eye-hand coordination. However, we believe that conceptual ability was probably the main factor as most children could copy one or two designs successfully which suggests that eye-hand coordination only became a problem for the children who failed to completely grasp the rationale of a particular design. The test and its scoring scheme are reproduced in the Appendix.

English Picture Vocabulary Test (EPVT)

This is an adaptation by Brimer and Dunn (1962) of the American Peabody Picture Vocabulary Test. Although designed to be a test of listening vocabulary, i.e. the comprehension of spoken words, the EPVT is strongly associated with general cognitive ability and has a correlation of .34 with the Copying Designs test. Further details of the test are given in the Appendix.

The ten-year follow-up included many tests and assessments designed to cover a wide range of abilities and educational attainment. These are described in some detail in an unpublished report to one of the government departments that funded this follow-up (Butler *et al.*, 1982). For the purposes of the present study, however, four tests and one assessment of the children's educational and cognitive progress were selected. All the tests were administered by class teachers.

British Ability Scales (BAS)

Four scales, of which two were verbal and two non-verbal, were selected from the British Ability Scales (Elliott *et al.*, 1979) with some modification appropriate for teacher administration. These scales were word definitions, recall of digits, similarities and matrices. A total BAS score was computed from these four scales which provided a measure of general cognitive ability and reasoning.

Picture Language Test

This was created specifically for the CHES ten-year follow-up and, like the five-year EPVT, provided a measure of listening vocabulary.

Reading test

A shortened version of the Edinburgh Reading Test composed of items selected from Stages 2, 3 and 4 of the Edinburgh Reading Tests (Godfrey Thompson Unit for Educational Research, 1977, 1980; Moray House College of Education, 1980) provided a measure of a wide range of reading ability. Elements of the test included: vocabulary, syntax, sequencing and comprehension.

Mathematics test

This test was also specially devised for the CHES ten-year follow-up. It consisted of 72 multiple-choice questions covering arithmetical processes (addition, subtraction, multiplication, division), number concept, geometry, algebra, trigonometry and statistics.

Communication

Teachers responded to a large number of items which rated the classroom behaviour of the study children. A subset of 8 of these items provided a scale of expressive language in terms of language structure, organisation of expressed thoughts, complexity of vocabulary, speech articulation, etc. This provided an additional assessment of linguistic competence to the listening vocabulary tests described above.

These 7 tests from the five- and ten-year follow-up surveys provided a broad picture of the cognitive and educational achievement of this sample of children which enabled us to check whether preschool education was more effective in some areas of development than others. It was felt that more confidence could be placed in results that were reproduced in several different tests than in only one or two.

Test scores and preschool groups

We explained in Chapter 3 that our analysis of the effects of early education was based on the subsample of children whose preschool experience was confirmed by matching with data in the Nursery/ Playgroup survey, plus those with no preschool educational experience. This subsample on which the main analysis was carried out is given in Table 4.1 where it can be seen that it included 9,132 of the total 13,135 in the five-year follow-up. This table does not provide estimates of levels of preschool utilisation, for this see Table 3.1. It is presented here to show the maximum numbers of cases in each preschool group on which the ensuing analyses were based. This is important for a full appreciation of the reliability of our statistics for specific preschool groups. The larger the number in a group, the more reliable will be the results for that group.

The table shows that there were four major groups; those who attended LEA nursery schools (N = 646), LEA nursery classes (N = 1,105) and hall playgroups (N = 3,169), and those with no preschool institutional experience (N = 3,719). The other preschool groups all had far fewer children in them; our independent nursery schools category totalled only 41 children.

The numbers of these cases with ten-year data were smaller because not all the five-year sample were successfully followed up at age 10 (see Appendix), thus analyses involving ten-year tests or other ten-year data are always based on the reduced numbers of cases given in the second column of Table 4.1.

The test means and standard deviations for the preschool study subsample are shown in Table 4.2. The basic test parameters for the five-year tests and ten-year communication were: mean = zero, standard deviation = one. The other ten-year tests had mean = 100 and standard deviation = 15. The subsample mean scores for the tests were all a little below the test means for the total CHES sample

Table 4.1 *Sample on which main analysis is carried out*

Main preschool placement	Number of cases in five-year survey	Number of cases in ten-year survey
No preschool	3,719	3,380
Maintained		
LEA nursery school	646	596
LEA nursery class	1,105	1,027
LA day nursery	119	105
Independent		
Nursery school	41	36
Day nursery	153	145
Hall playgroup	3,169	2,954
Home playgroup	180	166
Sub-sample on which multivariate analysis is based	9,132	8,409
Matched with other types of institutions but excluded from further analysis	26	24
Attended preschool but not matched with a nursery/ playgroup institution	3,825	3,516
No information on preschool experience	152	145
TOTAL SAMPLE	13,135	12,094

because the matched subsample had a slightly lower proportion of socially advantaged children than that in the total sample. As these excluded children had slightly higher than average test scores, their absence from the subsample resulted in a small decrease in the overall mean test scores. This in no way affected the validity of the comparisons between preschool groups, particularly when social differences were also taken into account as in the later analyses in this chapter.

The main body of Table 4.2 shows the deviation from overall mean for preschool groups for each test. Note that the absolute size of the deviation from overall mean is dependent on the standard deviation of the individual tests. Thus a deviation of .50 in a test with a standard deviation of one is the equivalent of a deviation of 7.50 in

Table 4.2 *Mean test scores for preschool groups*

Main preschool placement	Five-year		Ten-year				
	Copying Designs	EPVT	BAS	PLT	Reading	Mathematics	Communication
No preschool	-.15	-.19	-3.25	-2.56	-3.33	-2.90	-.23
Maintained							
LEA nursery school	.06	.00	.37	-.40	.95	.80	.14
LEA nursery class	-.07	-.10	-2.54	-2.11	-2.52	-2.72	-.10
LA day nursery	-.26	-.29	-.82	-2.47	-2.10	-2.64	-.08
Independent							
Nursery school	.11	.42	5.84	6.66	5.70	9.09	.49
Day nursery	.25	.12	3.14	1.57	3.91	3.47	.23
Hall playgroup	.16	.21	3.81	3.22	3.84	3.43	.23
Home playgroup	.51	.65	8.99	8.03	8.48	8.55	.48
Overall mean	-.04	-.04	99.56	99.90	99.55	99.65	-.03
Standard deviation	.98	.98	14.58	14.70	14.50	14.51	.96
TOTAL N	9,067	8,523	7,123	7,263	7,273	7,244	7,217

Note: Figures show deviation from overall mean.

a test with a standard deviation of 15. It is important to be aware of this difference when making comparisons between tests.

Several generalisations can be drawn from this table.

1. Children with no preschool experience and those who had attended maintained institutions had lower test scores than those who had attended independent or voluntary institutions.

2. The lowest five-year test scores were obtained by children who attended LA day nurseries and the lowest ten-year scores by those with no preschool experience.

3. The highest test scores were achieved by children who went to home playgroups with the exception of mathematics and communication in which the highest mean scores were associated with attendance at independent nursery schools.

4. Children who attended LEA nursery schools consistently scored higher than children who attended other types of maintained preschool institution, but never as high as children who attended institutions in the independent sector.

The results in Table 4.2 are the actual mean test scores of groups of children who had different types of preschool experience. They show that children who attended independent institutions were more advanced cognitively and had better vocabulary at 5 years, were better readers and mathematicians and more skilled verbally at 10 years than those who attended maintained institutions or had no preschool experience. We cannot say, however, that these differences were a *consequence* of their differing preschool experiences because we have already established that there were large social and family differences between children in the separate preschool groups, and such differences would also play a significant part in determining children's test scores. In order to estimate the unique contribution of preschool education to children's cognitive and educational achievement, it is necessary to take account of these intervening social and family factors.

Intervening variables

The CHES data sets contain a very large number of variables any of which could potentially be an important intervening variable in the relationships between children's preschool experience and their test scores. Our first task, therefore, was to identify the variables that were likely to be most important in this context. A subset of variables was selected on the basis of prior knowledge about the factors likely to have a bearing on the type of preschool experience children have. Most of these variables were described in Chapter 3 where their association with children's preschool experience was investigated. In order for these factors to be important as intervening variables, however, they must also be associated with the children's test performances. To identify variables which were most strongly predictive of test scores, one-way analyses of variance were carried out in which differences between categories of the five-year social variables described in Chapter 3 were tested with respect to all the above five-year and ten-year tests. We used the percentage of variance explained as our criterion for the strength of an association between independent and dependent variables. This method of selecting the key intervening variables makes it harder for the preschool variable to explain additional variance. Thus if the association between children's preschool experience and a given outcome remains statistically significant after taking account of variables which explain a relatively large proportion of the variance in the outcome variable, then greater confidence may be placed in the observed association between preschool experience and that outcome. In other words, the objective was to find the intervening variables likely to have the most damaging effect on any association found between preschool experience and children's ability.

Five-year independent variables which were found to explain a minimum of 2% of the variance in at least one five- or ten-year test or behavioural assessment are listed in Table 4.3. All these factors were also found to be related to the type of preschool experience the child had received and therefore, because they were related to both preschool experience and test scores, were potentially important intervening variables in the association between children's preschool experience and their test scores.

It would have been useful in this study to have had a measure of the child's general ability prior to starting preschool education as a base against which any changes attributable to preschool experience could be compared. However, apart from the methodological difficulty of measuring the IQ or cognitive aptitude of a national sample of 3-year-olds, the additional cost of such an exercise was prohibitive. To compensate for this lack of a measure of initial ability, we used the child's height at 5 years as a partial index of

Table 4.3 *Five-year independent variables*

Social Index score:	mean = 50, standard deviation = 10
Maternal depression:	mean = zero, standard deviation = 1.0
Child's height (cms):	mean = 108.8, standard deviation = 5.2
Neighbourhood:	1 Urban poor
	2 Urban average
	3 Urban well-to-do
	4 Rural
Number of children:	1 One
	2 Two
	3 Three
	4 Four or more
Child's gender:	1 Boy
	2 Girl
Mother's age:	1 <25 years
	2 $\geqslant 25 <30$ years
	3 $\geqslant 30 <35$ years
	4 $\geqslant 35$ years
Family type:	1 Both natural or adoptive parents
	2 Not both natural or adoptive parents
Ethnic origin:	1 Both parents of British origin
	2 One or both parents not of British origin
Country:	1 England
	2 Wales
	3 Scotland
Handicap:	1 No handicap
	2 Has mental or physical handicap
Maternal employment:	1 Never employed before child's fifth birthday
	2 Employment full-time or part-time outside the home before the child's fifth birthday

intelligence. The justification for this use of child's height is the known association between height and IQ (e.g. Rutter *et al.*, 1970, p. 82) attributable at least in part to genetic factors.

The family's socio-economic position as measured by the five-year Social Index was the factor which explained the greatest amount of variance in the cognitive and educational test scores at 5 and 10 years. The mother's educational level was also strongly related to test scores but as this was one of the Social Index items it explained little additional variance over and above that of the Social Index. Two other variables which consistently explained relatively high proportions of test variance were the type of neighbourhood in which the child lived and the number of children in the family. The strong interrelationship between Social Index, type of neighbourhood and size of family meant that there was some degree of overlap between them in the variance they explained in the dependent variables. Nevertheless, because of the considerable differences between preschool institutions in the types of neighbourhood in which they were located we decided that the type of neighbourhood in which the child lived was a potentially important intervening factor. Also, the number of children in the family is not in itself a socio-economic factor, like the Social Index, even though it has socio-economic implications. Therefore, we included this too as a principal intervening variable. These three variables, Social Index score, type of neighbourhood in which the child lived and number of children in the family, emerged by this process as the 'basic intervening variables' in all our subsequent analyses.

Analytical approach

It is important at this stage that we describe the procedure used to explore the actual effect of the intervening variables on the relationship between children's preschool experience and their test scores. Analysis of variance was selected as the most appropriate statistical method for our purposes because it is a powerful and robust statistical technique which can test the associations between independent variables and an outcome variable whilst simultaneously adjusting for the effects of the other independent variables in the analysis.

Our procedure was to carry out an initial analysis of variance in which the mean test scores for the preschool groups were statistically adjusted for the independent effects of the three basic intervening variables (Social Index, type of neighbourhood and number of children in the family). This resulted in the differences in mean scores between preschool groups being substantially reduced. The proportion of test variance explained by preschool experience was also reduced after adjustment for the three basic intervening variables.

The next step was to identify other variables that reduced still further the difference in mean scores between preschool groups or reduced the statistical significance of the preschool effect. This was done by repeating the analyses of variance with the preschool variable, the three main intervening variables (Social Index, neighbourhood and number of children) plus one additional independent variable.

The mean test scores for the preschool groups were then compared with those obtained before the addition of the extra independent variable to check whether there was a significant change. The object was to find those variables having the most damaging effect on the association between the preschool variable and the test score in question. This could be a reduction in the size of the difference in mean test scores between preschool groups or a reduction in the proportion of variance in test score explained by the preschool variable. This process was repeated for all the five-year independent variables listed in Table 4.3 and for all five- and ten-year test scores which resulted in 9 analyses of variance for each of seven tests, or 63 analyses of variance in all at this stage. Exactly the same procedure was adopted for all the behavioural assessments described in Chapter 5.

Preschool education and test scores allowing for intervening factors

Table 4.4 shows that mean test scores varied significantly between children with different preschool education and day care experience after adjustment for the basic intervening variables (Social Index, type of neighbourhood, number of children). The maximum difference between preschool means varied from a quarter to a half of a standard deviation depending on the test outcome, and the addition of the other intervening variables (listed in Table 4.1) made little difference to the mean scores or variance explained by the preschool variable after adjustment had first been made for the three basic intervening variables. The largest shifts in mean scores were found among children who attended LA day nurseries; their EPVT, BAS and Picture Language Test mean scores tended to increase after adjustment for mother's age or type of family. However, these shifts were small compared with the substantial changes in mean test scores that were found after adjustment for the three basic intervening variables.

The test variance explained by the main preschool placement was substantially reduced after adjustment for the basic intervening

Table 4.4 *Mean test scores by main preschool placement*

Main preschool placement	Five-year		Ten-year				
	Copying Designs	EPVT	BAS	PLT	Reading	Mathematics	Communication
No preschool	−.05	−.07	−1.25	−.73	−1.37	−1.06	−.10
Maintained							
LEA nursery school	.07	.01	.58	−.23	1.10	1.11	.15
LEA nursery class	.02	.00	−.49	−.16	−.67	−.89	.01
LA day nursery	−.15	−.16	1.33	−1.03	−.16	−.46	.04
Independent							
Nursery school	−.14	.15	1.37	2.06	.67	4.49	.20
Day nursery	.11	−.04	.80	−.80	1.58	1.47	.06
Hall playgroup	.02	.07	1.19	.82	1.31	1.01	.06
Home playgroup	.22	.34	3.05	2.79	3.19	2.89	.12
Overall mean	−.04	−.03	99.61	99.94	99.60	99.68	−.02
TOTAL N	8,670	8,158	6,802	6,939	6,947	6,919	6,890
Significance	p<.0005	p<.0005	p<.0005	p<.05	p<.0005	p<.0005	p<.0005

Note: Analysis of variance; figures show deviation from overall mean after adjustment for Social Index score, type of neighbourhood and number of children in the household.

variables but remained relatively unaltered by the addition of any one of the other intervening variables, so that the statistical significance of the difference in test scores between children with different types of preschool experience remained at the p < .0005 level. The only exception to this was the analysis for ten-year Picture Language Test in which the main preschool placement was generally significant at only the .05 level but increased to p < .005 after adjustment for the child's gender.

Our conclusion from these analyses was that the three basic intervening variables (Social Index, type of neighbourhood, number of children) accounted for a large part of the differences in social background between children who attended different types of preschool institution or who had no preschool experience, and that other five-year socio-economic and family factors had only marginal effects on the association between the child's preschool experience and test outcomes. Other factors such as parental attitudes and involvement in the child's preschool institution, changes in social and family circumstances between the five- and ten-year follow-ups and the child's junior school experience are investigated in later chapters. At this stage, however, we describe a little further the general pattern of results from what can be called the 'basic model'.

Whilst there were some variations in the results depending on test outcome, a general pattern can be discerned in Table 4.4. Children with no preschool experience had scores which were below average on all the tests. Attendance at LA day nurseries was also associated with lower scores in five of the tests and these children did not differ markedly in their mean scores from the children with no preschool experience. British Ability Scale scores of LA day nursery children, however, were notably higher than average. Children who attended LEA nursery schools achieved higher than average scores in all tests, except the ten-year Picture Language Test, with the highest mean scores occurring in the reading and mathematics tests. By contrast, children who went to LEA nursery classes had lower than average ten-year test scores though not so low as children with no preschool experience. These differences between LEA nursery schools and classes were not anticipated as it was assumed that the educational experience in the two types of LEA institutions was likely to be similar. It was possible, however, that at this stage of our analysis the relatively poor performance of children who attended LEA nursery classes might have been due to other factors yet to be built into the model.

In the independent sector the children in the most important group numerically were those who attended hall playgroups. These children had above average mean scores on all the tests and were comparable to the LEA nursery school children in their five-year tests and ten-year reading and mathematics scores. The mean BAS and PLT scores achieved by hall playgroup attenders were marginally higher than those of children who went to LEA nursery schools. Considering the differences between LEA nursery schools and hall playgroups in their staffing and general organisation, it is perhaps surprising that the test scores of children who attended these preschool institutions were so similar once the differences in home background were taken into account.

Attendance at independent nursery schools was associated with higher than average test scores for all tests except Copying Designs. These children in fact had the highest mean mathematics score. However, there were only 40 children in this group and the variation in test scores across the tests suggests that whilst the general pattern is clear, particular results for any one test might be less reliable than for other preschool groups containing more cases. Children who attended independent day nurseries had above average scores in cognitive and educational tests but their vocabulary test scores at five- and ten-year stages were below average. Finally, children who attended home playgroups were found to have the highest mean scores of all in every test except mathematics. The consistently high test performance of the home playgroup attenders suggests that this effect had not occurred by chance, and that at this stage of analysis home playgroups were associated with the greatest increase in cognitive and educational attainment at the ages of 5 and 10. Nevertheless, it was still possible that this effect was really due to other factors associated with home playgroups that were as yet not part of the model.

Interaction between preschool and other intervening variables

When evaluating the effects of preschool experience, an important consideration is whether some groups benefit relatively more from such experience than others. For example, do socially disadvantaged children gain more from attending a particular type of nursery than do advantaged children? In order to describe our approach to this question it is necessary to explain our method of analysis in a little more detail.

The basic model in all our analyses of variance is a main effects one, i.e. it is assumed that the effects of the different independent variables are additive. Occasionally, however, factors are found to 'interact' so that the effects on a dependent variable of two factors in combination are significantly larger, or smaller, than the sum of their independent effects obtained in the main effects analysis. When interactions appear in the analysis of variance it means that the actual test scores of children in a particular combination of social or family circumstances differ in some way from the scores predicted by the main effects analysis. Special care was taken in the performance of the analyses of variance to ensure that any such interactions involving the main preschool placement were identified.

In most analyses of variance no significant interactions occurred. There were, however, some interactions which required further investigation: Social Index interacted with preschool placement with respect to EPVT and reading scores, and type of neighbourhood interacted with preschool with respect to BAS, reading and mathematics scores.

As the Social Index score was included as a covariate rather than a factor, in our analyses of variance, the interactions between Social Index score and main preschool placement with respect to EPVT and reading scores were investigated in two ways: firstly, by a regression technique, and secondly by grouping the Social Index score into three categories (scores = 19–43, 44–55 and 56–73) and repeating the analysis of variance with Social Index as a factor rather than a covariate. Both methods showed similar interaction effects. We should also mention that the results of the main effects analysis of variance using the grouped version of the Social Index did not differ markedly from those obtained with Social Index score analysed as a covariate.

The interaction between Social Index score and main preschool placement with respect to EPVT score was due to differences in mean scores between socially advantaged and disadvantaged children who attended LA day nurseries. Socially advantaged children who had been to LA day nurseries had a mean EPVT score which was .72 points higher than expected whilst the score of socially disadvantaged LA day nursery children was .17 points lower than expected, thus the difference between these two groups was .89 EPVT points greater than expected from the main effects model. When children who attended LA day nurseries were excluded from the analysis, there was no significant interaction between Social Index and preschool placement.

The interaction between Social Index score and main preschool placement was more complex with respect to the children's reading score at 10. The same LA day nursery effect was present—with advantaged children doing markedly better than expected and disadvantaged children worse, the difference between these groups being 11 points greater than that expected from the main effects model. In addition, however, socially disadvantaged and average children who attended independent nursery schools performed less well than the main effects model predicted but socially disadvantaged children in home playgroups did better than expected.

Significant interactions were also found between the type of neighbourhood in which a child lived and her main preschool placement with respect to BAS, reading and mathematics. The LA day nursery effect observed in the Social Index analyses was apparent here also: children living in well-to-do neighbourhoods who attended LA day nurseries performed significantly better in these tests than the main effects model predicted. There was also some indication that children who lived in poor neighbourhoods performed relatively less well than expected if they attended independent nursery schools or independent day nurseries.

All these interactions affected very small numbers of children and for this reason the interactions associated with independent nursery schools and independent day nurseries should be treated with some caution. The LA day nursery effect however was found in all these analyses and warranted some further investigation.

Only 13 socially advantaged children attended LA day nurseries and, as it is unusual for children from advantaged homes to attend this type of institution, we first of all checked that there were no errors of classification. No such errors were found; the information provided by the mothers and the institutions attended by the children confirmed that they were indeed LA day nurseries. We then compared these day nurseries with those attended by children in other social groups using the types of institutional variables described in Chapter 2. Only one significant difference emerged; the LA day nurseries attended by the socially advantaged children in the CHES sample were less likely to be located in areas rated as 'poor' by the person completing the Nursery/Playgroup question-naire. We were unable to discover any other reason for the interactions.

This investigation of interactions did not provide convincing evidence of differentiation between social groups in the advantages gained in terms of increased test scores attributable to attendance at different types of preschool facilities. However, in Chapter 10 the same question is pursued using a different analytical approach which results in somewhat different conclusions.

Children with special educational needs

Our findings thus far suggested that attendance at a preschool institution was associated with increased test achievement. Apart from the difference in test scores between socially advantaged and socially disadvantaged children who attended LA day nurseries, it appeared that children from all types of social background were likely to benefit equally from preschool education. However, in order to check whether this was true for the most vulnerable children, an analysis was carried out on three special subsamples:

1. Severely disadvantaged children; defined as those with a Social Index score of 36 or under (N = 919)
2. Children of Afro-Caribbean origin (N = 137)
3. Children of Indian/Pakistani origin (N = 187)

There was some overlapping between the socially disadvantaged group and the two ethnic minority groups. As many as 34.4% of the Afro-Caribbean and 12.7% of the Indian/Pakistani children were also in the most disadvantaged Social Index group; this compared with 8.6% of the European (British origin) children.

For these subsamples, comparisons were made between children with no preschool experience and children who went to LEA nursery schools or classes or hall playgroups. There were too few children in the subsamples who had attended other types of pre-school institution for them to be included. Analyses of variance were carried out with all seven cognitive and educational dependent

variables and statistical adjustment was made for type of neighbourhood and number of children in family. For the ethnic minority subsamples, adjustment was made for Social Index score also.

In the socially disadvantaged subsample, three of the seven
analyses achieved statistically significant results. Attendance at
LEA nursery school was associated with a markedly higher mean
five-year EPVT score (p < .0005) and ten-year communciation
(p < .05), whilst hall playgroup children had a higher ten-year
mean mathematics score compared with the other preschool groups
(p < .05). Attendance at LEA nursery schools or hall playgroups
was associated with higher Copying Designs score, BAS score and
reading score compared with non-attenders but none of these
achieved statistical significance after adjustment for neighbourhood
and number of children. Nevertheless, the general trend across all
the tests was for socially disadvantaged children who attended LEA
nursery schools or hall playgroups to achieve higher scores than
children with no preschool experience. In contrast, children who
attended LEA nursery classes tended to perform *less* well than
average for this group; in particular their reading and mathematics
scores were very low.

For the Afro-Caribbean subsample all the analyses of variance
were non-significant. This was partly due to the small number of
these children who had attended LEA nursery schools or hall
playgroups and no consistent pattern emerged from the analyses.

The numbers were small for the Indian/Pakistani subsample also,
but the BAS and reading analyses did achieve significant findings.
These showed higher mean BAS and reading scores (p < .05 and p
< .005 respectively) for Indian/Pakistani children who attended
LEA nursery schools or hall playgroups. Similar results were
obtained in the mathematics analyses although statistical significance was not achieved. In all three of these analyses, Indian/
Pakistani children who attended LEA nursery classes had *lower*
mean BAS, reading and mathematics scores than children with *no*
preschool experience. It is worth pointing out that Indian/Pakistani
children had a very low five-year mean EPVT score (− 1.56)
compared with either the Afro-Caribbean children (− 0.73) or the
socially disadvantaged group (− 0.60) and it is possible that they
had greater difficulty adjusting to and communicating within
nursery classes where there were often more children than in the
LEA nursery school or playgroup. Clearly, children who speak little

or no English need considerably more attention and help from an understanding adult than the average preschool child and this applied to a high proportion of Indian/Pakistani children (Osborn and Butler, 1985, pp. 46–7).

These analyses that focus on specific groups of special educational concern do not point to any definite conclusion about effectiveness of preschool education in improving the cognitive and educational attainment of socially disadvantaged or ethnic minority children. Nevertheless, within the limits of the analyses there are signs that LEA nursery schools and hall playgroups did achieve small gains for these vulnerable groups.

Conclusions

The purpose of this chapter has been to describe our methodological approach and to develop an analytical model which would establish the basic associations between various types of preschool experience and children's test scores at the ages of 5 and 10 years. The socio-economic and family differences in the composition of maintained and independent preschool institutions, as a result of social variation in rates of utilisation, constituted important intervening factors in these analyses. A series of analyses of variance designed to test the effect of twelve social and family factors on the association between preschool experience and seven five- and ten-year test outcomes, showed that most of the social variation between preschool groups could be accounted for by three independent variables; the Social Index, type of neighbourhood in which the child lived and the number of children in the household. These we have termed the 'basic intervening variables' and they are routinely included in the analyses described in subsequent chapters.

The main results at this stage suggested that children's preschool experience was associated with variation in their test performance up to the age of 10. Children who had no preschool experience or who attended LA day nurseries had lower than average scores in most of the tests. Children who attended LEA nursery schools or hall playgroups achieved higher than average scores. Attendance at LEA nursery classes, however, was *not* associated with higher test scores and, indeed, these children had lower than average scores in some tests. The children with the best record of achievement were those who attended home playgroups.

Care was taken to check for interactions between the preschool variable and the intervening variables in relation to the test outcomes. Such interactions would indicate that a particular type of preschool experience was associated with higher test scores in one social group than in another. Some interactions were found which centred mainly on children who attended LA day nurseries. Socially advantaged children who attended LA day nurseries had relatively higher scores in some of the tests than socially disadvantaged children. An examination of the relevant questionnaires did not help to explain this interaction which involved only 13 children. In general, however, interactions did not affect the conclusions from the main effects analyses of variance.

Finally, an analysis was carried out on three small subsamples representing groups of special educational concern. These were socially disadvantaged chilren, Afro-Caribbean children and Indian/Pakistani children. The object was to compare the test scores of vulnerable children with no preschool experience with those who had attended LEA nursery schools or classes or hall playgroups. The small number of cases in these subsamples resulted in few statistically significant results, especially for the Afro-Caribbean children. The general pattern of results across all the analyses, however, suggested that attendance at LEA nursery schools or hall playgroups was associated with higher test scores than those achieved by children with no preschool experience. There was little evidence that attendance at LEA nursery classes increased the test scores of these vulnerable groups.

5

Preschool experience and behavioural adjustment

Behavioural problems in young children continue to be of concern to psychiatrists and a source of worry and frustration to parents and teachers. However, whilst considerable attention has been given to the aetiology of conduct disorders (Barron and Earls, 1984) and their correction (Mortimore *et al.*, 1983), little research has been carried out to find ways in which the risk of behavioural problems might be reduced. The preschool environment provides an opportunity to help children with behavioural problems (Chazan *et al.*, 1983) and it is possible that such experience can result in reduced risk of deviance in later years (Schweinhart and Weikart, 1980). In this chapter, therefore, we examine the association between children's preschool experience and various patterns of behaviour at the ages of 5 and 10 years.

The analytical approach adopted was exactly as for the analysis of achievement test scores which was fully described in Chapter 4. The object was to find intervening variables having the most damaging effect on the association between children's preschool experience and assessments of their behaviour in the home at age 5 and in school at age 10. These intervening variables were then incorporated into further analyses exploring the effects of other factors on the children's behaviour which are described in subsequent chapters. The question that was being pursued throughout was whether or not any residual effects of preschool experience on children's behaviour remained after taking account of all the relevant intervening factors.

In the CHES five-year survey mothers completed a scale of child behaviour based on the Rutter A scale (Rutter *et al.*, 1970, Appendix 6). This consisted of 27 items which were subjected to principal components analysis resulting in two behavioural dimensions which measured antisocial and neurotic behaviour in the home.

The antisocial behaviour scale consisted of 11 items which identified children who were disobedient, destructive, aggressive, irritable, restless or given to temper tantrums. The neurotic behaviour scale consisted of 9 items which identified children who were worried, miserable, fearful, fussy or complained of aches and pains. (Further details of these scales are given in the Appendix.)

Information was obtained on the chldren's behaviour in school and in the home at the age of 10. For the purposes of this study, however, we used only the data on school behaviour, on the grounds that teachers were likely to provide a more objective assessment of children's behaviour than were their mothers, even though the teacher's evaluation would be based on the general behavioural characteristics of all the pupils he or she teaches, with the corollary that what is deemed deviant in one school is an acceptable norm in another. Our ten-year behaviour scales, therefore, assess each child's behaviour in relation to that of his peers at school rather than to absolute behavioural norms. We also recognise that in many instances a particular behaviour pattern is situation-specific; that is to say, a child's behaviour at school may differ significantly from his behaviour at home or elsewhere. School behaviour, however, can have important consequences for educational progress and vice versa, and it is essential to recognise that the association between behavioural deviance and educational attainment is a two-way process. Inattentiveness in the classroom may contribute to poor achievement, but inability to cope with school tasks may result in frustration and rebellious behaviour (Schultz and Heuchert, 1983).

Behavioural scales completed by the child's class teacher included items from the Rutter B scale (Rutter *et al.*, 1970, Appendix 5) and the Connors teacher rating scale (Connors, 1969). A total of 76 items were subjected to correlational, principal components, and semantic analysis which resulted in the creation of seven behavioural scales (see Appendix). These scales are described briefly below.

Conduct disorder (10 items)

Identifies children who tease, interfere or quarrel with others, complain about things, are destructive or bullying, have temper tantrums or who suddenly change mood or become sullen.

Hyperactivity (6 items)

Strongly associated with conduct disorder (r = .75). Identifies children who are excitable, impulsive, squirmy, fidgety, restless, overactive, make odd vocal noises or make rhythmic tapping.

Application (15 items)

Identifies children who are unable to concentrate on or persevere with school tasks, are readily distracted and often do not complete tasks they start.

Extroversion (6 items)

Identifies children able to talk easily with friends or teachers and are not shy.

Peer relations (4 items)

Identifies chilren who are popular and have a number of friends with whom they are cooperative rather than being solitary.

Anxiety (9 items)

Similar to the five-year neuroticism scale. Identifies children who are fearful, nervous, worried, miserable, fussy or obsessional.

Clumsiness (12 items)

Identifies children who are clumsy in gross or fine motor movements, trip or bump into things, tend to have accidents or drop things.

All five- and ten-year behaviour scales were scored to give a mean of zero and a standard deviation of one. The intercorrelations between the behaviour scales and their correlation with the attainment test scores are given in the Appendix. Not surprisingly certain behavioural traits were found to be associated with each other. Children with conduct disorders were very likely to be hyperactive and to have greater difficulty in applying themselves effectively to their schoolwork. Poor application was also associated with reduced self-expression (communication) and both these types of behaviour predicted lower scores in the ten-year cognitive ability and attainment tests. These associations cannot be interpreted as indicating one-way causal relationships, since conduct disorders and disaffection with school goals may stem as much from low achievement as vice versa. Nevertheless, one of the more frequently mentioned purposes of preschool experience is to ease the transition into full-time attendance at infant school and its role in this respect could result in better adjustment to the school regime and ultimately lead to better educational performance.

We examine first the simple associations between preschool experience and children's behaviour at 5 and 10 years.

Behaviour and preschool groups

Table 5.1 shows the deviation from overall mean scores for the preschool groups as defined in Chapter 4 (Table 4.1) for the two scales of behaviour in the home at 5 years as assessed by the mothers, and for the seven scales of behaviour in the school at 10 years as assessed by the class teachers. A strong relationship was found between preschool experience and behaviour for all the scales except five-year neuroticism.

Comparison of the general pattern of results across all the behavioural scales shows one persistent effect. Children who attended LA day nurseries were more deviant than other preschool groups with respect to every behavioural attribute. The LA day nursery children were prone to antisocial and aggressive behaviour, were hyperactive and unable to concentrate on school work, did not get on well with others at school, were clumsy and anxious. There was no other group that showed a consistently opposite tendency to this, although children who had attended home playgroups were least likely to be antisocial or have conduct disorders and were more likely to be disciplined in their approach to school work.

The explanation for the high level of behavioural deviance in the LA day nursery children is clearly that many of these children were severely disadvantaged and the adverse home circumstances that lay behind the reasons for their being placed in day nurseries also provoked their deviant behaviour. However, it should be noted that children who attended other maintained institutions or had no preschool experience were also socially disadvantaged, though not, perhaps, to the same extent as LA day nursery children, yet they did not show the same high risk of deviance. Thus it is possible that the children's preschool experience contributed a small part to these

Table 5.1 *Mean behaviour scores by main preschool placement*

Main preschool placement	Five-year		Ten-year						
	Anti-social	Neurotic	Conduct disorder	Hyper-activity	Appli-cation	Extro-version	Peer relations	Anxiety	Clumsiness
No preschool	.08	−.04	.02	.03	.12	−.09	−.05	.05	.05
Maintained									
LEA nursery school	.04	.05	−.01	−.10	−.06	.08	.09	−.07	−.02
LEA nursery class	.09	.00	.13	.11	.07	.05	−.01	.05	.07
LA day nursery	.41	.09	.37	.42	.27	.22	−.29	.23	.32
Independent									
Nursery school	−.32	−.07	.00	−.09	−.15	.02	.06	.05	.07
Day nursery	.04	.10	.13	.01	−.07	.09	−.05	.07	−.08
Hall playgroup	−.13	.03	−.08	−.08	−.14	.05	.05	−.06	−.08
Home playgroup	−.30	−.10	−.12	−.07	−.29	.02	.09	−.06	−.10
Overall mean	.02	.00	.00	.00	.02	−.02	−.01	.02	.01
Standard deviation	1.00	1.00	1.01	1.00	0.99	1.00	1.00	1.01	1.00
TOTAL N	9,077	9,082	7,228	7,228	7,229	7,230	7,226	7,228	7,228
Significance	p<.0005	ns	p<.0005	p<.0005	p<.0005	p<.0005	p<.0005	p<.0005	p<.0005

Note: Figures show deviation from overall mean.

behavioural outcomes. The contribution of home background factors to the mean behaviour scores, however, must be taken into account as intervening factors before the possible behavioural consequences of children's preschool experience can be assessed.

Intervening factors and behaviour

The same set of social and family factors were examined in terms of their associations with all the five- and ten-year behavioural outcomes as were given in Table 4.3 but with a slightly different pattern of results. Certain factors were more strongly associated with the children's behaviour than with their educational test performance.

The Social Index was, with one exception, the factor most strongly associated with both five- and ten-year behaviour scores. The exception was the marked association between the child's gender and the hyperactivity score; gender explained 5.6% of the variance in hyperactivity compared with 1.6% for the Social Index score. Boys were more likely to be described as hyperactive than were girls, the difference in mean score amounting to .47 standard deviations. Girls, in contrast, were reported as being able to work with greater concentration at school than were boys. These results suggested that the child's gender should be included as an intervening variable even though the association between gender and type of preschool experience was relatively weak.

Maternal depression was strongly predictive of a number of behaviours, particularly five-year antisocial and neurotic behaviour. The fact that mothers completed both the behaviour and depression scales in the five-year survey contributed much to this correlation; mothers who saw depressive symptoms in themselves were likely to also see signs of behavioural deviance in their children. Also, however, in situations where depressed mothers have to cope with difficult children each tends to exacerbate the other's problems. Thus there are both real and methodological explanations for the correlation between behavioural deviance and maternal depression.

Type of neighbourhood, family size and type of family were the only other variables which explained a significant proportion of the variance in the behavioural scores and, with Social Index, gender, and maternal depression, were expected to be the principal inter-

vening variables in our analysis of the association between preschool experience and behaviour scores.

Behaviour at age five

We continued to follow the same procedure with our analysis of the
behavioural outcomes as was used with the educational and cognitive tests. Using analysis of variance to statistically adjust for the
effects of Social Index, type of neighbourhood and number of
children in the family (the basic model) we then introduced each of
the other independent variables in turn into the analysis and
observed the effect on the preschool groups' mean scores; the aim,
as we have stated, being to try to eliminate the associations between
children's preschool experience and their behavioural scores.

After statistical adjustment for the three basic variables, the
association between the child's main preschool placement and antisocial behaviour in the home, as rated by the mother, was substantially weakened, and after further adjustment either for type of
family (two-parent, single-parent, etc.) or maternal depression, was
reduced to statistical non-significance. Neurotic behaviour did not
vary between preschool groups prior to adjustment for the effects
of intervening variables, but when maternal depression was added
to the analysis a significant difference occurred between children
who attended LA day nurseries and those who went to hall playgroups (p < .05); the former were at reduced risk of neuroticism.
Such an effect, however, could be a spurious result of 'over-adjust-
ment' as a consequence of the fairly strong association between
neuroticism and maternal depression (r = .34) due, in part, to the
fact that the mothers completed both scales.

In general, these analyses of the five-year behavioural scales did
not suggest that attendance at preschool institutions either
increased or decreased the risk of five-year behaviour problems in
the home.

Behaviour at age 10

There were several reasons why we investigated the associations
between preschool experience and ten-year behaviour, even though
its relationship with the five-year behavioural outcomes was weak
after adjustment had been made for salient social and family

factors. Firstly, the ten-year measures were assessments of behaviour at school, rather than at home. Secondly, there were a number of additional behavioural dimensions obtained at age 10 but not at age 5 to which preschool experience might have been relevant. Thirdly, we were aware of the so called 'sleeper effect' on child development and behaviour attributable to preschool experience. This concept has been invoked in response to findings from a number of American longitudinal studies demonstrating long-term gains which were attributed to early education despite the lack of early effects (Brown (ed.), 1978; Kagan and Moss, 1962). More recently, however, the concept of the 'sleeper effect' has been subjected to some criticism (Clarke and Clarke, 1981) and is giving way to the idea of a transactional and cumulative explanatory model to account for this emergence of later educational gains after preschool intervention (Clarke, 1984 (a) and (b); Schweinhart and Weikart, 1980).

A general pattern could be discerned across all the analyses of the associations between preschool experience and ten-year behaviour although only three of the seven remained statistically significant after adjustment for the intervening variables. The most favourable behavioural outcomes were associated with children who had no preschool experience or who had attended LEA nursery schools, and the least favourable outcomes were associated with LA day nursery attendance. This general pattern was best exemplified in the analyses for conduct disorder, hyperactivity and extroversion (see Table 5.2) in which the preschool effect retained its statistical significance.

The similarity between the analyses for conduct disorder and hyperactivity was not surprising given the strong correlation between these types of behaviour ($r = .75$). In both these analyses there were marked gender differences with boys being far more likely to show conduct disorder and hyperactive behaviour than girls. Adjustment for the child's gender tended to increase the differences between children classified according to their type of preschool experience, whereas adjustment for social and family factors tended to reduce the preschool effects. If the mean conduct disorder scores for the main preschool placement are examined after statistical adjustment for the three basic variables plus child's gender and type of family (Table 5.2), we are led to the conclusion that the effect was entirely due to the higher mean scores of the

Table 5.2 *Mean adjusted behaviour scores for preschool groups*

Main preschool placement	Ten-year		
	Conduct disorder	Hyperactivity	Extroversion
None	−.05	−.03	−.06
Maintained			
LEA nursery school	−.02	−.01	.08
LEA nursery class	.08	.08	.07
LA day nursery	.20	.27	.15
Independent			
Nursery school	.20	.03	.03
Day nursery	.19	.09	.02
Hall playgroup	.01	−.01	.02
Home playgroup	.04	.04	.00
Overall mean	.00	−.01	−.02
TOTAL N	6,871	6,871	6,873
Significance	p< .005	p< .05	p< .05

Note: Figures show deviation from overall mean after adjustment for Social Index, type of neighbourhood, number of children in the family, child's gender, and type of family.

children who attended LA or independent day nurseries or independent nursery schools. In the analysis of hyperactivity the effect could be attributed only to the children who went to LA day nurseries. Omission of the LA day nursery group from these analyses reduced the association between type of preschool experience and behaviour to statistical non-significance.

The extroversion scale correlated at a low level with the conduct disorder and hyperactivity scales and, unlike the latter, was unrelated to the child's gender. High scorers on the extroversion scale were talkative with peers and teachers and were bold and confident in their relationships with others. These children were likely to be popular and cooperative with their friends (r = .43 with peer relations scale), and extroversion was positively, though not very strongly, associated with ten-year test performance (r = .11 to .13). Conceptually, extroversion differs from the other behaviour dimensions in that both tails of the hypothesised distribution contain deviant cases—high scorers are over-talkative or garrulous and low scorers silent and withdrawn. The other behaviour dimensions are more unidimensional with increasing degrees of conduct disorder, hyperactivity or whatever the particular scale measures. Thus both exceptionally high and exceptionally low scorers on the extroversion scale might be deemed deviant—this could explain the relatively low correlations with the test outcomes if the associations between extroversion and educational tests are in fact non-linear.

In the analyses of preschool experience related to the introversion–extroversion dimension we found children with the lowest mean scores were those with no preschool experience and the highest mean scores were for children who attended LA day nurseries (Table 5.2). The overall difference between these extremes was .21 standard deviations after adjustment for the relevant intervening factors. This difference was comparable with those for the Social Index, type of family and family size. This analysis suggested that preschool educational experience was a significant factor in the introversion–extroversion dimension.

Self-esteem and locus of control

Our analysis thus far has examined the children's behaviour at home and in the school as perceived by their mothers and teachers.

We have found that preschool education influenced certain kinds of behaviour, but not others. Our final discussion in this chapter describes how preschool experience affected the children's own self-image.

Two scales, designed to assess locus of control and self-esteem, were created for this purpose, and these are described in detail in the Appendix. Locus of control is a concept which has been devised by educationalists concerned with classroom studies who have found that children who are self-directed are more successful educationally than those who are other-directed. 'Other-directedness' is akin to the fatalistic attitudes, frequently attributed to working-class culture, which are believed to be a contributory factor in social class differences in school performance (Lefcourt, 1972; Gammage, 1975). The locus of control measure (CARALOC) used in this study was assembled by Philip Gammage, a British authority in this field. The scale consists of 15 items which are scored and standardised to give a mean of 100 and a standard deviation of 15. Low scores indicate children who were fatalistic and felt they were other-directed, and high scores indicate children who were inner-directed.

Self-esteem was assessed by means of the Lawrence Self-Esteem Questionnaire (LAWSEQ, Lawrence, 1973, 1978) which consists of 12 items which were scored and standardised to give a mean of 100 and a standard deviation of 15. Low scores were achieved by children who had a poor opinion of themselves and believed that they were not much liked by others.

The CARALOC and LAWSEQ scales were positively correlated (r = .35) so that children with a poor self-image also tended to believe that they were ineffectual in their relations with others and in their schoolwork. A similar degree of correlation was found between the CARALOC scale, the ten-year attainment test scores and the 'application' behavioural dimension (details given in the Appendix). Thus there was a tendency for self-directedness, good communication, a positive attitude to school work and high achievement to coincide.

Our analysis of the relationship between children's preschool experience and their locus of control and self-esteem was carried out in the same way as for the other behavioural analyses, but no significant associations were found after adjustment was made for the relevant intervening variables. Thus if preschool education is

expected to increase a child's self-confidence and self-deter-
mination, there is no evidence from our data that such an effect
persists to the age of ten.

Conclusions

Behavioural assessments were made at 5 and 10 years using screen-
ing instruments that consisted of a number of behavioural scales
analysed and scored by means of principal components analysis.
Mothers completed the five-year behavioural scales on their children and two scores were computed to provide indices of antisocial
and neurotic behaviour in the home. When the children were 10,
behavioural items were completed by their class teacher and 7
indices of behaviour in the school were computed. Finally, the
study children completed a questionnaire themselves which incorporated scales designed to measure locus of control and self-esteem.

A detailed analysis was carried out designed to minimise the
possibility that any associations between the child's type of preschool experience and his behaviour could be attributed to other
socio-economic or family factors. It was found that children's
preschool experience was significantly associated with only 4 out of
the total of 9 behaviour scales. These were five-year neuroticism
and ten-year conduct disorder, hyperactivity and extroversion.

The strongest association, after adjustment for intervening social
and family variables, was with ten-year conduct disorder, and
children who attended LA or independent day nurseries or private
nursery schools were found to be the most deviant. Also children
who attended LA day nurseries were more likely than non-
attenders to show hyperactive or extrovert behaviour at school. It is
possible that full-time attendance and long hours at day nurseries
may have been contributory factors in these results and this is
investigated in Chapter 7.

These results suggest that the type of preschool experience a child
is exposed to can influence some but not all aspects of her later
behaviour. However, the associations were relatively weak and
could be due to intervening factors that at this point we have not
identified. This is in sharp contrast with the results for the cognitive
and educational tests reported in Chapter 4 which retained a strong
association with preschool experience after following a similar
analytical process.

6

Home and school experience between five and ten years of age

As children grow older their home and family circumstances change in many ways, but the precise pattern of change is liable to vary from child to child. In general things tend to improve with passage of time; incomes may rise and a mode of family life becomes established which the young child understands and can depend on. Despite this, most families are susceptible to events which can disrupt this familiar way of life; a younger sister is born, an older brother leaves home, the family moves house. Normally the parents are able to prepare their children for these minor changes and help them adjust to the new circumstances, but other events may occur that are more traumatic and can have a lasting effect on the child's developmental progress and behaviour; the father is made redundant, the family is evicted from their home, the marriage breaks up, a parent dies.

While all families experience such changes at some time, certain social groups are more vulnerable to stress-provoking life events than others. Many single-parent families, for example, experience downward social mobility (Osborn *et al.*, 1984, pp. 49–53), socially disadvantaged families are more likely to have a greater number of children and are at increased risk of marital breakdown compared with socially advantaged families. Given that this propensity for family change varies between different social groups and that the type of preschool placement in which a child is enrolled is partly determined by family circumstances, we can expect that the changes in home life to which some children in our study were subjected between the ages of 5 and 10, might constitute intervening factors in the relationship between their preschool experience and educational attainment and behaviour at the age of ten. In this chapter, therefore, we examine the significance of certain social and family changes for the associations we have described in Chapters 4 and 5 between preschool experience and subsequent child development.

This is done with respect to four factors: (1) change in Social Index score as an indicator of upward or downward social mobility of the family; (2) change in type of family; (3) change in family size; (4) type of junior school attended.

Social mobility

Children in upwardly mobile families might be expected to perform better in attainment tests than those who are downwardly mobile or whose social circumstances remain unchanged. However, it should be noted that the possibilities for mobility are dependent partly on a family's initial position in the social hierarchy; those at the top can only go down and those at the bottom can only go up—this results in the well-known 'regression to the mean' effect.

For the purposes of the present study, social mobility has been defined as the arithmetic difference between the five- and ten-year Social Index scores. The result of this computation is summarised in Table 6.1 which shows that 26% of the sample changed by no more than 1 point in Social Index score over the five years. Almost half the families were upwardly mobile by at least 2 Social Index points and more than one in four by a minimum of 5 points which represents a change equivalent to half a standard deviation in Social Index score. Another 26% of the sample experienced downward mobility of at least 2 Social Index points, and 9% had scores reduced by at least 5 points.

To examine the effect of social mobility on children's ten-year test scores this variable was added as an independent factor in an analysis of variance together with the basic independent variables (five-year Social Index score, type of neighbourhood, number of

Table 6.1   *Change in Social Index score between five and ten years*

	N	%
More than 4 points fall	1,011	9.3
2 to 4 points fall	1,779	16.3
Within 1 point of five-year score	2,861	26.2
2 to 4 points rise	2,340	21.4
More than 4 points rise	2,933	27.8
TOTAL	10,924	100.0

Note: A fall in Social Index score between five- and ten-year surveys indicates a decline in socio-economic circumstances, a rise in the score indicates an improvement.

children in the family and main preschool placement) for each of the ten-year tests and assessments in turn. This showed a very consistent pattern in which children from upwardly mobile families achieved higher scores than those in downwardly mobile families. It is important to note that the five-year Social Index score was included in the analysis of variance so that the higher test scores achieved by upwardly mobile children represented a change from that predicted by their 1975 Social Index position. In concrete terms, a group of children who were socially disadvantaged at 5 years of age would have lower mean test scores at ten than socially advantaged children. But those in the five-year disadvantaged group who were upwardly mobile had higher ten-year test scores than the others in this group whose families were not mobile. However, the upwardly mobile group were unlikely to achieve test scores on a par with the children who were socially advantaged over the whole period.

The effect of social mobility on children's behaviour at school was less clear cut than for the educational tests. Upwardly mobile children were on better terms with their peers than were down-wardly mobile children and there were weak associations with the application and anxiety scales. All the other behaviour scales, however, were not significantly associated with social mobility.

Clearly the analysis of children's test performance related to social mobility is a complicated issue. For present purposes, how-ever, it is sufficient to note that mobility has an important effect on children's educational test scores with possible implications for the associations we have been describing between children's preschool experience and educational attainment. These implications are examined later in this chapter after first considering the effects of other types of change between 5 and 10.

Change in parental situation

One of the most emotionally disturbing events that can affect a young child is the change or loss of a parent figure, and this is something that is happening to greater numbers of children than hitherto (Study Commission on the Family, 1980). Five years is a relatively short period, yet in the CHES sample one child in ten had experienced some kind of change in his or her parental situation between their fifth and tenth birthdays (Table 6.2). The total

Table 6.2 *Type of family (1980) by type of family (1975)*

Type of family (1980)	Type of family (1975)						
	Two parents			One parent		Neither natural parent (fostered or with grandparents)	All
	Both natural parents	Adoptive parents	Step-family	Supported single parent	Lone parent		
Two parents							
both natural parents	84.4	0.0	0.1	0.1	0.1	0.0	84.8
adoptive parents	0.0	0.6	0.0	0.0	0.0	0.0	0.6
step-family	2.1	0.0	2.1	0.7	1.3	0.0	6.2
One parent							
supported single parent	0.9	0.0	0.1	0.7	0.3	0.0	2.0
lone parent	3.4	0.0	0.3	0.4	1.8	0.0	5.9
Neither natural parent	0.1	0.0	0.0	0.0	0.0	0.3	0.5
All	90.9	0.7	2.6	1.9	3.5	0.4	100.0

Note: Figures denote percentages of grand total N = 11,299. Sign test: Chi square = 252.3 (1df) p<.0005.

proportion of children living with both natural or adoptive parents declined from 91% in 1975 to 85% in 1980. The proportion of children who moved from a two-parent family situation in 1975 to a one-parent family in 1980 was 5%, whilst 2% changed from a one-parent to a two-parent situation.

For the purposes of the present analysis the complex pattern of change in Table 6.2 needed to be considerably simplified. Thus we assumed a classification of types of family that formed a hierarchy from the optimal situation (both natural parents present) to the least desirable from the child's point of view (foster-parents or grandparents). This entailed making a value judgement about the benefit for the child of different family situations, but we felt the assumptions were justified. Generally speaking, it is better for the child to be with both natural parents than to have one parent replaced by a stepparent; if that is not possible a stepfamily is usually preferable to a one-parent family, and finally, it is better to be with one natural parent than to be in foster care. These assumptions will not stand up in every case, and a tranquil stepfamily could provide a more desirable situation than a family which consists of both natural parents but is fraught with tensions and hostility. However, the child in the stepfamily would have been subjected to a disruption in her family life not experienced by most children who continue to live with both natural parents.

If we accept this assumption of a hierarchical relationship between the categories of the family classification, then those cases falling below the diagonal (7%) can be said to have experienced a change for the worse between the ages of 5 and 10, whilst those above the diagonal experienced a change for the better (3%). The balance (90%) were in the same parental situation on both occasions.

Using the same method as described above for social mobility, we investigated the association between change in type of family and ten-year tests and assessments. For these analyses, the child's type of family at age 5 was also included as an independent variable to provide a base against which the change in family situation could be compared.

Change in type of family was significantly associated with only one of the five ten-year cognitive and educational tests—reading, and this was at a relatively low level of statistical probabilty ($p < .05$). A change for the worse in parental situation was associated with lower reading scores, whereas a change for the better predicted a higher score. In general, however, change in family type as defined here had little effect on test scores after adjustment for the other independent variables.

Previous analyses demonstrated that type of family was more strongly associated with children's behaviour than with their cognitive abilities, and the findings for conduct disorder and hyperactivity agreed with this general pattern. A change for the worse in family type was associated with increased risk of conduct disorder and hyperactivity whereas this risk decreased with a change for the better. There were no significant associations between change in family situation and any of the other behavioural assessments.

Change in family size

It is well known that children from large families perform less well in educational tests than those from families of one or two children, and the National Child Development Study has demonstrated that small changes in reading and arithmetic scores can follow a change in family size between a child's seventh and eleventh birthdays (Fogelman and Goldstein, 1976).

In the present study 72% of the children were from families in which the total number of children was the same at the five- and ten-year follow-ups; 40% of the sample being in two-child families on both occasions. Some of these families would have experienced some change, as older children became 'adults' on their eighteenth birthday and were replaced by other children; for example, step-siblings that entered the family when a parent remarried. These more complex aspects have not been investigated further for the purposes of the present study, and the main categories of change studied were those that involved a net increase or decrease in family size. Between the ages of 5 and 10, 15% of the families increased in size by at least one additional child; only 2% had increased by two or more children. Almost the same proportion of families had decreased in size, 8% had one and 5% at least two fewer children (Table 6.3).

Change in family size was found to be significantly related to all five ten-year test scores. The main effect was that an increase in family size, especially of two or more children, reduced the child's test score. Change in family size had no effect on the behavioural assessments.

Table 6.3   *Change in family size*

	N	%
Decrease of two or more children	573	5.1
Decrease of one child	948	8.4
Same number of children	8,120	71.9
Increase of one child	1,448	12.8
Increase of two or more children	211	1.9
TOTAL	11,300	100.0

Type of junior school attended

It was highly probable that parents who had paid for their children to attend private nursery schools or home playgroups would be the ones most likely to wish to send their children to independent junior or preparatory schools, and to be in a position to do so. To the extent that independent schools are more achievement-orientated than maintained schools, this was an obvious factor to be tested as an intervening variable.

Three-quarters of the children in our sample were, at the age of 10, attending schools that were fully maintained by the LEA (Table 6.4). Less than 4% attended Direct Grant or independent schools, the remainder attended voluntary controlled or voluntary aided schools (9% and 13% respectively). As expected there were substantial social differences between the children who attended different types of school. There was a trend across Social Index groups from 81% of the most disadvantaged children who attended maintained schools to 62% of the most advantaged. Opposite trends were found in the proportions of children who attended voluntary-controlled and Direct Grant or independent schools.

Table 6.4   *Type of junior school attended*

	N	%
Maintained	8,960	74.6
Voluntary controlled	1,100	9.2
Voluntary aided	1,524	12.7
Direct Grant	108	0.9
Independent	311	2.6
TOTAL	12,003	100.0

Table 6.5   Main preschool placement by type of junior school at ten years

Main preschool placement		Type of junior school				
		Maintained	Voluntary-controlled	Voluntary-aided	Direct Grant/Independent	N = 100%
No preschool	%	74.2	9.3	14.8	1.8	2,757
Maintained						
LEA nursery school	%	75.3	6.9	15.2	2.7	481
LEA nursery class	%	83.1	4.7	11.0	1.2	829
LA day nursery	%	72.3	6.0	20.5	1.2	83
Independent						
Nursery school	%	65.6	9.4	9.4	15.6	32
Day nursery	%	69.4	12.4	16.5	1.7	121
Hall playgroup	%	73.6	11.3	11.3	3.8	2,417
Home playgroup	%	72.0	9.8	10.6	7.6	132
All	%	74.9	9.3	13.1	2.7	6,852

Note: This table is based on the matched sub-sample. Chi square (21 df) = 116.1 p<.0005.

There was also some continuity between the type of preschool experience the child had and her subsequent schooling (Table 6.5). In particular children who went to private nursery schools and home playgroups were more likely to be attending independent schools at age 10 than were children with other types of preschool experience. The findings, however, suggested that subsequent schooling was not likely to be an important intervening factor in the association between preschooling and ten-year tests and assessments because of the relatively small proportion of children who attended independent schools.

The mean test scores at age 10 associated with type of junior school after adjustment for other independent facors showed attendance at Direct Grant and independent schools to be associated with increased test scores, particularly BAS and reading. However, children who attended voluntary controlled or voluntary aided schools achieved similar test scores to those who went to maintained schools. The type of school the children attended was unrelated to their behavioural assessments at 10.

The effect of social and family change on the associations between preschool experience and ten-year cognitive and educational ability

The main purpose of this chapter is to check whether the children's experiences between the ages of 5 and 10 had any appreciable effect on the associations we have found between the type of preschool education they received and their ability, attainment and behaviour at 10. This was achieved using the same procedure as described in Chapter 4: a series of analyses of variance were carried out so that mean test scores associated with different preschool groups in a basic analysis of variance could be compared with those obtained after an additional independent variable was added. The change factor that was itself associated most strongly with test scores was change in Social Index score and it was expected because of this to be the most significant intervening change variable in the preschool-test associations. However, even this variable had very little impact on the effects attributable to the child's preschool education. In the analysis with British Ability Scale score as dependent variable, change in Social Index score increased the mean score of children with no preschool experience by .09 points, and decreased the mean score of children who attended home playgroups by .01 points which are very small amounts given that the BAS standard deviation is 15. Also, these two groups still had the lowest and highest mean BAS scores respectively and the preschool effect retained its statistical significance (p < .0005).

Change in type of family or in family size slightly increased the differences in mean scores between preschool groups for BAS, Picture Language Test and reading. The significance of the association between preschool experience and PLT was also increased to p < .005. The association between main preschool placement and mathematics score was unaffected by any of the change variables.

Finally, differences in communication skills which were attributable to children's preschool experience were slightly reduced by changes in their socio-economic circumstances between the ages of 5 and 10. This mainly affected children who had attended LA day nurseries whose mean score increased by .07 points after adjustment for Social Index change which represents a small improvement in expressive language for this group. The mean communication score of children who had attended independent nursery schools decreased by .05 points after adjustment for change in Social Index, which indicated a reduction in the advantage attributable to attendance at this type of preschool institution. As a result of this the mean communication score of LEA nursery school attenders was the same as that of children who went to independent nursery school, after taking account of the social change which had occurred between 5 and 10. This was the only instance, however, where small improvements in mean scores of children with different types of preschool experience due to changes between 5 and 10 resulted in a change in ranking of the preschool groups.

From these analyses we conclude that although changes in the child's social and family circumstances after the age of 5 resulted in small alterations in the effects of preschool experience on ten-year test scores, the main preschool effects persisted.

The effect of social and family change on the associations between preschool experience and ten-year behavioural assessments

The only behavioural assessments which were significantly related to children's preschool experience after adjustment for the basic five-year intervening factors were conduct disorder, hyperactivity and extroversion (see Chapter 5). The other behavioural dimensions—application, peer relations, anxiety and clumsiness—were reanalysed with the change variables added to the basic analyses of variance to check whether unmeasured social change between ages 5 and 10 had been effectively eliminating any association, but this did not lead to new conclusions regarding these outcomes.

We noted above that change in type of family was strongly associated with conduct disorder and hyperactivity; a change for the worse in the parental situation increased the risk of these types of behaviour. When five-year type of family and family change variables were added into the analysis of variance for conduct disorder, there was a reduction in the risk of conduct disorder attributed to attendance at LA day nurseries. Most of this effect, however, was found to be due to five-year family type and change in family type resulted in only small adjustments in the mean conduct disorder scores for preschool groups.

Exactly the same interpretation was made for the analysis related to hyperactivity. Differences in risk of hyperactive behaviour in 10-year-olds that were attributable to the type of preschool placement they had experienced were in fact largely due to their parental circumstances at the age of 5, and family change betwen 5 and 10 made little further difference to the preschool effect. Family and social change between five- and ten-year surveys made no difference to the association between preschool groups and extroversion.

An alternative analytical approach

It is often the case that social circumstances of children at the time of testing are more strongly related to their performance than are earlier events and conditions of life. Thus it was possible that by basing all our analyses on children's circumstances at the age of 5, less of the variance in ten-year test scores was being explained than if ten-year independent variables were used. The reason why five-year social variables feature so much in our analysis is that they were more relevant to variation in utilisation of preschool services. The purpose of the present chapter is to take account of the ten-year situation of the children by creating the change variables we have described and examining their effect in addition to that of the five-year independent variables. We consider this to be the most appropriate longitudinal approach. However, we decided to test whether children's preschool experience could explain any of the residual variance in ten-year test scores in regression analyses containing only ten-year variables (apart from the preschool variable itself).

The independent variables included in these regressions were: ten-year Social Index, maternal depression, child's height, child's gender, any handicap in the child, type of family, family size, country of residence, age of mother, type of junior school attended, parental interest in the child's education and the preschool variable. Dependent variables were BAS, Picture Language Test, reading, mathematics and communication. The preschool variable retained a high degree of statistical significance ($p < .0005$) with respect to all tests except PLT ($p < .005$) and the mean scores for the preschool groups were remarkably similar to those reported in Chapter 4.

This alternative approach adds weight to the conclusion that social change and educational experience after the preschool period were not responsible for the preschool effect on later achievement.

Conclusions

Changes in social and family circumstances between the five-year and ten-year studies were investigated as possible intervening factors in the associations between preschool experience and children's educational attainment and behaviour at 10 years shown in previous chapters. Four types of change were analysed: change in Social Index score as an indicator of social mobility, change in type of family, change in size of family and the type of junior school attended at age 10.

Factors which had a significant effect on ten-year educational and cognitive test scores were: change in Social Index score, change in family size, and type of junior school. Change in type of family made no appreciable difference to these test scores.

Associations between change variables and the ten-year behavioural assessments are less easily summarised. Change in Social Index score showed a weak association with the application, peer relations and anxiety scales. Change in type of family was an important factor in the analyses of conduct disorder and hyperactivity scales. Changes in family size and type of junior school attended were in the main not associated with any of the behavioural assessments after adjustment for other relevant intervening variables.

An examination of how the change variables affected the relationships between children's preschool experience and their ten-year test results and behavioural assessments concluded that there was little evidence that these relationships were a spurious result of the child's experiences between 5 and 10. The analysis of the communication scale, however, did show that adding change of Social Index score to the basic analysis of variance resulted in a slight reordering of the preschool categories. After taking into account change in Social Index score, the children with the highest mean communication score were those who attended LEA nursery schools or independent nursery schools.

An alternative analytical approach, in which several ten-year independent variables plus the preschool variable were introduced into regression analyses with the ten-year tests as dependents, provided further evidence that the preschool effects persisted.

This chapter has shown that children's experiences between ages 5 and 10 did not undermine the preschool effects on ten-year test scores. However, those variables which had even a small influence on the preschool effects were used in the final analytical models described in Chapter 10 to check whether all such factors in combination could finally eliminate the preschool effect.

7

Frequency and duration of attendance at preschool institutions and age at infant school entry

The finding that children's attendance at preschool institutions apparently results in improvement in their cognitive ability and educational attainment immediately raises questions about the *amount* of preschool education required to achieve this result. Is it the case, for example, that children who attend a nursery school for a year gain twice as much in terms of improved test scores as children who attend the same nursery school for only six months, all other things being equal? Such a question is very hypothetical since it rarely happens that all other things are in fact equal. However, even on its own terms the simple quantitative approach to nursery education is probably wrong because there must be an age below which children are simply unable to benefit from attending a preschool institution. It would be a remarkable 2-year-old who could benefit from nursery experiences designed for 3- and 4-year-olds, yet in order to have two years' preschool experience a child would need to start attending before the age of 3 in most instances because the majority of children enter infant reception classes before their fifth birthday. Thus the length of time a child spends in a preschool placement depends in part on the normal school entry age in the area where she lives as well as her age when she first starts attending the preschool institution. Sometimes, however, a child is admitted to infant school earlier than the average child because, having spent a period at a preschool institution, she is considered by parents and head teacher to be ready for school. Thus the duration of a child's preschool education and the transition into infant school are integrally linked. It is evident from this that behind a simple concept like 'length of time in the preschool facility' lies a network of factors depending on parental wishes and preschool, school and local authority policies which affect the age at which children start attending both preschool placements and infant schools. These factors in turn, vary according to the area where the family lives, the types of preschool provision available and the socio-economic position of the family. This complexity creates difficult problems for any analysis designed to measure the effects of duration of children's preschool experience on their subsequent development.

The second dimension of 'quantity' in which there is a lot of interest is the frequency of attendance at preschool institutions. It is important to know whether or not children who attend institutions full-time progress differently from those who attend part-time. Again there are difficulties in that patterns of attendance depend on the type of institution the child attends (see Chapter 2), the proximity of the preschool institution to the child's home, and the need for all-day care for special reasons—for example where both parents have full-time jobs. Finally, many children start attending their preschool placement for only a few sessions and by degrees increase the frequency of attendance. The information from our survey describes the final pattern of attendance prior to starting infant school and we do not know for how long this had applied.

In this chapter we describe in more concrete terms the various patterns of attendance of children in the CHES sample and then attempt to assess the implications of this for their later development.

Patterns of attendance

We have said that the length of time a child spends in preschool education is complicated by local variations in age at infant school entry as well as by other factors; but in addition some children attend more than one placement consecutively. 30% of children whose main preschool placement was a LEA nursery school or class had attended another placement prior to the main one and in most instances this was an independent preschool institution. A typical sequence was for a child to start by attending a playgroup and then move to the LEA nursery school or class when a place became available. This is one means by which mothers are able to control the way their children are introduced into the preschool system, with the child starting at playgroup at a relatively young age and for fewer sessions per week than at nursery school, then graduating to more frequent attendance in the formal educational setting provided by the LEA nursery school or class before finally entering infant school. This process is only possible, of course, where such a combination of facilities is available.

For more than 85% of children who attended independent institutions the main preschool placement was their only placement. The majority of children who had attended a preschool placement prior to the main one went to other independent institutions; very few attended maintained nurseries and then went on to an institution in the independent sector.

A very small number of children had attended more than one institution concurrently and these were excluded from the preschool classification because of the complications that would have resulted from having a small group of children matched with more than one preschool institution. Children who attended two preschool institutions usually went to two playgroups, probably because the playgroups operated only 1 or 2 sessions a week and the mother wished her child to attend more frequently.

Table 7.1 shows the age at which children started attending their main preschool placement. More than half of those who went to LA day nurseries and 37% of those attending independent day nurseries started before 3 years of age. Very few LEA nursery school or nursery class children started so young (7% and 2%) although about one in five playgroup children first attended before the age of 3. The majority of children who went to nursery schools

Table 7.1 *Age started main preschool placement by main preschool placement*

Main preschool placement		Age started main preschool placement			N
		< 3 yrs	≥ 3 yrs < 4 yrs	≥ 4 yrs	
Maintained					
LEA nursery school	%	7.2	65.4	27.4	642
LEA nursery class	%	1.7	55.5	42.8	1,091
LA day nursery	%	53.4	31.4	15.3	118
Independent					
Nursery school	%	12.5	62.5	25.0	40
Day nursery	%	37.3	48.7	14.0	150
Hall playgroup	%	19.9	66.7	13.4	3,137
Home playgroup	%	19.7	69.1	11.2	178

and classes or playgroups, however, started between the ages of 3 and 4. The children who were most likely to have started preschool late were those who went to LEA nursery classes (43%). However, 28% of this group had previously attended other institutions.

The end of preschool education usually coincided with the start of infant school. As the children in the CHES sample were all born in April 1970, they were legally required to start school at the beginning of the Summer term 1975. About one-third of the children who attended a preschool placement started infant school at age 5 compared with a quarter of those with no preschool experience (Table 7.2).

Table 7.2   *Age started school by main preschool placement*

Main preschool placement		Age started infant school				N
		≤ 4yrs 4m	> 4yrs 4m ≤ 4yrs 7m	> 4yrs 7m ≤ 4yrs 11m	> 4yrs 11m	
No preschool	%	6.5	37.6	30.8	25.1	3,651
Maintained						
LEA nursery school	%	5.1	25.4	39.3	30.2	623
LEA nursery class	%	8.1	22.6	35.7	33.5	996
LA day nursery	%	4.5	32.4	26.1	36.9	111
Independent						
Nursery school	%	5.4	18.9	40.5	35.1	37
Day nursery	%	2.7	28.0	32.0	37.3	150
Hall playgroup	%	4.4	27.8	36.3	31.6	3,125
Home playgroup	%	6.7	29.2	35.4	28.7	178

Children without preschool experience were the ones who were most likely to start infant school at the beginning of the school year (September) following their fourth birthday. This reflected the policy in some areas such as the North and North West of England and Wales to admit children to infant reception classes early as a

Table 7.3 *Duration of attendance by main preschool placement*

Main preschool placement		Duration of attendance in months					N
		≤ 6m	> 6m ≤ 12m	> 12m ≤ 18m	> 18m ≤ 24m	> 24m	
Maintained							
LEA nursery school	%	15.6	36.6	28.6	16.4	2.7	639
LEA nursery class	%	25.7	38.1	22.5	12.5	1.2	1,076
LA day nursery	%	14.5	21.4	17.9	12.0	34.2	117
Independent							
Nursery school	%	7.7	25.6	25.6	33.3	7.7	39
Day nursery	%	7.3	22.7	25.3	22.0	22.7	150
Hall playgroup	%	10.9	20.4	27.6	31.6	9.5	3,119
Home playgroup	%	5.6	25.3	30.9	29.8	8.4	178

Note: This gives duration of attendance at the child's main preschool placement. Some children also had prior placements and thus the total length of time in preschool institutions for these children was longer.

means of meeting a demand for educational provision for under-fives (Osborn *et al.*, 1984, Chapter 6).

The variation in age at starting preschool education or day care and age at infant school entry resulted in substantial variation in the length of time children spent in preschool institutions. Once again this depended also on the type of preschool institution the child attended. One third of the children who attended LA day nurseries and a fifth of those who went to independent day nurseries had done so for more than two years (Table 7.3). Fewer than 10% of children who went to other independent institutions, and fewer than 3% of those in LEA nursery schools and classes had attended for more than two years. Most children who attended LEA nursery schools and classes did so for no more than one year (52% and 64% respectively). In the independent sector, however, at least two-thirds attended for over a year. This is an important difference between the maintained schools and the independent sector and reflects the differences in age composition between the types of institution described in Chapter 2. However, it is necessary to remember that some 20% of the children who attended LEA nursery schools and classes had previously also attended play-groups or private nurseries.

The pattern of weekly attendance was the thing that varied most according to the type of preschool institution the child attended (Table 7.4). The majority of children who went to LEA nursery schools or classes attended 5 sessions a week (60% and 70%

Table 7.4   *Number of sessions attended by main preschool placement*

Main preschool placement		Number of sessions attended per week				N
		1–2	3–4	5	6–10	
Maintained						
LEA nursery school	%	1.1	1.0	60.2	37.7	620
LEA nursery class	%	1.6	1.1	70.1	27.2	1,013
LA day nursery	%	2.9	5.8	5.8	85.6	104
Independent						
Nursery school	%	12.5	20.0	47.5	20.0	40
Day nursery	%	16.3	19.1	26.2	38.3	141
Hall playgroup	%	53.0	31.8	14.4	0.8	3,107
Home playgroup	%	32.0	33.7	32.0	2.2	178

respectively) and nearly all the remainder attended 10 sessions. Of those who attended LA day nurseries 86% went full-time; by contrast in independent day nurseries only 38% attended full-time and 26% half time. More than half of the children who went to hall playgroups attended no more than 2 sessions a week and only 15% attended for 5 or more sessions. These results parallel the hours of opening of the different types of preschool institutions described in Chapter 2.

In sum, it can be seen that attendance at LEA nursery schools and classes tended to be full-time or part-time (5 sessions a week) for no more than a year, whereas in hall playgroups, the main form of independent provision, children attended fewer sessions but over a longer period. It would be unwise to attach too much importance to the fact that these two different attendance patterns provided the children with equal amounts of preschool education, because clearly the response to this experience would be different for 3-year-olds and 4-year-olds. The results are best seen as further evidence of the fundamental differences between types of preschool institution which could have important implications for the children who attend them.

Patterns of attendance and test scores

We have investigated two kinds of question regarding the effects that patterns of attendance have on children's behaviour, cognitive development and educational attainment. Firstly, do such factors help to explain the differences in children's test scores and assessments that we have thus far attributed to different types of institutions? Secondly, what effect, if any, does the pattern of attendance itself have on the child's development?

To examine the effect of patterns of attendance on the association between the main preschool classification and test scores we adopted the same analytical procedure that was described in Chapter 4; this was a series of analyses of variance in which the basic analysis (with Social Index score, type of neighbourhood and number of children in family as intervening variables) was repeated with additional factors describing the child's pattern of attendance. The additional variables were: the age when the child started her first preschool placement, her main preschool placement and infant school; the duration of the child's attendance at her main preschool placement; the number of sessions the child attended. These variables were not included all together in one analysis but were added one at a time and in selected combinations to the basiç analyses of variance. Dependent variables were the five-year Copying Designs test and EPVT, and the ten-year BAS, Picture Language Test, reading and mathematics. The variables 'age started main preschool placement' and 'duration of attendance at main preschool placement' were found to be unrelated to any of the test outcomes, whereas, in contrast, the variables 'age started first placement' and 'age started infant school' did achieve statistically significant results.

The present analysis excluded children who had no preschool experience because, clearly, the question of patterns of attendance did not apply to them. This necessary omission of non-attenders immediately reduced the analyses related to British Ability Scales and Picture Language Test to statistical non-significance and this was not altered in any way by the addition of the pattern of attendance variables. This suggests that the performance of children in these tests did not differ according to the type of preschool institution attended, and therefore the important contrast in terms of BAS and PLT scores was between children with and without preschool experience.

The analyses for the other test outcomes did show statistically significant differences between the preschool groups that persisted when non-attenders were excluded. For some outcomes, however, the pattern of attendance variables reduced the level of statistical significance of the preschool effect. The addition of number of sessions attended reduced the significance of the association between preschool and EPVT to $p < .005$, and mathematics to $p < .05$. The addition of any one of the pattern of attendance variables reduced the significance of the preschool association with reading score to $p < .05$. In none of these analyses, however, were the mean scores for children who attended different preschool placements substantially altered. Thus although statistical significance was reduced, the main effects of the preschool experience relating to these outcomes remained relatively unchanged when the age the child started at preschool, age at infant school entry or the number of sessions attended were added. This, however, says nothing about the effects of these factors themselves on the test outcomes which are discussed later in this chapter.

Patterns of attendance and behaviour

Using the same analytical approach as for the test outcomes described above, the associations between the child's main preschool placement and the five-year behavioural assessments were examined after adjustment for the age the child started preschool, age at infant school entry and the number of sessions attended. This analysis could be performed only for those children who had attended a preschool institution and it showed that children who attended LA day nurseries had significantly higher antisocial behaviour scores than did children who attended other types of preschool institutions; there was, however, no statistically significant difference in neurotic behaviour score between children with different types of preschool experience.

In the antisocial behaviour analysis, the addition of 'age started first placement' and 'age of entry to infant school' reduced the mean score of children who had attended LA day nurseries. When the number of sessions attended had been added an even greater effect was found which in fact reduced the association between main preschool placement and antisocial behaviour to statistical non-significance. However, although the association between the number of sessions attended and antisocial behaviour was itself non-significant in this analysis, it became significant if the main preschool placement was excluded. Thus differences in antisocial behaviour could be attributed either to the type of institution the child attended or to the number of sessions attended. The fact that particular types of preschool institutions were homogeneous in regard to the number of sessions children attended meant that the two effects were difficult to separate out. A further examination of this problem is presented below in the section on frequency of attendance related to test scores.

Age at entry to infant school

A higher proportion of children with *no* preschool experience had started infant school at an early age than children who *had* attended preschool institutions (Table 7.2) and we checked whether this had any effect on the association between children's preschool experience and test outcomes or behavioural assessments. The results showed that the effects of preschool education remained and for two outcomes, Copying Designs and Picture Language Test, were strengthened, although the mean scores for the preschool groups barely changed.

An examination of the mean scores of children who started infant school at different ages did not reveal a consistent picture across all the five- and ten-year tests and assessments (Table 7.5). After adjustment for the main preschool placement, Social Index score, type of neighbourhood and number of children in the family, we found the association between age at infant school entry and the outcome was non-significant for BAS, PLT, mathematics and anti-social behaviour at age 5. Late entrants to infant school (after fifth birthday) had markedly lower Copying Designs scores than those who started attending before 4 years 8 months. However, early infant entry was associated with *lower* mean EPVT scores than those achieved by children who had started school after age 5. Children starting infant school before 4 years 5 months had the highest mean ten-year reading score, but the lowest mean reading score was associated with the rising five entrants. Finally, children who started infant school after 5 were less neurotic than were the early school entrants.

In order to check whether children who had not attended any type of preschool institution might have benefited by being admitted early to infant school instead, analyses of variance were performed on the subsample of such children with all the same outcome variables. After adjustment for Social Index, neighbourhood and number of children in the family, a very similar pattern of results was obtained to that given in Table 7.5. This confirmed that the insignificant effect of early entry to infant school on children's test scores was much the same irrespective of whether or not they had attended a preschool placement.

Thus after taking into account socio-economic and family factors, and the child's preschool experience, we found no conclusive or consistent evidence to suggest that there was any educational or behavioural advantage or disadvantage for children who entered infant reception classes before the statutory age. This finding contrasts markedly with the consistently positive effects that our results showed were associated with attendance at preschool institutions, and it strongly suggests that whilst the preschool curriculum, with its emphasis on learning through play and social contact with staff and other children, can have definite cognitive

Table 7.5 *Age started infant school and test scores*

Age started infant school	Five-year tests		Ten-year tests				Five-year behaviour	
	Copying Designs	EPVT	BAS	PLT	Reading	Mathematics	Antisocial	Neurotic
≤ 4y 4m	.13	−.03	.75	.45	1.27	.62	.04	.00
> 4y 4m ≤ 4y 7m	.16	−.05	−.30	.14	.10	.04	−.02	.04
> 4y 7m ≤ 4y 11m	.03	.01	−.01	.18	−.62	−.35	.00	.02
> 4y 11m	−.23	.04	.19	−.45	.38	.25	.01	−.06
Overall mean	−.03	−.03	99.63	99.97	99.65	99.70	.01	.00
Significance	p< .0005	p< .005	ns	ns	p< .05	ns	ns	p< .005

Note: Analysis of variance; figures show deviation from overall mean after adjustment for main preschool placement, Social Index, neighbourhood and number of children in the family. This table includes children with no preschool experience.

and behavioural benefits, the regime in the normal infant reception class may be less appropriate for all under-fives. However, it is important to recognise that at any age children vary in their ability to cope with a particular type of educational environment, mainly because the rate of cognitive development is faster in some children than in others, due to differences in genetic endowment, and the extent to which social and family background can accelerate or retard a child's cognitive growth.

Age of starting preschool education

We have shown that the age at which a child started attending a preschool institution varied substantially from one type of institution to another; furthermore, we have said that this fact made little difference to the association between a child's preschool placement and his test scores or behaviour. We now go on to consider the association between the age when the children started their preschool placement and the results they achieved in our set of tests and assessments (Table 7.6).

The analyses include only those children who attended a preschool placement, and the mean scores were statistically adjusted for the main preschool placement, Social Index score, type of neighbourhood and number of children in the family. The majority of this group of children (about two-thirds) started their first preschool placement between the ages of 3 and 4 years and the balance was about equally divided between those who started before 3 or after 4 years of age. Fewer than 2% of all the children in the sample attending preschool institutions started before the age of 2 years, therefore the under-3 category can reasonably be interpreted as meaning between 2 and 3 years of age,with the average age being nearer 3 than 2 years.

A fairly consistent pattern emerged in which the children who started their preschool placement before 3 years of age (but usually after 2) had higher test scores at the ages of 5 and 10 than those who did not start until after they were 4 years old. This association achieved statistical significance for the five-year Copying Designs test, and ten-year BAS, Picture Language Test and reading. Age of starting preschool was not associated with the five-year behavioural assessments. When age at infant school entry was added into the analyses, however, the age of starting preschool lost its statistical

Table 7.6 *Age started preschool education and test scores*

Age started first placement	Five-year tests		Ten-year tests				Five-year behaviour	
	Copying Designs	EPVT	BAS	PLT	Reading	Mathematics	Antisocial	Neurotic
< 3 yrs	.05	.00	.90	.27	.54	-.02	.05	-.04
< 4 yrs	.02	.01	.05	.27	.30	.26	-.01	.00
≥ 3 yrs								
≥ 4 yrs	-.10	-.04	-1.00	-1.22	-1.54	-.88	.00	.03
							-.04	.02
Overall mean	.07	.09	101.82	101.66	101.85	101.64		
Significance	p<.005	ns	p<.05	p<.05	p<.005	ns	ns	ns

Note: Analysis of variance; figures show deviation from overall mean after adjustment for main preschool placement, Social Index, neighbourhood and number of children in the family. If age started infant school is added to the analysis all the associations in this table except the reading analysis become non-significant.

significance for all the tests except the ten-year reading test, although the tendency for children to have lower scores if they started preschool after their fourth birthday was still apparent.

It is not easy to see why the child's age at infant school entry should affect the association between age of starting first preschool placement and the test outcomes. Part of the explanation, however, is that children who started preschool early were also likely to start infant school early (correlation = .19; p < .0005), so the two variables tended to cancel each other out. The arithmetical difference between these two ages was approximately equivalent to the length of time the child spent in the preschool placement before starting school. However, analysis of the duration of attendance in months, related to test outcomes, did not lead to more conclusive results than those we have reported. We suggest, therfore, that the methodological difficulties stemming from the associations between the type of preschool placement, age of starting preschool, age of entry to infant school and duration of preschool attendance, mean that it is impossible to identify the separate and unique effects of all these variables. What is evident, however, is that the basic association between the type of preschool experience children had and their test scores was remarkably stable, no matter what combinations of these intervening factors were built in.

Frequency of attendance

If there are long term educational advantages attributable to children's attendance at a preschool institution it appears logical to assume that children who attended more frequently would, as a consequence, derive more benefit. Our findings, however, did not support this assumption. The achievement of children who attended 1 or 2 sessions a week was not significantly different from that of children who attended more than 5 sessions a week.

A child's frequency of attendance did appear to have an effect on his behaviour. Those who attended for more than 5 sessions a week were more likely to show antisocial behaviour at home (p < .05). This effect disappeared, however, when the type of preschool experience was taken into account. Inspection of the results led us to the conclusion that the children who were antisocial were mainly those who attended LA day nurseries, most of whom attended full time (10 sessions a week) and probably for long hours each day and over a long period. It was very likely, therefore, that it was a combination of factors associated with LA day nurseries which produced the observed behavioural effect. No such effects were found, however, for neurotic behaviour.

The lack of any significant result for the effects of frequency of attendance on children's test scores prompted us to try a different analytical approach. We thought that the close association of particular patterns of attendance with specific types of preschool institutions might have been distorting the results in some way. We therefore carried out separate analyses on two subsamples: children who attended LEA nursery schools and children who attended hall playgroups. We excluded from these analyses all the children who had attended more than one preschool placement and also those who were said to have started attending their main preschool placement before the age of 3 years. Analyses of variance were carried out for each of these two subsamples separately with the following independent variables: Social Index score, type of neighbourhood, number of children in the family, age at entry to infant school, duration of attendance at the preschool institution and the number of sessions per week the child attended. The last variable was grouped 1–5 and 6–10 sessions per week for the children who attended LEA nursery schools, and 1–2, 3–4 and 5–10 sessions per week for the children who attended hall playgroups in keeping with the main groupings for the two types of institution.

The results from these analyses of variance are presented in Table 7.7 where it can be seen that, with one exception, frequency of attendance was unrelated to any cognitive test or behavioural assessment. The one significant result indicated that more frequent attendance at playgroup increased five-year Copying Designs score. However, the lack of any consistent pattern of results across all the tests suggests that this one significant finding probably occurred by chance.

Our conclusion after sifting all the evidence is that our data do not suggest that attending a preschool institution more frequently will necessarily help a child obtain higher levels of educational achievement. Such a conclusion flies in the face of common sense and it must be accepted that there may yet be methodological problems, due to the complexities to which we have alluded, which perhaps we have been unable to overcome completely in our analytical approach.

Table 7.7 *Analysis of number of sessions attended and test scores*

| | Five-year tests | | Ten-year tests | | | | Five-year behaviour | |
	Copying Designs	EPVT	BAS	PLT	Reading	Mathematics	Antisocial	Neurotic
LEA nursery school sessions attended								
1–5	.00	.05	.55	–.48	.42	.52	.01	–.02
6–10	.01	–.10	–1.08	.95	–.81	–1.01	–.01	.04
Overall mean	–.03	–.11	97.91	97.85	98.91	99.12	.11	.06
Significance	ns	ns	ns	ns	ns	ns	ns	ns
Hall playgroup sessions attended								
1–2	–.05	–.02	–.33	–.53	–.02	–.07	–.04	–.02
3–4	.06	.03	.79	.53	.19	.53	.04	.04
5–10	.05	.01	–.39	1.04	–.37	–.91	.07	–.02
Overall mean	.13	.16	103.12	103.06	103.26	102.93	–.11	–.04
Significance	p<.05	ns	ns	ns	ns	ns	ns	ns

Note: Analysis of variance; figures show deviation from overall mean after adjustment for Social Index, neighbourhood, number of children in the family, infant entry age and duration of attendance at main preschool placement (months). The analyses were carried out on two sub-samples: LEA nursery school attenders and hall playgroup attenders. Children with more than one preschool placement or who started attending before 3 years of age were excluded.

Conclusions

There are many policy, institutional and parental decisions which influence the particular pattern of attendance followed by an individual child. The age at which a child starts attending a preschool institution, the frequency of attendance and the age at which he starts at infant school are determined by different factors all of which may have implications for his developmental progress. It has therefore been very difficult to formulate any definite conclusions as to which is the ideal age for starting preschool and the optimal number of sessions a week to attend.

Firstly, we established that most children in our sample utilising LEA nursery schools and classes started soon after their fourth birthday and attended for either 5 or 10 sessions a week. Day nursery children started at a much younger age and usually attended full-time (10 sessions a week). In contrast, many playgroup children started soon after their third birthdays but few attended for more than 4 sessions a week.

Analyses which examined the association between the type of preschool placement the child attended and his cognitive educational and behavioural development, revealed that the child's age when starting preschool, age at infant school entry and the number of sessions attended made virtually no difference to the basic associations between the type of preschool attended and the outcomes. Thus pattern of attendance did not emerge as a major factor in differences in test scores between children with different types of preschool experience.

There was some evidence that children who started their preschooling young did slightly better in the tests than those who started late in the preschool period. The number of sessions attended weekly appeared unrelated to test outcomes, except that children attending 10 sessions a week were more antisocial in their behaviour. However, children who attended LA day nurseries were also more inclined to antisocial behaviour, and it was not possibe to separate out the different effects attributable to the day nursery experience or to the number of sessions spent in a preschool institution *per se*. This was a constant problem in these analyses in which the strong associations between the independent variables made it impossible to determine the main cause of the various effects.

Another explanation for this lack of significant associations between the frequency and duration of children's attendance at preschool institutions and their subsequent intellectual growth is that parents enroll them in their nursery or playgroup when they are judged to be ready for this experience and, since children acquire the necessary degree of emotional independence at different chronological ages, the optimal age for first attending a preschool placement also varies between children. Those who are seriously distressed in a preschool setting are likely to leave, or attend fewer sessions until they become accustomed to the new regime. This process of fitting the pattern of attendance to suit the needs of the individual child will inevitably result in reducing variation between children in their cognitive development due to differences in duration and frequency of attendance at preschool institutions.

Finally, we were unable to find conclusive or consistent evidence that there were any educational or behavioural advantages for children who entered infant reception classes before the statutory age. This is important in view of the policy in some Local Education Authorities to admit children early to infant school rather than setting up nursery schools or classes. In contrast, the finding that children who attended preschool institutions performed better in cognitive and educational tests up to the age of 10 years was sustained irrespective of the age at which they started infant school.

8

The preschool institutional environment

The purpose of our analysis in previous chapters has been to examine thoroughly factors in the home background of the children which might explain away the associations we have found between their preschool educational experience and subsequent cognitive ability and behaviour. Our conclusion, on the basis of this analysis, is that the preschool effects we have found are real to the extent that we have been unable to attribute them entirely to any of a large number of other independent variables, and, by extension, we are of the opinion that other unmeasured independent social or family factors are unlikely to account for these effects. In this chapter we shift the emphasis away from the children's home environment and focus instead on the charcteristics of the preschool institutions they attended.

We have already shown, in Chapter 2, that the structure and organisation of the various types of preschool institution differed quite considerably and such differences might reasonably be expected to have consequences for the way they influence children's subsequent cognitive skills. In this chapter, therefore, we examine the association between institutional factors, as provided by the preschool institutions themselves, and the children's five-year Copying Designs test and English Picture Vocabulary Test scores. The object is to assess whether particular features of the preschool setting such as staffing, curriculum and the social background of the group of children attending the institution have any measurable effect on children's test performance. In addition, we will check whether variation in children's test scores according to the type of institution attended could be explained by these institutional factors.

Before describing these analyses, a cautionary note on the methodological limitations of this part of our study is necessary. The Nursery/Playgroup survey, from which all our institutional information was obtained, was carried out at the same time as the cohort study when many of the children in our sample had already left their preschool placements to start school (see Appendix). Thus the descriptions of a preschool institution could have been obtained as much as a year after the study child had left and during that period some changes may have taken place. Such changes as did occur were unlikely to be an important source of bias but they could have increased random variation in the data, and thereby reduced the likelihood of finding statistically significant associations with the outcomes. The absence of such associations, therefore, should not be taken to mean that an institutional variable is unimportant.

A second methodological problem stems from the fact that certain types of preschool institution were homogeneous in some respects. Child–adult ratios, for example, followed closely the recommendations of the responsible authorities—LEA nursery schools having ratios of 10:1, and LA day nurseries 5:1. Thus results from analyses of children's test scores in terms of the child–adult ratios of the institutions they attended simply tended to replicate those obtained in analyses based on the main preschool categories. The lack of variability of certain factors within different types of institution meant that the independent effects of such factors could not readily be assessed.

Table 8.1 *Selected preschool institutional factors for analysis*

---

1. Average number of children per session
2. Percentage of children attending 1–4 sessions
3. Percentage of children attending 5 sessions
4. Percentage of children attending 10 sessions
5. Percentage of staff with nursery or infant teaching qualifications
6. Percentage of staff with other teaching qualifications
7. Percentage of staff with nursery nursing qualifications
8. Child–adult ratio
9. Percentage of children of Indian/Pakistani origin
10. Percentage of children of Afro-Caribbean origin
11. Percentage of children who speak little or no English
12. Proportion of children from homes with some difficulty, e.g. overcrowding, only one parent, marital difficulties, family ill-health, poor standard of child-care, etc.
13. Problem Index, defined in Chapter 2
14. Skills curriculum scale, defined in Chapter 2
15. Language curriculum scale, defined in Chapter 2
16. Finding-out curriculum scale, defined in Chapter 2
17. Gross motor curriculum scale, defined in Chapter 2

Institutional factors and five-year test scores

The relationships between 17 institutional factors (listed in Table 8.1) and five-year Copying Designs and EPVT scores were investigated in a series of analyses of variance in which statistical adjustment was made for the effects of the type of preschool institution attended by the study child, Social Index score, type of neighbourhood, and family size. It is important to note that the descriptions of the institutions attended by the study children were obtained from the personnel in charge of the institutions, whereas the other independent variables in the analyses of variance describe the survey child's own social and family circumstances as provided by his mother. As interest centres on differences in regime within preschool institutions, these analyses necessarily exclude children who had no preschool education or day care experience.

Of the 17 institutional variables investigated, only 5 were found to be significantly associated with Copying Designs (Table 8.2) and 2 with EPVT scores (Table 8.3). It will be seen that in all but one of these analyses a low level of statistical significance was achieved, and in most instances it is difficult to draw any general conclusions from the results. For example, children who attended preschool institutions where at least one member of staff (but no more than 40% of all staff) had a nursery-nursing qualification, achieved slightly higher Copying Designs scores than did children in institutions with no nursery nurses, or more than 40% nursery nurses. Similar problems of interpretation were encountered in results from the analyses of the gross motor curriculum scale related to Copying Designs, and the proportion of children attending 10 sessions a week related to EPVT.

Study children who attended institutions which included children of Indian or Pakistani or Afro-Caribbean origin or children who could speak little English obtained higher Copying Designs test scores than did children who attended institutions with no children from these groups.

In these analyses statistical adjustment was also made for the study child's own ethnic origin. The consistency of this effect of ethnic composition on Copying Designs score across these three variables inspires more confidence in the validity of this finding than the results for the other institutional factors described above. The implication is that preschool institutions attended by ethnic minority group children provide a better learning environment than

Table 8.2 *Institutional factors and five-year Copying Designs score*

1. Percentage of staff with nursery-nursing qualifications

	None	< 40%	> 40%	Overall mean and Total N	Significance
Deviation from overall mean	−.01	.07	−.04	.07	p< .05
N	2,537	1,217	1,101	4,855	

2. Percentage of children of Indian/Pakistani origin

	None	< 10%	> 10%	Overall mean and Total N	Significance
Deviation from overall mean	−.03	.07	.05	.08	p< .05
N	3,178	1,142	264	4,584	

3. Percentage of children of Afro-Caribbean origin

	None	< 10%	> 10%	Overall mean and Total N	Significance
Deviation from overall mean	−.02	.04	.21	.08	p< .05
N	3,704	725	155	4,584	

4. Percentage of children who speak little or no English

	None	< 10%	> 10%	Overall mean and Total N	Significance
Deviation from overall mean	−.02	.08	.07	.07	p< .05
N	3,687	907	217	4,811	

5. Percentage of Gross motor Curriculum scale

	0–3	4–6	7–9	> 10	Overall mean and Total N	Significance
Deviation from overall mean	−.05	.02	.03	−.07	.07	p< .05
N	136	1,084	2,525	1,139	4,884	

Note: Five analyses of variance, each adjusted for main preschool placement, Social Index score, neighbourhood, number of children in the family and (for 2, 3 and 4 only) ethnic origin of study child.

Table 8.3 *Institutional factors and five-year English Picture Vocabulary Test*

1. *Percentage of children attending 10 sessions*

	None	< 50%	> 50%	Overall mean and Total N	Significance
Deviation from overall mean	−.01	.09	−.06	.10	p< .05
N	3,242	685	471	4,398	

2. *Percentage of staff with other teaching qualifications*

	None	< 40%	> 40%	Overall mean and Total N	Significance
Deviation from overall mean	−.03	.09	.07	.10	p< .005
N	3,716	976	163	4,855	

Note: Three analyses of variance, each adjusted for main preschool placement, Social Index score, neighbourhood, and number of children in the family.

those with no such children. It should be noted that this effect was not limited to children from ethnic minorities but applied to *all* children in the CHES cohort who attended these institutions, and we can postulate that the presence of children from a number of ethnic groups in the preschool institution creates a richer, more culturally diverse setting from which all children in the institution can benefit.

Finally, the presence in the institution of at least one member of staff with a teaching qualification other than in nursery/infant education was associated with significantly increased EPVT scores (p < .005) We know from Chapter 2 that independent nursery schools and home playgroups were more likely than other types of preschool institution to have staff with 'other' teaching qualifications, and that the children attending these types of preschool institution achieved the highest EPVT scores. It is tempting to conclude from this that these two findings are linked in some way; this should be resisted, however, because the analyses of variance adjust for the effects of both staff qualifications and type of preschool institution. It is worth noting that children who attended institutions having nursery/infant teaching staff also scored higher in Copying Designs and EPVT tests although the differences failed to achieve statistical significance.

Thus our analysis of institutional factors resulted in only two reliable conclusions; (1) children who attended institutions where there were ethnic minority group children had slightly higher Copying Designs scores, and (2) children who attended institutions where there were qualified teachers achieved higher EPVT scores. In general, however, specific institutional factors appeared to have little impact on the children's level of attainment at 5 years.

Institutional factors as intervening variables

Our second approach to evaluating individual institutional factors was to see whether their inclusion in analyses of variance altered the associations we found between the type of preschool placement a child attended and his or her test scores. For example, if the staffing of one type of institution differed significantly from that of another, and staffing was an important factor contributing to differences in test scores between children who attended the two types of institution, then the inclusion of staffing in the analyses of variance might affect the observed association between type of preschool and test scores. In short, although institutional factors might not have strong independent associations with test outcomes, they may nevertheless be important intervening variables.

The same analytical approach was adopted as in previous chapters. Each institutional variable was added in turn to the basic analysis of variance and the strength of the association between the main preschool placement and the test scores was checked. Any reduction in the percentage of variance explained by the main preschool placement would indicate that the institutional variable in question was an important intervening factor in the association between preschool placement and test outcome. Similarly, a marked change in the mean score for a particular preschool category would suggest that an institutional factor was of some importance.

This approach revealed that some institutional factors had a small, measurable effect on the association between preschool placement and test scores. The first finding was that adjustment for

the proportion of staff with teaching or nursery-nursing qualifications reduced the Copying Designs and EPVT mean scores of
children who attended independent nursery schools. This suggests
that the mean test scores achieved by children who attended independent nursery schools could be attributed to the typical pattern
of staff qualifications in this type of institution. However, as
explained in Chapter 2, this is a complex issue because of the
varying number of staff and varying numbers of qualifications held
by individual staff members. It would require a very extended
anlaysis of the data to decide the optimal combination of staff with
particular qualifications within an institution and such an analysis
is not warranted. Nevertheless, the presence of qualified staff in the
institution made a significant contribution to the achievement of
cognitive gains in young children who attended preschool
institutions.

The second finding was that adjustment for the proportion of
children from difficult homes who attended the institution reduced
the preschool effect on Copying Designs score to statistical non-
significance, and EPVT score from $p < .0005$ to $p < .05$. This
mainly affected LA day nurseries of which 80% reported that more
than three-quarters of their children came from difficult homes
(Chapter 2). In the EPVT analysis the mean score for the LA day
nursery children increased after adjustment for the proportion of
children in the institution who were from difficult homes, whereas
the mean EPVT score of children who attended independent day
nurseries decreased. This had the effect of reducing the difference
between the highest mean EPVT score, achieved by children who
went to home playgroups, and the lowest, achieved by those who
attended independent day nurseries, from .51 to .36 standard
deviations. The implication of this finding is that institutions with a
high proportion of socially disadvantaged children were less likely
to succeed in promoting cognitive development in the children who
attended, than were other institutions which had no disadvantaged
children. It is important to note that our method of analysis takes
into account the child's own social background, when examining
the effect on these scores of the social composition of the institution
he attended.

Minor effects attributable to various other institutional factors
could be discerned in the findings but staff qualifications and social
composition of the institution emerged as the most significant ones.

Social composition of LEA nursery schools and hall playgroups

In Chapter 2 we showed how the social composition of preschool institutions varied between the different types of institution. Generally speaking, LEA schools and LA day nurseries had higher proportions of socially disadvantaged children than did institutions in the independent sector. In the previous section in this chapter we described the reduction in differences in EPVT scores between children who attended different types of preschool institution when the social composition of the institution was taken into account. This leads to the hypothesis that successful teaching in an institution which has a high proportion of socially disadvantaged children may be more difficult than in institutions which have no children with social problems. To explore this hypothesis further, a detailed analysis was carried out on two of the major providers of preschool education: LEA nursery schools and hall playgroups. Limitations of time and resources necessitated restricting these analyses to only these two types of institution and the two five-year cognitive tests. The results obtained also did not warrant the continuation of the analysis to all the other types of preschool institution, ten-year tests and behavioural assessments as we were of the opinion that the conclusions reached would be similar for all types of preschool institution.

For the purposes of this analysis, three indices were selected which described the social characteristics of the children who attended the preschool institution:

1. the proportion of children in the institution who were from difficult homes;
2. Problem Index score; and
3. the proportion of children in the institution who spoke little or no English.

These variables are defined in Chapter 2.

Analysis of variance was used to test the difference in mean Copying Designs and EPVT score between categories of these three institutional variables, firstly for children who attended LEA nursery schools, and secondly for those who went to hall playgroups. In all these analyses statistical adjustment was made for the study child's Social Index score, type of neighbourhood and number of children in the family. There were no significant differences in mean test scores between children who had attended LEA nursery schools with different proportions of children requiring special attention. This was true both before and after statistical adjustment for the child's own home background. This suggests that LEA nursery schools with a high proportion of socially disadvantaged children are as effective in promoting cognitive development as LEA nursery schools with few such children.

The results for hall playgroups were less clear-cut than for LEA nursery schools in that they varied according to the particular institutional factor and test criterion involved. Children who attended hall playgroups with a high proportion of children from difficult homes achieved *lower* mean Copying Designs and EPVT scores than did those who attended playgroups with no such children. However, this difference in mean Copying Designs score was eliminated after statistical adjustment for the child's own home background, and although a difference in mean EPVT score remained after adjustment for home background factors this was non-significant.

A comparison of hall playgroup children in terms of the institutional Problem Index also showed that poor unadjusted mean test scores associated with playgroups having a Problem Index score of one or more became non-significant after adjustment for the child's own social and family circumstances. The most surprising results were those for hall playgroups attended by children who could speak little or no English. The mean Copying Designs score of children who attended these institutions was significantly higher than that of children who went to playgroups where there were no

Table 8.4 *Copying Designs scores of children attending hall playgroups according to the proportion of children who could speak little or no English*

Proportion of children in hall playgroup who could speak little or no English	N	Unadjusted deviation	Deviation adjusted for Social Index, neighbourhood, and number of children
None	2,648	−.03	−.03
Up to 10%	403	.18	.19
More than 10%	46	−.08	.04
Overall mean		.12	.12
Significance		p< .0005	p< .0005

children who spoke little English (Table 8.4). This difference persisted after adjustment for the child's own background and retained a high degree of statistical significance (p < .0005). Table 8.4 shows that the highest mean Copying Designs score was achieved by children who attended playgroups where at least 1% but no more than 10% of the children spoke little or no English. Where there were more than 10% non-English speakers the mean score was above average as a consequence of the statistical adjustment for the child's own social and family circumstances.

This association of higher mean Copying Designs score with attendance at an institution where there were children who could speak little English conforms with the findings for all preschool institutions described earlier in this chapter. It is possible that the cultural diversity in the preschool institution might create an atmosphere which is positively conducive to cognitive development. Without further very detailed analysis, however, a conclusive explanation for this interesting effect cannot be offered.

These results highlight an important methodological difficulty when trying to assess the possible effect of the social composition of preschool institutions on the developmental progress of the children who attend them. This difficulty stems from the fact that institutions which accommodated a high proportion of socially disadvantaged children were more likely to be attended by socially disadvantaged children in the CHES sample. Thus poor test scores associated with attendance at an institution which accommodated a high proportion of socially disadvantaged children could be attributed either to this institutional factor or to the child's own social background. In other words, the social composition of the institution a child attends becomes confounded with the child's personal circumstances. Although the analysis of variance adjusts for these two independent effects, it is very likely that the more powerful effect of a child's home background on his test performance negates the relatively weak influence of the institutional factors.

Comparison of LEA nursery schools and hall playgroups

LEA nursery schools and hall playgroups between them provided preschool places for nearly three-quarters of all the children in our sample who had attended a preschool placement. Attendance at both types of institutions was also consistently associated with

increased test performance at 5 and 10 years of age. It was important to know, therefore, whether the small differences in mean test
scores between children who attended these two major types of
preschool institution were statistically significant. We also needed
to establish whether test scores of children who attended LEA
nursery schools with a high proportion of socially disadvantaged
children differed from the scores of children who went to playgroups having a similar social mix. In other words we wanted to
find out whether playgroups were more or less sucessful than LEA
nursery schools when they accommodated numbers of socially
disadvantaged children who were likely to be more demanding on
the staff.

Tables 8.5 and 8.6 show no significant difference in Copying
Designs or EPVT mean scores between children who attended LEA
nursery schools and hall playgroups, after adjustment was made for
the child's main home background factors.

Table 8.5 *Copying Designs score of children who attended LEA nursery
schools or hall playgroups according to social composition of the
institution*

	LEA nursery schools		Hall play- groups		Overall mean	Signifi- cance
	Deviation	N	Deviation	N		
1. All institutions	.03	626	−.01	3,033	.10	ns
2. Institutions with at least one child from a difficult home	−.01	465	.01	409	.01	ns
3. Institutions with Problem Index score of one or more	.04	353	−.04	402	.05	ns
4. Institutions with at least one child who spoke little English	−.03	300	.02	434	.20	ns

Note: Four analyses of variance; deviation from overall mean adjusted for Social
Index, type of neighbourhood, and number of children in the family.

Table 8.6   *EPVT score of children who attended LEA nursery schools or hall playgroups according to social composition of the institution*

	LEA nursery schools		Hall play-groups		Overall mean	Signifi-cance
	Deviation	N	Deviation	N		
1. All institutions	−.06	578	.01	2,888	.15	ns
2. Institutions with at least one child from a difficult home	.02	427	−.02	394	.00	ns
3. Institutions with Problem Index score of one or more	−.01	324	.01	382	.02	ns
4. Institutions with at least one child who spoke little English	−.04	284	.03	418	.09	ns

Note: Four analyses of variance; deviation from overall mean adjusted for Social Index, type of neighbourhood, and number of children in the family.

In view of the contrast between these two types of institution in their staffing and general organisation, it is surprising that the level of achievement of children who attended LEA nursery schools was so similar to that of playgroup children. Even when the analysis was restricted to institutions with socially disadvantaged children the differences in mean scores between children who had attended LEA nursery schools and hall playgroups were still non-significant after adjustment for the home circumstances of the study children. This gives further weight to the findings described in Chapter 4 which suggested that socially disadvantaged children who attended either LEA nursery school or hall playgroups achieved higher scores at 5 and 10 years than did those with no preschool experience.

We suggest that the widening of the young child's experience beyond the home, the contact with other children in a group setting and the interaction with adults other than his own parents are themselves important elements in his development. Differences in the organisational features of the preschool environment seem to have only marginal effects on children's subsequent development, although it is possible that particular combinations of such factors may be of some importance (Lazar, 1985).

Finally, it is essential to recognise that the child's educational and behavioural development is not the only criterion on which the evaluation of preschool provision should rest. Playgroups typically operate for 3 or 4 sessions a week, with many children attending only 2 or 3 sessions, and this type of facility cannot give the much needed service that LEA nursery schools, through their half-time and full-time pattern of attendance, can provide. The availability of preschool provision within the maintained sector which is free to the families who use it is vital for those families who cannot pay playgroup fees because of financial hardship. LEA nursery schools are also better resourced to help handicapped children or those with behaviour problems than are many playgroups. For these kinds of reasons it is essential to retain, and indeed continue to expand, the provision of LEA nursery schools, so that the service can reach the one child in four who has no organised preschool experience and who, because of this, is at a developmental disadvantage when compared with children who attend nursery schools and playgroups.

Conclusions

In this chapter we have attempted to identify features of the preschool institution which contributed to the preschool effects described in earlier chapters. For this purpose we selected 17 representative variables from the data obtained in the Nursery/Playgroup survey which covered patterns of attendance, staffing, ethnic and social composition of the institution and curriculum.

Generally speaking, institutional variables were found to have little significant independent effect on children's cognitive ability at 5 years, but there were two exceptions to this general conclusion; first, all children who attended institutions where there were children from ethnic minority groups achieved higher Copying Designs scores; and second, higher EPVT scores were associated with institutions where the staff had teaching qualifications other than in nursery/infant teaching. This second finding appeared to be an explanatory factor in the higher-than-average EPVT scores achieved by children who attended independent nursery schools.

Nearly 80% of LA day nurseries, compared with fewer than 5% of any other type of institution, recorded that more than three-quarters of their children came from difficult homes, and this might have been a major factor contributing to the lower test scores of children who attended this type of institution. When statistical adjustment was made for the proportion of children from difficult homes, the EPVT score of children who had attended LA day nurseries increased substantially, although this effect was not found for Copying Designs score.

Further investigation of the effect of the social composition of the institutions showed that LEA nursery schools with socially disadvantaged children were as effective as those with none. In hall playgroups, deficits in children's test scores associated with the presence of socially disadvantaged children in the playgroup were eliminated after adjustment for the child's own home circumstances. A notable exception to this was the higher Copying Designs scores achieved by children who went to playgroups where there were children from ethnic minority groups. The cultural diversity in these institutions could have been a contributory factor in increasing cognitive development. An alternative explanation for this finding could be that staff in multicultural preschool institutions adopt different teaching methods from those of staff in institutions with no children from ethnic minority groups.

Comparisons of LEA nursery schools and hall playgroups with and without socially disadvantaged children showed that children's attendance at either type of institution was associated with increased test scores. It is important to note, however, that LEA nursery schools provide a comprehensive and free service to families in special need which could not be offered within the independent sector and our results should not be taken to indicate that playgroups could do the same work as LEA nursery schools, nor ought they to replace them.

In conclusion, a methodological observation should be made concerning the social composition of preschool institutions. If a preschool institution accommodated a high proportion of socially disadvantaged children, there was an increased probability that a child in our study who attended that institution came from a socially disadvantaged home. Thus when adjustment was made in an analysis of variance for the child's *own* social background much of the difference in scores attributable to *institutional* factors was likely to be lost because of the more powerful direct influence of the child's personal circumstances. We suspect, therefore, that our methodological approach minimised any institutional effects on the child's development that may actually have been quite important.

9

Parental involvement

Parental involvement in preschool education is a complex and often controversial concept. It is without doubt a central plank of the playgroup movement and is written into the constitution of the Preschool Playgroups Association whose aim is '... to promote community situations in which parents can with growing enjoyment and confidence make the best use of their own knowledge and resources in the development of their children and themselves'. (Published in every issue of *Contact*, the official journal of the PPA.)

Lady Plowden in her speech as retiring president of the Preschool Playgroups Association, stated that she would back playgroups and the playgroup philosophy with its emphasis on the importance of parental involvement, in preference to LEA nursery education (Plowden, 1982). However, not all parents wish to be involved in their child's preschool placement, especially those who have career or occupational commitments and therefore prefer their children to attend more frequently than is possible at most playgroups.

Parents originally conceived the idea of playgroups and many playgroups today are managed by parent committees. Nevertheless, only a minority of parents is involved in playgroups in this way. For the most part parental involvement in playgroups means helping with the children during the sessions on a regular, though usually not frequent, basis. Some voluntary playgroups depend entirely on mothers agreeing to help on a rota system which means being available once or twice a term to assist the playgroup leader in running the sessions. From the point of view of a child attending a playgroup run mainly by rota parents, he will meet a succession of different parent helpers from session to session, and his own mother will be there only once or twice a term. In this set-up the playgroup leader is inevitably a very important figure, since she is the one familiar person who is present at every session and whom the child will come to recognise as the one consistent stable factor in his new environment.

It is vital for young children that their preschool placement, whether it be a playgroup, nursery school or day nursery, become a familiar, friendly and non-threatening place, because embarking on preschool education represents the first step into the world beyond the family home that the child makes on his own. The need for handling this transition from home to preschool with great care is recognised by parents and professionals alike and most institutions encourage mothers to remain with the child until he is settled in. In the playgroup setting this may lead to mothers continuing to help out on a regular basis after their children are settled. Thus the mother's initial concern for her own child's integration into the group can become transformed into providing a service for the group as a whole.

This need for a preschool institution to become familiar to the child and to provide continuity and stability from session to session, at the same time as it creates sufficient diversity for the child to develop new ideas, concepts and skills, may be less easily achieved if the helpers in the group are constantly changing. This implies that the optimal situation is for an institution to be staffed by the same people continuously in order to provide an effective learning environment for the child. However, through her involvement in the activities of the group and social contact with others, a mother might learn skills, acquire knowledge and develop an increased sense of personal well-being that ultimately benefits her own child, which asset is lost if the child attends an institution in which there is limited scope for parental involvement of the type we have been discussing. Thus there is an inherent contradiction in this concept of parental involvement between the two objectives of providing an optimal learning environment for all the children in the group through staff continuity, and encouraging the participation of parents who can improve their parenting skills through this experience of managing children, and so ultimately benefit their own children.

There are other ways in which parents become involved in their children's preschool institutions besides giving direct help in the sessions. These include: management, consultative and administrative collaboration, and assisting with such activities as fund-raising and outings. Analysis of the Nursery/Playgroup data has shown that direct help in sessions and management activities was most frequently found in hall playgroups and least so in LA day nurseries. In LEA nursery schools, on the other hand, parental support and fund-raising, etc. were the predominant modes of help (van der Eyken *et al.*, 1984, pp. 111–13).

Lazar and Darlington (1982) concluded from their analysis of the combined results of the American Consortium studies, that the direct involvement of parents in intervention programmes was an important element in the children's improved functioning later on, and that the provision of services for the whole family resulted in even more gains for the children. Parental involvement was a central feature of the intervention on which the success of one of these schemes was believed to depend (Weikart *et al.*, 1978). Here the preschool intervention was carried right into the child's own home and the mothers played an active part at home and in the preschool centre. The focus of attention in these programmes was the whole family, not just the child, and the family received a considerable amount of professional attention. This degree of involvement was associated with outstanding personal and educational gains for the child in later life compared with children from similar backgrounds who had no preschool intervention.

Few, if any, children in the CHES cohort would have experienced the kind of experimental preschool programme described in these Consortium studies, and in our sample the degree and type of parental involvement varied quite considerably. In our analysis we have focused on four specific questions. These are:

1. What is the effect on children who attend preschool institutions staffed by parents compared with those who went to institutions with no parental input?

2. Do children whose own parents are involved in the preschool institution achieve different test results from those achieved by children of non-involved parents?

3. To what extent are any apparently beneficial effects of parental involvement due to greater parental interest in their child's educational progress?

4. Do differences in parental involvement between types of institutions explain variation in children's test scores hitherto attributed to their preschool experience?

Before proceeding to the investigation of these questions we shall review some of the institutional differences in patterns of parental involvement.

Institutional differences in parental involvement

In the Nursery/Playgroup survey we asked: 'How many members of staff do you have who are parents of children currently attending your institution and work/help with the children during the sessions? Include parent helpers.' The respondent was asked to give the number of parent staff/helpers who work/help:

(a) every session open during the week,
(b) at least one session per week but not every session,
(c) at least one session per term but less than once a week.

The question was designed in this way so that it could be answered by all types of institutions, irrespective of how many sessions they operated. A similar question elicited the number of non-parent staff. From the answers to these questions it was possible to determine the total number of staff and parent helpers who were present in the institution at least once a term; this, of course, included those present every session. This total number inevitably exceeded the number of staff and helpers present at any one session, unless all the staff and helpers were there every session. In playgroups which operated a parent rota the total count of helpers involved at any time could actually exceed the total number of children who attended if all the parents were on the rota and there were also one or two regular staff. In the discussion that follows, therefore, it is important to recognise that the fundamental differences in the patterns of staffing between maintained institutions and playgroups have a bearing on the indices of parental involvement that we have used. This complexity is minimised, however, in the approach we have adopted in the analyses of variance presented later in this chapter.

There was one other methodological problem which pertained to the interpretation of the staffing questions by the survey respondents; namely the possibility that some institutions having, say, one parent helper each session will have recorded this as one parent every session, even though it was a different parent each time and should, therefore, have been recorded as the total number of individual parents involved according to the frequency of their personal involvement. The questions were worded and ordered on the questionnaire in such a way as to reduce the risk of this misinterpretation and it is unlikely to seriously affect our conclusions. It is important, however, that we draw attention to this possible source of error, of the extent of which we have no knowledge.

In Table 9.1 we show the percentages of preschool institutions which received parental help with the children during the sessions. Parents who helped at least once a week we have termed 'regular helpers' and those who helped at least once a term but less than once a week, 'rota helpers'. As some institutions had both regular and rota help, the percentages do not total 100%.

Table 9.1 *Percentage of preschool institutions with parent helpers*

Type of institution		Regular help	Rota help	No parental help	N = 100%
Maintained					
LEA nursery school	%	23.3	9.4	71.8	710
LEA nursery class	%	16.5	8.3	78.5	1,928
LA day nursery	%	27.1	1.7	72.6	543
Independent					
Nursery school	%	27.2	6.5	68.8	189
Day nursery	%	29.7	4.5	68.3	700
Hall playgroup	%	68.0	28.8	22.8	11,523
Home playgroup	%	30.0	16.8	63.4	1,215

Note: Information from the Nursery/Playgroup survey.

As many as 68% of hall playgroups had regular parental help and 29% rota help; only 23% of these institutions had no parental help at all. No other type of preschool institution approached this degree of parental involvement in running the sessions the children attended. The other types of institution in the independent sector, however, were also more likely than maintained institutions to have parent helpers. LEA nursery classes were the least likely to have regular help from parents (17%) but the amount of rota help they received (8%) was similar to that of LEA nursery schools (9%). These differences, however, were insignificant compared with the contrast between the level of parental involvement in hall-based playgroups and that in the other types of preschool institution.

Parents could be involved in ways other than helping with the children during the sessions and some of these types of involvement

Table 9.2 *Percentage of preschool institutions with parents who help in other ways*

Type of institution		Percentage of institutions in which at least one parent is involved in the way specified				
		Practical help	Attending social events	Planning and management	Consultative committee	Attending discussions
Maintained						
LEA nursery school	%	94.0	73.3	37.5	19.1	47.5
LEA nursery class	%	90.2	75.1	22.5	29.3	46.9
LA day nursery	%	69.8	55.9	2.2	3.2	14.8
Independent						
Nursery school	%	60.3	73.0	18.5	19.9	19.4
Day nursery	%	41.8	37.8	9.2	5.9	10.7
Hall playgroup	%	85.4	68.1	52.2	20.1	31.2
Home playgroup	%	44.6	40.6	7.8	3.4	15.0

Note: Information from the Nursery/Playgroup survey.

are described in Table 9.2. These types of parental help or contact were:

1. giving practical help: fund-raising, mending equipment, helping with outings or parties for children, etc.;
2. attending social events where parents and staff meet;
3. taking part in planning and management as members of parent or management committee, etc.;
4. taking part in consultative committees with no executive powers;
5. attending talks and discussions about parentcraft, education, etc. especially arranged for groups of parents.

The role of parents in maintained institutions centred mainly on giving practical help with fund-raising, mending equipment and helping with outings or parties for the children. 94% of LEA nursery schools, 90% of LEA nursery classes and 70% of LA day nurseries reported that they had parental involvement of this type. However, 85% of hall playgroups also had this sort of help. Organising social events was another way in which 75% of LEA schools and 56% of LA day nurseries achieved contact between parents and staff, but a similar pattern was found for hall playgroups (68%) and independent nursery schools (73%). LEA nursery schools and classes were more likely than other types of institution to organise educational talks and discussions for parents (47%). Over half of the hall playgroups had at least some parental involvement in the planning and management of the group, which was more than other types of institution had, although 38% of LEA schools reported that parents were involved in planning and management. Day nurseries, both maintained and independent, showed little sign of parental involvement in planning, management or consultation. Finally, we found that home playgroups had very low levels of parental involvement of any kind, with the exception of rota help, and the contrast with hall-based playgroups in this respect was most marked. This was probably because home playgroups were usually small with few staff and consequently had less scope for significant parental involvement. An alternative explanation is that those who ran playgroups in their own homes preferred to maintain their independence and to run the group in their own way.

The overall picture of parental involvement obtained from the Nursery/Playgroup survey was one in which substantial numbers of hall playgroups had parents helping in the sessions and also participating in management activities. In the maintained sector parents were more likely to be involved in supporting the institution in practical ways with the professional staff being responsible for teaching and management. In independent day nurseries and home playgroups there was very little evidence of parental involvement in any form.

The next question we look at is how these institutional differences were reflected in the involvement of the parents of the CHES cohort children who attended different types of preschool institution.

The parental point of view

We have been describing so far the proportions of different types of preschool institution in which parents were involved in various ways. The next step is to describe the extent to which parents of children in the CHES sample became involved in the nurseries or playgroups the children attended, and to consider whether some social groups were more likely to be involved than others. Table 9.3 shows the proportion of mothers in different Social Index groups who helped in their children's preschool facility and the frequency of their involvement. Socially disadvantaged mothers were less likely to be involved in their children's preschool institution than were those who were not socially disadvantaged. Of the mothers in the most disadvantaged Social Index group, 16% helped in some way compared with 38% of the advantaged Social Index group. One explanation for this difference was that socially advantaged children were more likely to attend playgroups, where there was greater opportunity for parental involvement, than maintained institutions. However, we still found social differences in the proportion who helped within the group of mothers whose children attended hall playgroups. We suggest that the stresses experienced by socially disadvantaged mothers effectively reduced their willingess to cope with the additional responsibility incumbent upon involvement in nursery or playgroup activities. For those beleaguered mothers especially, the child's preschool placement offered a brief respite from immediate responsibility and provided

Table 9.3 *Maternal help by Social Index group*

Social Index group		Maternal help				N = 100%
		Directly with children		Other type of help	Did not help	
		At least once a week	Less than once a week			
Most disadvantaged	%	4.1	7.4	4.6	83.9	367
Disadvantaged	%	5.6	15.5	3.3	75.7	859
Average	%	6.9	19.8	5.8	67.5	2,019
Advantaged	%	8.1	24.0	6.1	61.8	1,156
Most advantaged	%	8.4	20.0	8.1	63.5	655
ALL	%	6.9	19.1	5.7	68.3	5,056

Note: Sample = children who attended a preschool placement.

leeway for coping with other pressing problems. If one objective of involving parents with the children was to increase their skill in handling their own child and so help them to cope better with this parental task, it is ironic that mothers most in need of this help and support were least likely to be in a position to obtain it.

Table 9.3 also shows that socially advantaged mothers were more likely than disadvantaged mothers to help in sessions, either on a weekly basis or less often, and to provide types of help other than working with the children during sessions. Variation in levels of maternal involvement according to the type of preschool institution the child attended conformed to the expected pattern in that mothers whose children went to hall playgroups were the ones who were most likely to help in some way—9% helped with the children at least once a week, and 29% less often (Table 9.4). Mothers whose children attended LA day nurseries were the least likely to help in any way (6%), and fewer than 17% of the mothers whose children attended other types of institution were involved.

It was more common for mothers of playgroup children to give direct help with the children but the proportion of mothers providing other types of help did not differ so much according to the preschool institution attended by their children. The exception was LA day nurseries and home playgroups where only 3% of mothers helped.

The main reason given by non-helping mothers for not having been involved in their child's preschool institution was that their help was not required. As many as 72% of the most disadvantaged mothers and 53% of the advantaged mothers gave this reason for not helping. About one mother in ten whose child attended a preschool placement said that she was too busy or preferred not to help, and, again, socially disadvantaged mothers were more likely to give this reason (13%) than were the most advantaged mothers (7%).

Mothers whose children attended hall playgroups were less likely to report that their help was not required (45%) than were mothers whose children attended other types of preschool placement of whom about three-quarters gave this explanation for non-involvement. The distinction between hall playgroups and other types of preschool facility reflected the general pattern of parental involvement found in the institutions themselves in which hall playgroups were markedly more likely to provide the opportunity for parents to be involved.

Table 9.4 *Maternal help by main preschool placement*

Main preschool placement		Maternal help				N = 100%
		Directly with children		Other type of help	Did not help	
		At least once a week	Less than once a week			
Maintained						
LEA nursery school	%	3.2	4.2	5.5	87.2	600
LEA nursery class	%	3.2	5.8	4.1	86.8	1,019
LA day nursery	%	0.0	2.9	2.9	94.2	103
Independent						
Nursery school	%	5.1	2.6	7.7	84.6	39
Day nursery	%	4.3	1.4	4.3	90.1	141
Hall playgroup	%	9.4	28.7	6.4	55.4	3,030
Home playgroup	%	4.1	9.9	2.9	83.0	171
ALL	%	6.9	19.2	5.6	68.3	5,103

Note: Sample = children who attended a preschool placement. Chi square = 625.5 (18 df) p< .0005.

Clearly these responses from the mothers in the study were very subjective and there was a likelihood that the mothers tended to believe that their help was not required, rather than admitting that they were too busy or, perhaps, not sufficiently interested to help. Nevertheless, the contrast between hall playgroups and all the other types of institution implies a fair degree of validity in the responses and suggests that more might be done to provide for parental involvement and participation in preschool activities for those parents who would like to be actively involved in their child's preschool institution.

The pattern of maternal participation in the preschool facilities attended by children in the CHES cohort as revealed by these figures followed that of the institutions themselves described above: hall playgroups offered the most scope for involvement and mothers of children who attended these institutions were the ones who were most likely to have been involved. In total, however, fewer than one in three of the mothers in our study had been involved in any way in her child's preschool placement.

Parental interest in the child's education

In the ten-year follow-up survey the children's class teachers were asked to rate the parents' interest in their child's education on a four point scale from 'very interested' to 'uninterested': After adjustment for several home background factors this variable was found to be strongly associated with children's educational test performance, the obvious inference being that parental interest in the child's education enhanced her progress at school. So strong was this association that we thought it could be an important intervening factor in the associations we have found between children's preschool experience and their test scores. In particular we hypothesised that parents who were interested in their child's education would have been more likely to: (1) find them a good preschool placement and (2) become involved in that institution. If this were true, then it may transpire that parental interest was the factor underlying the educational success we have hitherto attributed to the child's preschool experience.

Before examining these possibilities we should explain why we decided not to use the teacher's rating of parental interest and to create instead an alternative index which is described below. We felt that class teachers were probably aware of the relative educational ability of the study child and that this could influence their judgement on how interested were the parents in their child's education. In other words, if a child was doing better than his peers at school, then a teacher might subconsciously attribute this in part to parental interest. Equally, there was the possibility that teachers attribute a greater degree of interest to middle-class, articulate parents than to less well-off parents who have difficulty expressing their thoughts and concerns about their child to teachers. This comment is not a criticism of teachers' objectivity, judgement or attitude towards lower social class groups; rather we are highlighting the fact that social differences and professional beliefs can shape individual perceptions and, in the situation under discussion, any actual link between active parental interest and a child's attainment is further enhanced by the subjective judgements made by the class teachers.

For this reason we decided to create an index of parental interest by making use of information, also provided by the class teachers, in the ten-year educational survey. Teachers were asked to estimate the total amount of time a child's parent(s) had been in contact with school staff during the previous school term, and for what proportion of this time they had discussed the child's educational progress. These two pieces of information were compiled into an index given in Table 9.5. This shows that 29% of the parents had not seen the staff at school at all in the previous term, 45% had spent less than

Table 9.5   *Scale of parental contact with junior school staff in previous term*

Category	N	%
0. Did not see staff	3,474	28.5
Saw staff for less than ½ hour and time spent discussing educational progress was:		
1. < 90%	2,561	21.0
2. > 90%	2,863	23.5
Saw staff for at least ½ hour and time spent discussing educational progress was:		
3. < 90%	2,127	17.5
4. > 90%	1,154	9.5
TOTAL	12,179	100.0

parents may still have an insecu.

half an hour with school staff and 27% had spent at least half an hour with the staff. Since the child's educational progress was usually the major topic of conversation between parents and staff, we have divided the sample into those for whom education was virtually the only topic discussed (more than 90% of the time) and those who also discussed other things (up to 90% of the time on education). The most important two groups in this scale are those who did not see the staff in the previous term, and those who spent half an hour or more discussing their child's educational progress, these being the two most extreme groups.

This scale provides a more objective indication of parental interest or concern with a child's education than the teacher's rating. However, we should not overlook one reason why parents and teachers might spend a lot of time discussing the child's educational progress; namely that a child is not doing as well at school as he should be. Also, less time might be spent discussing education if there are other pressing concerns such as behavioural or health problems which also might have implications for the child's educational progress.

A comparison of this scale of parental interest with the teacher's rating of the mother's interest in her child's education provided a partial check on the validity of using the amount of parental contact with school staff as an index of the parents' interest in their child's education. Only 9% of parents whom the teacher judged to be very interested in their child's education had not met the school staff during the previous term compared with 88% of those who were judged by the teacher to be uninterested. This strong association between two indicators of parental interest in the child's education increases confidence in the validity of the scale based on parental contact with the school staff. We are aware, however, of further methodological constraints, namely that teachers may have been more inclined to attribute an interest in children's education to those parents he or she had seen most often and if parents had not been seen at school the teacher may have assumed that this reflected a lack of interest. Notwithstanding all the methodological problems, parental interest is of central importance for the child's school progress and, as we have argued, may be a key factor in our analysis of the effects of preschool education.

We found large social differences in the proportion of parents who had been in touch with the staff at their child's school; as many as 43% of the most disadvantaged parents had not visited the school during the previous term compared with only 14% of the most advantaged parents. The reverse trend (4% to 20%) was found for those who spent a lot of time discussing educational issues. Such trends were expected and reflect the typical class differences in the way concern for children's educational progress is expressed.

Table 9.6 relates the child's preschool experience to the scale of parental contact in the junior school when the child was 10. High proportions of parental non-contact, with the implication of little interest in the child's education, were associated with children who had never attended a preschool placement (37%), LEA nursery class attenders (33%) and LA day nursery attenders (34%). Parents who were most likely to have had at least minimal contact with the junior school staff were those whose children had attended home playgroups, hall playgroups and independent day nurseries. Parents who paid for their children to go to home playgroups were also the ones who were most likely to spend a lot of time discussing the child's education at school (15%). Parents who were frequently in contact with junior school staff for other reasons as well as their children's education, were those whose children had attended independent nursery schools or day nurseries. A good part of the reason for these differences was the social class variation between children who attended different types of preschool institution. Socially advantaged parents were more likely to send their children to playgroups, and also to display an interest in their subsequent education.

Mothers who were involved in the preschool institution attended by their child were somewhat more likely than those who were not involved to subsequently show an interest in their child's educational progress. Again, this can be seen as another aspect of the general configuration of factors we have been describing, with very contrasting pictures. One child grows up in a comfortable home with parents who are interested in his educational prospects and who find a stimulating playgroup for him to attend in the preschool phase. Because playgroups offer the greatest opportunity for parental involvement, the child's mother is likely to be recruited to help in some way, and through this involvement, her interest in her child's education will be further stimulated. In contrast, another child grows up in poor and cramped housing conditions where the

Table 9.6 *Parental interest by main preschool placement*

Main preschool placement		Parental interest: scale of contact with junior school staff					N = 100%
		Did not see staff	Saw staff for less than ½ hour and time spent discussing educational progress was:		Saw staff for at least ½ hour and time spent discussing educational progress was:		
			< 90%	> 90%	< 90%	> 90%	
None	%	37.4	19.7	21.1	14.3	7.5	2,790
Maintained							
LEA nursery school	%	24.1	21.1	24.9	21.5	8.3	493
LEA nursery class	%	33.1	20.5	22.8	16.5	7.0	842
LA day nursery	%	34.2	19.0	19.0	20.3	7.6	79
Independent							
Nursery school	%	25.8	12.9	16.1	35.5	9.7	31
Day nursery	%	20.9	24.3	18.3	24.3	12.2	115
Hall playgroup	%	20.1	23.2	27.9	18.5	10.4	2,447
Home playgroup	%	17.8	17.0	31.1	19.3	14.8	135
ALL	%	29.1	21.1	24.1	17.0	8.7	6,932

Note: Chi square = 250.7 (28 df) p< .0005.

stresses of life and more demanding and immediate problems make it difficult for the parents to express special interest in his education. Financial constraints may compel his mother to go out to work and, if she works full-time, the child to attend a LA day nursery if a place is available; otherwise he may be left with a childminder which can effectively bar the child from attending a nursery school or playgroup. In these circumstances, even if the child is found a preschool placement, the mother is unlikely to have either the time or the energy to become involved in the institution's activities in any way.

These two thumb-nail sketches portray the two extremes of the social situations that underlie the data we have described. It is important to recognise the interrelatedness of all these factors and the complex ways in which they can combine to either support or impede a child's educational progress. Each child is unique in the particular developmental path she follows yet some general principles can be discerned in the tangle of data which help to explain how some children succeed and others fail. In the remainder of this chapter we explore further how the parental attitudes that we have been discussing enter into the equations relating preschool experience to later educational attainment.

Parental involvement and children's test scores

We have pointed out that there are two separate questions to consider when evaluating the possible effect on child development and educational achievement of parental involvement in preschool institutions. These are: (1) are institutions that utilise parent helpers as effective, less effective or more effective than institutions which do not, and (2) do children whose own mothers help in the preschool institution they attend fare better than those whose mothers are not involved?

To explore these questions we have adopted the same analytical procedure as described in earlier chapters; namely a series of analyses of variance in which the independent effects of our parental involvement variables on selected outcomes are tested after statistical adjustment for the main intervening variables (i.e. main preschool placement, Social Index score, type of neighbourhood and number of children in the family). For this purpose we have limited our analysis to two five-year and two ten-year tests. These are

Copying Designs test, English Picture Vocabulary Test, reading test and communication assessment. The ten-year reading and communication scores were selected from all the ten-year tests and assessments because they were the two which were the most strongly associated with children's preschool experience and one of the objectives of the present chapter is to ascertain whether the preschool association with these ten-year outcomes was partly due to institutional differences in parental involvement. Firstly, however, we examine the independent effects of the following factors:

1. institutions with and without rota parents;
2. institutions with and without regular parent help;
3. involvement of the study child's own mother in the institution the child attended;
4. parental interest in the child's educational progress.

A comparison between children in the CHES cohort who attended preschool institutions where there was at least one parent who helped on a rota basis and children who attended institutions with no rota parents, for each of our four test scores, found no significant differences in mean scores after adjustment for the main intervening variables. Children who attended institutions where there was regular parent help (parents helping at least once a week) achieved slightly higher scores in all four tests than did children who went to institutions without regular parent help, but none of these differences achieved statistical significance.

These results indicate that the presence of parent helpers in the preschool institution attended by the study children neither enhanced nor retarded their test scores when compared with those children who attended institutions without parents helping in the sessions. It is important to recognise, however, that the methodological limitations of these analyses, described in Chapter 8, might obscure any real effects of having parents as staff in the preschool institution.

The comparison of children whose own mothers helped in the preschool institution they attended with children whose mothers were not involved showed fairly conclusively that maternal involvement of any kind was associated with increased test scores in three out of the four tests, Copying Designs being the only non-significant result (Table 9.7). The type or frequency of help seemed unimportant; the main contrast being between children whose

Table 9.7 *Maternal help and children's test scores*

Maternal help	Copying Designs	EPVT	Reading	Communication
Directly with children:				
at least once a week	.08	.17	0.58	.06
less than once a week	−.02	.08	1.02	.08
Other type of help	.05	.17	1.53	.08
Did not help	−.01	−.06	−0.48	−.04
Overall mean	.07	.10	102.00	.14
Significance	ns	p< .0005	p< .05	p< .05

Note: Sample = children who attended a preschool placement. Analysis of variance; figures show deviation from overall mean adjusted for main preschool placement, Social Index score, neighbourhood, and number of children in the family.

mothers helped in any way and those whose mothers were not involved. We hypothesised that this result could be attributed to the fact that mothers who became involved in their children's preschool placement had a higher level of interest in their subsequent education. However, statistical adjustment for this additional factor did not affect the associations between maternal help and the child's test scores. Further analysis indicated, moreover, that these effects applied only to children who attended hall playgroups. Children whose parents were involved in the LEA nursery schools they attended did not differ in their test scores from those whose mothers were not involved. Thus in playgroups, contact with the child's parent might have been an important element in his success. This will be explored further later in this chapter.

Parental interest in the child's education has been shown to increase the probability that a mother helped in her child's preschool institution but it also had a direct independent effect on the child's developmental progress. The extent of this effect in our study is shown in Table 9.8 in which parental interest in a child's

Table 9.8 *Parental interest and children's test scores*

Parental interest: scale of contact with junior school staff	Copying Designs	EPVT	Reading	Communi- cation
Did not see staff	−.06	−.09	−2.04	.16
Saw staff for less than ½ hour and time spent discussing educational progress was:				
< 90%	−.05	.00	−0.55	−.13
> 90%	.11	.05	2.20	−.22
Saw staff for at least ½ hour and time spent discussing educational progress was:				
< 90%	−.03	.00	−0.75	.03
> 90%	.08	.13	3.49	−.26
Overall mean	−.02	−.01	99.64	.02
Significance	p< .0005	p< .0005	p< .0005	p< .0005

Note: Analysis of variance: figures show deviation from overall mean adjusted for main preschool placement, Social Index score, neighbourhood, and number of children in the family.

education at age 10, using our scale of parental contact with junior school staff described in Table 9.3, is analysed in terms of the four test scores. In all four analyses the mean scores of children whose parents had *not* been in contact with the junior school were significantly poorer than those whose parents *had* spent a lot of time at the school discussing their educational progress. Children whose parents spent relatively little time with the junior school teachers but spent most of that time discussing educational progress also had better than average test scores. Thus the parents' concern about the child's educational progress was the main consideration rather than the amount of contact they had with the class teacher. In the analyses related to the five-year Copying Designs and EPVT scores it was necessary to assume that parents who were interested in their children's education at the age of 10 were likely to have had similar attitudes during the child's preschool years. The ensuing results justified this assumption in that those obtained for the five-year tests followed a very similar pattern to those for the ten-year tests. However, the percentages of test variance explained in the former were somewhat lower than for the latter, which implied that some change in parental attitudes occurred between the five- and ten-year surveys.

It can be seen that the association between parental *interest* and the test scores was stronger than that between parental *help* in the child's preschool institution and the test scores for all the tests except EPVT. This was partly because the parental involvement analyses could only be computed for those children who had attended a preschool placement, whereas the question of parental interest in their child's education was applicable to all children including those with no preschool experience. For purposes of comparison, therefore, parental interest in a child's education was reanalysed with the same four tests but excluding the children with no preschool experience. This confirmed that parental interest was more strongly associated with Copying Designs, reading and communication test scores than was parental help, whereas for EPVT the reverse was true.

Analyses of variance which included both parental help *and* parental interest (as well as the three basic intervening variables) did not alter the pattern of results we have described. Parental interest was strongly associated with three of the tests but not EPVT, whereas parental help in the preschool institution was most strongly associated with EPVT. It is possible that contact with a preschool institution heightens a mother's awareness of the importance of language and vocabulary skills with measurable consequences for her child's vocabulary development at 5 years but not general conceptual ability as measured by the Copying Designs test. An analysis based on a subsample consisting only of children who attended hall playgroups, found that those whose mothers helped at the playgroup did better in the ten-year Picture Language Test than the children whose mothers did not help (p < .0005). This supports the hypothesis that children's vocabulary skills were enhanced in some way if the mother had been involved in the preschool playgroup. This type of advantage could underlie the other long-term, though weaker, associations between maternal involvement and the child's ten-year reading and communication skills. The lack of any association between parental interest in the child's education and EPVT in this analysis is inexplicable, particularly as a strong association was found in the analysis which included children with no preschool experience (Table 9.8).

Yes

Effect of parental involvement on the association between preschool experience and test scores

Maternal involvement in the child's preschool placement and also parental interest in the child's educational progress have been shown to be associated with both the child's test performance and also the type of preschool placement he had. Therefore such factors are likely to account for some of the variation in test scores between children who had attended different types of preschool institution. To examine the extent of such effects on the association between children's main preschool placement and their test performance, the same procedure was adopted as described in previous chapters; a series of analyses of variance was carried out which computed the differences in mean test scores between preschool groups after statistical adjustment for the three basic intervening variables (Social Index, type of neighbourhood and number of children in the family) plus the following additional variables in various combinations:

1. the presence of rota parents in the institution;
2. the presence of regular parent helpers;

3. maternal help in the institution her child attended;
4. parental interest in the child's educational progress at 10 years.

The object of these analyses was to examine the changes in statistical significance and mean scores for preschool groups when these additional independent variables were added into the analysis of variance. Except for an analysis involving only parental interest in the child's education, these analyses excluded children with no preschool experience as, clearly, they would be unaffected by issues centring on parental involvement in preschool institutions.

The first finding was that differences in mean test scores between children who attended different types of preschool institution were reduced to statistical non-significance in the Copying Designs and reading analyses after certain of the parental involvement variables were added in.

In the Copying Designs analysis the addition of parental interest in the child's education at 10 years had the effect of improving the mean score of children who attended LA day nurseries. This resulted in the observed differences in Copying Designs scores between preschool groups becoming non-significant. In the ten-year reading analysis no appreciable changes in mean scores occurred for individual preschool groups when adjustment was made for the parental involvement variables. The small shifts which did occur, however, resulted in the differences in reading scores between groups being reduced to statistical non-significance when both maternal help and parental interest were added to the analysis of variance. The variable which appeared to have the greatest effect on the test variance explained by the child's preschool experience was the involvement of the mother in her child's preschool institution. However, in both Copying Designs and reading analyses the decline in sample size, after adding in the ten-year parental interest variable, was also found to be a contributory factor in the reduction of the preschool effect to statistical non-significance.

Adjustment for parental involvement variables also reduced the differences in mean EPVT scores between preschool groups although, unlike Copying Designs and reading, the differences in mean EPVT scores between preschool groups remained statistically significant. The addition of the maternal help variable into the EPVT analysis of variance improved the mean scores of children who attended LA day nurseries so that the scores of these children differed little from those of children who went to independent day nurseries. Differences in communication score between preschool groups proved to be non-significant both before and after statistical adjustment for maternal involvement and parental interest, because of the exclusion of children with no preschool experience.

These analyses show that children whose parents were interested in their education and whose mothers helped in some way at the preschool institutions they attended achieved slightly better test scores than the children whose parents were less interested and did not take part in preschool activities. These factors were found to have a marginal effect on the variation in test scores between children who attended different types of preschool institution. Test scores were unaffected, however, by the presence or absence of parent helpers in the institution the child attended; the important factor was the involvement of the child's own parents. We have already explained that these analyses excluded children with no preschool experience because the maternal involvement variables were applicable only to those who had attended a preschool placement. The question of parental interest in the child's education, however, applied to all children and we have shown that this had a relatively strong effect on test scores (Table 9.8). We checked, therefore, whether this factor could account for the difference in test scores between children with and without preschool education. The findings were that after adjustment for parental interest, the differences in mean test scores between preschool groups remained statistically significant. Comparison between the analyses for the different tests before and after adjustment for parental interest showed no major shifts in the mean scores for the ten-year tests but there was an improvement in five-year test scores for children who attended LA day nurseries as described earlier in this chapter. We can conclude from this that differences in parental interest in the child's education between children in the different preschool groups does not account for the variation in mean test scores between attenders and non-attenders at preschool institutions.

Conclusions

The extent and nature of parental involvement varied considerably between types of preschool institution in our study. Although parental involvement is a central concept within the playgroup movement and more than three-quarters of all playgroups had parent helpers, fewer than half (45%) of the mothers whose children attended hall playgroups were involved in any way. Far more were involved in this type of facility, however, than in other types of institution. In LEA nursery schools 13% were involved and in LA day nurseries only 6%. In addition there was a sharp contrast between hall playgroups and other types of institution in the kind of help that was given by parents. Many hall playgroup mothers helped with the children in the sessions or served on management committees. This type of involvement occurred less often in nursery schools where fund-raising activities, practical help, assistance with outings and similar kinds of support were more typical. The reason most frequently given by the mothers as to why they were not involved in their children's preschool institution was that their help was not required. A minority of mothers said that they were too busy or did not wish to be involved.

Parental involvement in preschool education can be seen as an indication of parental interest in a child's development. Information obtained in the ten-year follow-up enabled us to create a scale of parents' interest in their child's education which was found to be strongly associated with children's test performances after taking account of other social background factors. Parents who helped in their children's preschool institution were also found to be interested in their educational progress at age 10. Thus parental interest in education was an important intervening factor in our analyses exploring the associations between parental involvement and children's test results.

Our analysis of the effects of parental involvement on children's cognitive and educational progress examined two questions: (1) what was the effect if she attended an institution where there were parent helpers, and (2) what was the effect if her *own* mother was involved?

We found that after adjustment for the type of institution attended and the child's own home and social background, children who attended institutions with parent helpers performed no differently in selected five- and ten-year tests than children who went to institutions without parent helpers. The implication of this is that parent helpers can be a valuable resource in the preschool setting and the fact that many such helpers do not have special training does not adversely affect the children in the group. The majority of parent helpers are mothers whose experience with their own children naturally provides them with the necessary skills to fulfil a role in the preschool context. We suggest, however, that the effectiveness of the system depends on the presence of a fully trained nursery teacher or playgroup leader within the classroom or group to ensure coordination and continuity.

Our second approach to the effects of parental involvement was to compare the educational attainment of children whose own mothers had been involved in their preschool institution, with that of children whose mothers had not been involved. This showed that the achievement of children whose mothers had helped in their preschool institutions was slightly better than that of children of non-involved mothers. This finding persisted after adjustment had been made for parental interest in the child's education, the type of preschool attended and home background factors. The effect of parental involvement was strongest in terms of the child's vocabulary skills and it is possible that this could have been due to the emphasis given to language development in many preschool institutions being transmitted to the mother who in turn encouraged her child's vocabulary development. This might have been achieved consciously by the mother deliberately introducing new words and concepts to her child, or unconsciously through increased conversation betweeen mother and child.

Finally, we investigated the possibility that differences between types of preschool institution in the extent and type of parental involvement might account for the variation in test scores that have been attributed to children's preschool experience. The main conclusion was that parental involvement and parental interest were of some significance in the association between test scores and children's preschool experience. Statistical adjustment for parental interest in the child's education reduced the differences between preschool groups in Copying Designs and reading scores to statistical non-significance but this was due partly to the unavoidable reduction in sample size. However, the differences in test scores between children who had attended a preschool placement and those who had not still persisted after parental interest in the child's education was taken into account.

We conclude, therefore, that parental involvement in a child's preschool institution can confer small benefits on the child in terms of her later educational development. The exact route by which this is achieved, however, is far from clear. One very strong possibility is that mothers who are interested in their child's education are more likely to become involved in the preschool institutions than are other mothers, and this involvement consolidates their educational interest and, perhaps, provides practical means whereby a mother can further her child's developmental progress.

10

Overview and main findings

The purpose of this chapter is to draw together the main findings and conclusions of the study by focusing sharply on the question of whether or not there are demonstrable long-term effects on children's cognitive ability and behaviour which can be attributed to their experience in preschool institutions. In doing so, we shall summarise some of the arguments which have been elaborated in previous chapters, and present the final analyses which bring together the main explanatory variables which have been identified.

Research background and methods

A number of studies of British preschool education have shown small gains in cognitive skills or educational attainment which have been attributed to children's attendance at preschool institutions. Reviewers of the research literature have interpreted such findings in different ways depending on the criteria they have used for the success or otherwise of preschool intervention. Barbara Tizard (1975), for example, concluded from her review of the research being carried out in the early 1970s that preschool education could not close the social class gap in achievement or prevent educational failure. It is doubtful, however, that anyone would expect preschool education to achieve such ambitious ends, and Smith and James (1977), after reviewing the same research concluded that preschool education *could* make an impact on children's cognitive development without suggesting that dramatic long-term educational gains might ensue. It is important, therefore, to recognise that *large* long-term effects attributable to early education should not be anticipated.

In America, in contrast to Britain, early disappointment in the apparent failure of Headstart programmes to increase the educational potential of socially disadvantaged children has been giving way to a more optimistic attitude following the widely publicised results from two research centres. The Perry Preschool Project directed by David Weikart at the High/Scope Educational Research Foundation in Michigan has followed the progress of 123 severely disadvantaged children of low IQ from preschool age in 1962 to adulthood (Clement *et al.*, 1984). The 58 children in this sample who attended a 'quality preschool' were found, in comparison with controls, to have better school attainment, to be less likely to need remedial education or to develop delinquent behaviour and to be more likely to complete their education to high school level and subsequently find employment. The results of this study are so impressive that it is difficult to comprehend how so much could be achieved by the comparatively simple and once-and-for-all expedient of preschool intervention. Whilst the integrity and expertise of the High/Scope researchers cannot be doubted we must not overlook the possibility that the continuity of interest that the research programme maintained with the sample over the years may have contributed to producing the results. We suggest that the most ardent advocate of preschool education would not expect attendance at even the very finest preschool nursery to increase the educational potential and life chances of children to the extent suggested by the Perry Preschool Project; there must have been contributory factors additional to the preschool intervention the children had experienced.

The Perry Preschool Project was one of eleven experimental preschool evaluation programmes originating in the 1960s which later collaborated in the 'Consortium for Longitudinal Studies' coordinated by Irving Lazar and Richard Darlington (1982). There were 2,100 children involved in the Consortium research, this being the total number traced and interviewed in two follow-up studies in 1976 and 1980. The main findings from this project suggested that attendance at a well-run preschool programme reduced the risk of school failure and increased the likelihood of completing secondary education and achieving employment success after leaving school.

The importance of these American studies is that they provide evidence that preschool education is capable of increasing children's intellectual capacity over considerable periods. It would be unwise, however, to claim on the basis of this that such intervention could close the social class gap in school achievement. To quote the words of one American researcher:

... few (if any) serious students of early education expect that a year or two of preschool, however well accommodated, will solve the educational problems usually associated with the low income minority experience. (Evans, 1985, p. 202)

It is essential, therefore, to keep in proportion the extent to which any single, transitory experience can be expected to have an effect on a child's developmental progress. This is not to deny, however, the importance of being able to demonstrate even small effects of preschool intervention as an indication of its valuable contribution to a child's education.

The American experience, demonstrated in these research programmes, cannot have direct implications for preschool education in Britain because the children who were followed up were mostly black, came from very poor homes, were of low IQ and had been involved in specially devised experimental preschool programmes (Woodhead, 1985). These, clearly, are not the characteristics of children at a typical nursery school or playgroup in Britain, but the importance of these American studies is that they provide strong evidence that early intervention can be effective in achieving long-term gains for disadvantaged children. The possibility that similar advantages might accrue to children who had attended British maintained and independent preschool institutions prompted the present critical evaluation of children's behaviour, development and attainment at 5 and 10 years of age in relation to their preschool educational experience. This was carried out using data from the Child Health and Education Study (CHES) which is a longitudinal survey of all children in Britain who were born during one week in April 1970. Comprehensive information about the child's preschool experience was provided by the mother at about the time of the child's fifth birthday, and details were obtained of the child's home and family background at 5 and 10 years that were to be a crucial part of the present study. Health visitors conducted developmental and vocabulary tests with the children at age 5, and teachers administered a battery of tests at age 10 which covered general ability, vocabulary, reading, mathematics and language skills. Children's behaviour was assessed by means of behaviour scales completed by their own mothers at age 5 and by class teachers at age 10.

In addition to the cohort study, a national survey of preschool institutions was carried out in 1975 (van der Eyken *et al.*, 1984). The object of this institutional study was to review preschool education and day care provision at that time and also to identify the institutions attended by the children in the cohort study. This survey provided a check on the validity of the mother's description of the type of institution her child attended and supplied details of the staffing and organisation of the institutions that were likely to have an influence on the educational experience the child had whilst attending.

Of the children in the cohort study who had attended a preschool institution almost 60% were successfully matched with the institution they had attended in the Nursery/Playgroup survey. This matching rate was better for children who had attended maintained institutions than for those who had attended independent nurseries or playgroups. Exact agreement between the mother's account of the institution and the actual type of institution attended by the child amounted to 84% of the matched subsample. Most of the discrepancies in the mothers' definitions were between institutions in the maintained sector, or between institutions in the independent sector; very few mothers confused maintained with independent institutions. Since the mothers' definitions of their children's preschool placement were not completely reliable, we decided to carry out our analyses on the cases which were successfully matched with an institution in the Nursery/Playgroup survey, plus those who had not attended preschool institutions. This resulted in a basic sample of 5,413 children with preschool education experience and 3,719 without.

Types of British preschool provision

The lack of any unified policy in Britain for preschool education and day care provision for children under 5 years of age has resulted in considerable diversity of types of provision. The characteristics of these different types of provision indicate response to the needs of children from different sections of the community, as well as following a particular educational tradition. The advent of playgroups which originated to meet the demand of mainly middle-class parents for a social experience for their preschool-age children, has resulted in maintained nursery schools and classes developing a responsibility for working class children, particularly those known to be at a social disadvantage. Local Authority day nurseries have been used to an even greater degree as places of care for children from families who are experiencing extreme stress and who have come to the attention of the Social Services Department. Thus there is considerable variation in the social composition of the different types of nurseries and playgroups.

The types of institution showed important staffing differences in that maintained nurseries were staffed mainly by professionally trained teachers and nursery nurses, whereas playgroups depended more on parent helpers, many of whom had no relevant formal qualifications. The physical environment also differed from one type of institution to the next, ranging from purpose-built nursery premises to church and community halls and to private homes. Another major difference was found in the pattern of attendance; maintained institutions operated five days a week and children attended full- or half-time, while in the independent sector many playgroups only operated two or three days a week and most children attended only 2 or 3 sessions.

The types of preschool institution we have investigated thus revealed many points of difference, and although there was variation *within* types of institution, this was small in comparison with the completely different experiences of children who went to hall playgroups, LEA nursery schools, LA day nurseries, home playgroups or who had no preschool experience. Thus the burden of our analysis centred on differences in educational attainment and behaviour found between children who attended different types of preschool institution and the non-attenders.

Social variation in utilisation of preschool services

Hall playgroups accommodated the largest proportion of children in our sample (45%) and a further 5% attended other types of independent institution. In the maintained sector, 7% and 12% respectively attended LEA nursery schools and classes, whilst only 1.3% went to LA day nurseries. A very small number (N = 49) attended special institutions for handicapped children. As many as 29% of the sample had no preschool education or day care experience at all, although three-quarters of this group started infant school before their fifth birthday compared with about two-thirds of those who attended preschool placements.

There was considerable social variation in the proportions of children utilising institutions in the maintained and independent

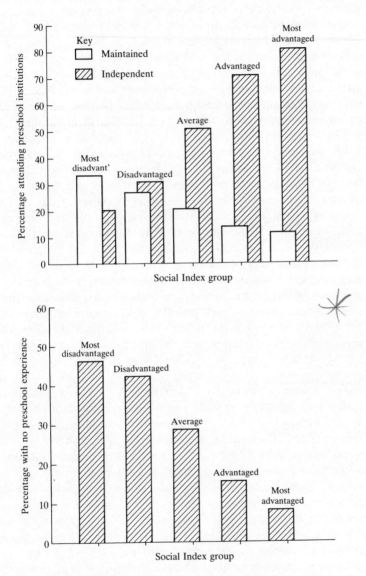

FIG. 10.1. Preschool experience by Social Index group

sectors. Using a composite index of socio-economic inequality we divided the sample into five groups from the most disadvantaged to the most advantaged Social Index groups. Figure 10.1 shows that the proportions of children who attended independent institutions ranged from 20% of the most disadvantaged to 79% of the most advantaged children. In the maintained sector the reverse trend occurred, with 33% of the most disadvantaged decreasing to 11% of the most advantaged children attending LEA nursery schools or classes or LA day nurseries. In consequence, as many as 46% of the most disadvantaged children had received no form of preschool education compared with only 10% of the most advantaged group.

This social inequality in the use of preschool education facilities is of considerable concern, implying as it does that the groups of children and their families with the greatest need for extra support were in fact least likely to obtain it. What is needed, therefore, is expansion of maintained nursery schools or classes or day nurseries, particularly by those authorities that currently have no such provision. The expansion of part-time nursery classes in infant schools over the decade between 1975 and 1985 (see Chapter 2) is an encouraging sign of official recognition of this need for more maintained preschool education facilities. However, findings from our study indicate the need to ensure that nursery classes are staffed and equipped in accordance with the educational requirements of the 3- to 4-year age-group, and are not simply run in the same way as infant reception classes. Some local education authorities are providing places in infant classes for 4-year-olds as an alternative to providing designated nursery classes. Whilst this policy helps to meet the parents' demand for their children to start school at an earlier age, our study strongly suggests that this type of provision does not result in measurable improvements in children's cognitive and educational achievement or behavioural characteristics. It is therefore the more important to continue to provide and develop nursery curricula appropriate to the under-five age-group.

The inequality of provision that existed both between local authorities and different types of residential neighbourhood was a significant factor in creating these social differences in preschool utilisation. More than a third of LA day nurseries were located in poor inner city areas, compared with only 6% of playgroups. Conversely, only 5% of LA day nurseries and 11% of LEA nursery schools and classes were in areas they deemed to be rural compared

[handwritten margin note: important that settings are designed to meet children's individual needs.]

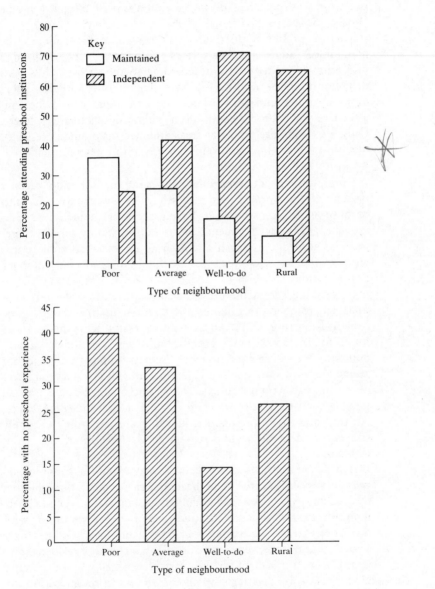

FIG. 10.2. Preschool experience by type of neighbourhood

with 36% of playgroups. This points up the fact that independent provision has tended to develop in areas where local authority provision was sparse and the population was predominantly middle class.

This geographical distribution of preschool provision in the maintained and independent sectors partly explains the variation in utilisation of such provision according to the study child's own neighbourhood of residence shown in Figure 10.2. Children living in poor residential neighbourhoods were the most likely to be non-attenders and those in well-to-do neighbourhoods the least likely. Only 9% of children in rural areas attended maintained preschool institutions but 64% went to playgroups or other types of independent provision.

Family size is an important consideration, not only because preschool utilisation varied according to this factor but also because it has been shown to have a profound influence on children's cognitive development. The size of the family should, therefore, be accorded as much attention as its socio-economic status when examining the effects of preschool education on children's test performance.

Figure 10.3 shows the preschool utilisation rates of study children according to the number of children in their family. The comparisons reveal differences that were not so great as those found for the Social Index groups, but nevertheless of children in families comprising four or more children, almost half had not attended a preschool institution compared with less than a quarter of the children with no siblings or only one. Socially disadvantaged families tend to have more children than do advantaged families, but the variation in preschool utilisation rates according to family size occurred at all socio-economic levels (Osborn *et al.*, 1984, p. 118).

Analysis of many other social and family variables from the five-year survey showed the same basic pattern, namely that children from socially disadvantaged or vulnerable families were more likely than advantaged children to attend maintained institutions, with the reverse trend occurring in independent nurseries and playgroups. Social Index score, type of neighbourhood of residence and family size were identified as variables of special importance because they were powerful predictors of test scores and also were strongly associated with the type of preschool experience the child

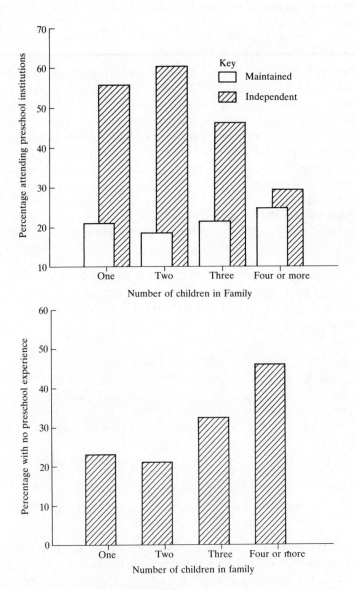

FIG. 10.3. Preschool experience by number of children in family

had. This made them important as intervening variables when we examined the associations between preschool experience and the child's subsequent achievement and behaviour.

Preschool experience and attainment

We have adopted an essentially Popperian approach in our evaluation of preschool education services by attempting to refute the proposition that attendance at a preschool institution has a positive effect on children's cognitive development and educational attainment. To this end we have attempted to find as many intervening variables as possible which reduce the size and statistical strength of the associations between children's preschool experience and their test scores. By 'intervening variables' we mean the social and family factors described in Chapter 3 which were associated with both children's preschool experience and their test scores.

We used two five-year and five ten-year test outcomes:

Five-years
1. Copying Designs test. A non-verbal test of cognitive ability based on spatial awareness and eye–hand coordination.
2. English Picture Vocabulary Test (EPVT). A test of vocabulary comprehension.

Ten-year
3. British Ability Scales (BAS). A test of cognitive ability incorporating verbal and non-verbal subscales.
4. Picture Language Test (PLT). A test of vocabulary comprehension.
5. Reading test. A shortened version of the Edinburgh Reading Test.
6. Mathematics test. Specially designed for the CHES ten-year follow-up covering the four rules of arithmetic, number concepts, measure, algebra, geometry and statistics.
7. Communication. A scale of expressive language based on assessments made by the child's class teacher.

An advantage of having several test outcomes is that the conclusions of the evaluation need not rest on only one or two test criteria, which might not be adequate for revealing aspects of cognitive development that are most susceptible to preschool experience.

Twelve factors were selected as potential intervening variables because of their strong association with both the preschool variable and test scores. These were: Social Index score, type of neighbourhood, number of children in the family, child's gender. and height, mother's age and employment status, maternal depression, type of family, ethnic origin, country of residence and handicap (see Table 4.3). The method of analysis was to examine the differences between mean test scores for children in each preschool group after making statistical adjustment for the effects of the first three of these intervening variables, plus each other intervening variable in turn in a succession of analyses of variance. This process enabled us to identify all the intervening variables which significantly reduced the preschool effect on the test scores. Since each intervening variable had a greater effect on some tests than on others the final results given in Figures 10.4 to 10.10 contain different subsets of independent variables. This, to repeat, is a consequence of our empirical approach to the selection of variables which had a maximal effect on reducing the strength of association between the preschool variable and the test scores.

Before describing the results of these analyses it should be noted that we also investigated the effects on the children's attainment of their social and educational experience between 5 and 10 years of age. In particular we looked at the type of primary schools the children attended, the social mobility of the family, change in family size, change in type of family (i.e. from two-parent to one-parent or vice versa) and the degree of parental interest in the child's education. Social mobility and parental interest in the child's education were found to be strongly associated with several test scores and, as intervening variables, caused a significant reduction in the differences between mean scores for preschool groups in relation to some of the tests. Thus these variables also appear in the relevant analyses in Figures 10.4 to 10.10.

All these figures describe the results of analyses of variance in which the differences between mean scores for each independent variable have been adjusted for the effects of all other independent variables shown in the analysis. The length of the bars represents the maximum difference between category means for each variable. This is especially important for the main preschool placement variable because there were eight different preschool categories and only the two with the most extreme mean scores are shown in the figure. The adjusted mean scores for *all* the preschool categories are shown in a separate table beneath the figure. These are arranged hierarchically from the type of preschool placement with the highest mean score to the one with the lowest mean score.

We do not propose to discuss each of these analyses separately as this would be tedious and the figures and tables themselves clearly show how the pattern of results differs from one analysis to the next. Instead we shall extrapolate the most important general points that relate to the associations between children's preschool experience and their later cognitive development.

First, the statistical associations between preschool experience and all but two outcomes—Copying Designs ($p < .005$) and

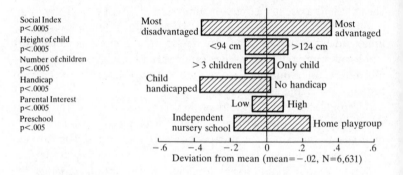

Preschool groups and five-year Copying Designs score

Main preschool placement	N	Deviation from mean
Home playgroup	132	.24
Independent day nursery	113	.11
LEA nursery school	473	.08
LA day nursery	75	.07
LEA nursery class	805	.03
Hall playgroup	2,369	.02
No preschool	2,637	−.06
Independent nursery school	27	−.18
OVERALL MEAN		−.02
TOTAL N	6,631	

Fig. 10.4. Preschool experience and five-year Copying Designs score

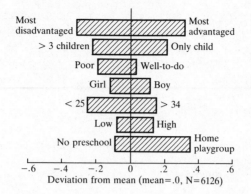

Social Index p<.0005	Most disadvantaged			Most advantaged
Number of children p<.0005	> 3 children		Only child	
Type of neighbourhood p<.0005	Poor	Well-to-do		
Child's gender p<.0005	Girl	Boy		
Mother's age p<.0005	< 25		> 34	
Parental interest p<.0005	Low	High		
Preschool p<.0005	No preschool		Home playgroup	

Deviation from mean (mean=.0, N=6126)

Preschool groups and five-year EPVT score

Main preschool placement	N	Deviation from mean
Home playgroup	123	.35
Independent nursery school	27	.17
Hall playgroup	2,214	.07
Independent day nursery	107	.03
LEA nursery school	436	.01
LEA nursery class	736	.01
LA day nursery	64	.01
No preschool	2,419	−.09
OVERALL MEAN		.00
TOTAL N	6,126	

FIG. 10.5. Preschool experience and five-year EPVT score

Picture Language Test (p < .05) were very strong (p < .0005) after statistical adjustment for all the intervening variables which most reduced the differences in mean scores and statistical significance between preschool groups.

Second, the overall differences in the children's mean scores according to their preschool experience were large relative to the effects of other social and family factors. This amounted to the equivalent of about one-third of a standard deviation in the tests which compared favourably with those differences attributed to the child's gender, maternal age, parental interest in the child's

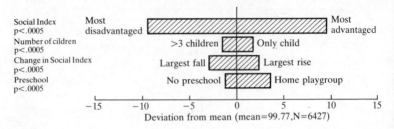

Preschool groups and ten-year British Ability Scales score

Main preschool placement	N	Deviation from mean
Home playgroup	127	3.54
Independent nursery school	28	2.33
LA day nursery	70	2.01
Hall playgroup	2,318	1.22
LEA nursery school	447	.78
Independent day nursery	110	−.06
LEA nursery class	768	−1.02
No preschool	2,559	−1.19
OVERALL MEAN		99.77
TOTAL N	6,427	

FIG. 10.6. Preschool experience and ten-year British Ability Scales score

education and family size. Socio-economic inequality as measured by the Social Index, however, remained the most powerful determinant of differences in cognitive and educational attainment in children. At the age of 10 the most disadvantaged children were the equivalent of one standard deviation in test scores behind the most advantaged children—after statistical adjustment for their other family circumstances.

Third, children who attended home playgroups had the highest mean scores in four out of the seven tests analysed and had the second highest score in the other three. Despite the relatively small number of children who attended home playgroups, the differences between their test scores and those of non-attenders achieved statistical significance in all the tests except communication. However, the statistical differences between the mean scores achieved by home playgroup attenders and those who went to LEA nursery schools or hall playgroups were generally non-significant. Nevertheless, the consistently high test scores of the home playgroup children across all the tests suggests that their results were not chance findings. Either home playgroups were singularly effective in promoting children's cognitive development or, despite all the statistical controls we have built into our model, they still represented a highly selected group of children of above average ability.

The factor which most distinguished home playgroups from all other types of preschool institution was their small size. The average number of children and staff present during a session was 13

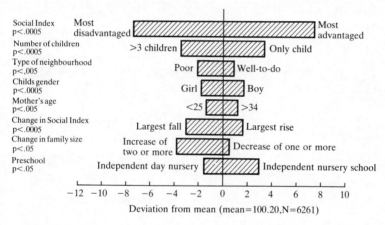

Preschool groups and ten-year Picture Language Test score

Main preschool placement	N	Deviation from mean
Independent nursery school	27	2.91
Home playgroup	123	2.80
LA day nursery	64	.72
Hall playgroup	2,260	.70
LEA nursery school	447	.11
LEA nursery class	767	−.34
No preschool	2,463	−.68
Independent day nursery	110	−1.55
OVERALL MEAN		100.2
TOTAL N	6,261	

FIG. 10.7. Preschool experience and ten-year Picture Language Test score

and 2 respectively in home playgroups compared with 23 and 4 in hall playgroups, and 30 and 3 in LEA nursery classes. By operating in a private house, the home playgroup was likely to have a homely atmosphere in which young children might respond more readily to the activities provided. Home playgroups were also the type of preschool institution that were the least likely to accommodate children having any kind of social or behavioural problem; the majority (81%) being located in well-to-do or rural areas where the prevalence of social problems was relatively low. Only 28% of home playgroups were attended by one child or more who had been referred by a social worker, health visitor or other professional, compared with 44% of hall playgroups and 85% of LEA nursery schools or LA day nurseries.

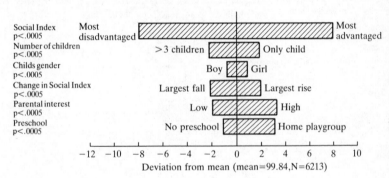

Preschool groups and ten-year reading score

Main preschool placement	N	Deviation from mean
Home playgroup	125	3.12
LEA nursery school	438	1.31
Independent day nursery	101	1.22
Hall playgroup	2,237	1.05
Independent nursery school	27	.72
LA day nursery	66	.03
LEA nursery class	751	−1.04
No preschool	2,468	−1.09
OVERALL MEAN		99.84
TOTAL N	6,213	

FIG. 10.8. Preschool experience and ten-year reading score

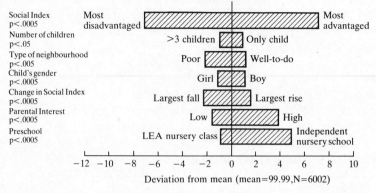

Preschool groups and ten-year mathematics score

Main preschool placement	N	Deviation from mean
Independent nursery school	26	4.95
Home playgroup	121	2.58
Independent day nursery	100	2.08
LEA nursery school	435	1.35
Hall playgroup	2,160	.67
LA day nursery	66	.14
No preschool	2,363	−.85
LEA nursery class	731	−.91
OVERALL MEAN		99.99
TOTAL N	6,002	

FIG. 10.9. Preschool experience and ten-year mathematics score

The combination of a homely atmosphere with a small number of children from socially advantaged, and probably stimulating, home backgrounds in home playgroups may well provide the optimal learning environment for very young children. It is interesting to compare home playgroups with childminders which, although similar in terms of scale, differ considerably in the service offered. Nevertheless, the results for the children who attended home playgroups in this study suggest the potential for childminders to perform a more overtly educational role:

Childminding is perhaps potentially the *best* form of day care for the preschool child, not the worst. The ideally small-scale setting, with each

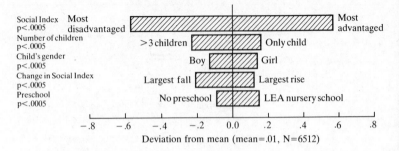

Social Index p<.0005	Most disadvantaged	...	...	Most advantaged
Number of children p<.0005		>3 children	Only child	
Child's gender p<.0005		Boy	Girl	
Change in Social Index p<.0005		Largest fall	Largest rise	
Preschool p<.0005		No preschool	LEA nursery school	

Deviation from mean (mean=.01, N=6512)

Preschool groups and ten-year communication score

Main preschool placement	N	Deviation from mean
LEA nursery school	455	.15
Independent nursery school	28	.12
Home playgroup	128	.12
LA day nursery	73	.11
Hall playgroup	2,332	.06
Independent day nursery	112	.00
LEA nursery class	791	.00
No preschool	2,593	−.09
OVERALL MEAN		−.01
TOTAL N	6,512	

FIG. 10.10. Preschool experience and ten-year communication score*

minder caring for no more than three children of varying ages; the continuity of care provided in a stable minding situation, far exceeding that possible in an institution; the situation of the minder and minded children as participants in the community, not isolated, sealed-off in the nursery; all these possibilities point to the potential advantages of good minding over other day care arrangements. (Raven, 1981, p. 155)

Fourth, the mean scores of children who attended LEA nursery classes were significantly higher than those of non-attenders only in the Copying Designs test and the communication scale. In the ten-year BAS, Picture Language test, reading and mathematics tests these children were indistinguishable in their level of achievement from the non-attenders. However, the cognitive and educational development of children who attended LEA nursery schools was enhanced relative to both non-attenders and children who went to

LEA nursery classes. Moreover, children who started attending infant reception classes from an early age also achieved test results that were no higher than those of children who started school after reaching their fifth birthday. The contrast between LEA nursery schools and nursery classes suggests that they differed in the educational experience they offered, and that nursery classes may have resembled infant reception classes in some respects. Evidence supporting this inference is the finding that child–adult ratios of more than 10 : 1 occurred in 36% of LEA nursery classes compared with only 3% of LEA nursery schools; and in 23% of LEA nursery classes, compared with only 10% of LEA nursery schools, all the children attended full-time. High child–adult ratios and full-time attendance are more typical of infant than nursery classes, and we suggest on the basis of these results that some children in our sample were attending nursery classes that were run more on the lines of an infant reception class than a class in a nursery school.

There is also another crucial difference between LEA nursery schools and classes in that the former enjoy full autonomy from the rest of the primary school system, whereas the latter are part of a larger school attended by a wider age-range of children. The implication of this for nursery teachers in primary schools is that they are frequently accorded lower status than teachers of infant- and junior-age children and perhaps receive a smaller share of the school's resources to spend on classroom equipment. Of possibly greater importance, however, is the relative isolation of the nursery class teacher from others teaching the same age-group, who as a result lacks the support and sharing of ideas with others which are so essential for sustaining enthusiastic and lively classroom practice.

Fifth, after statistical adjustment for the relevant socio-economic and family factors, the mean scores of children who attended LA day nurseries differed little from those of children who attended LEA nursery schools or hall playgroups. This is an important finding in view of the considerable social differences we have demonstrated between children who attended LA day nurseries and those enrolled in other types of institution. LA day nurseries accommodated many children whose families were experiencing serious social problems. Most of these children reach LA day nurseries on referral from social services or the health visitor and of necessity these nurseries accept children within a wide age-range up to

[handwritten margin note: why do purposely set up, separate nursery schools do better in this study than nursery classes in primary school?]

5 years. There is evidence that in the decade since our Nursery/ Playgroup survey was carried out in 1975, LA day nurseries have become even more the facility that provides day care for children from severely disadvantaged homes (van der Eyken, 1984). This suggests that children attending LA day nurseries were a highly selected group; nevertheless, within the limitations of our analysis (which can measure only some of the more important social differnces) our findings show that the scores of these high-risk children were on a par with those of children who attended other types of preschool institution in both the maintained and independent sectors, and on average higher than those of children without preschool experience. These conclusions are based not so much on the statistical differences between LA day nursery attenders and other groups, as on the similar pattern of results across all seven analyses of cognitive and educational achievement.

Finally, children who had no preschool placement achieved the lowest mean test scores in four out of the seven tests analysed and had the second lowest score in the other three. This suggests that attendance at most types of preschool facility can increase children's educational potential.

Further checks on the validity of the results

The procedures leading to the final models presented in Figures 10.4 to 10.10 were designed to minimise the strength and size of the preschool education effect on the test outcomes. The independent variables in these analyses were those having the most damaging effect on the association between children's preschool experience and their subsequent intellectual progress. However, to allay any lingering doubts as to the validity of our findings, we decided to check whether other analytical approaches might produce different results.

One alternative approach entailed carrying out multiple regressions in which the mean test score for each preschool group was statistically adjusted for all 17 independent variables which have already featured in at least one set of analyses described in other chapters (the variables are specified in Tables 4.3, 6.1 to 6.4 and 9.5). The introduction into the analysis of this large number of potential intervening factors in addition to the ones described in Figures 10.4 to 10.10 made no substantial difference to either the

Table 10.1 *Significance of difference between mean test scores for non-attenders and preschool groups*

Main preschool placement	p<	Five-year tests		Ten-year tests					Max. N
		Copying Designs	EPVT	BAS	PLT	Reading	Mathematics	Communication	
Maintained									
LEA nursery school	p<	.005	ns	.05	ns	.05	.05	.0005	398
LEA nursery class	p<	.05	ns	ns	ns	ns	ns	.05	666
LA day nursery	p<	ns	ns	ns	ns	ns	ns	ns	60
Independent									
Nursery school	p<	ns	ns	ns	ns	ns	ns	ns	22
Day nursery	p<	.05	ns	ns	ns	.05	.05	ns	93
Hall playgroup	p<	.05	.0005	.0005	.05	.0005	.005	.005	1,992
Home playgroup	p<	.005	.0005	.05	.05	.005	.05	ns	115

Note: Figures show the level of statistical significance of the difference between the mean test scores of non-attenders; and children who attended different preschool placements. These are results from multiple regression analyses in which the mean scores of the preschool groups were adjusted for the effects of 17 other independent variables.

statistical significance of the preschool effect, or the mean scores for the different preschool groups. Table 10.1 shows the statistical significance of the differences in mean scores between non-attenders and attenders at each type of preschool institution obtained in these regressions for all the five- and ten-year tests. The non-significant results associated with LA day nurseries and independent nursery schools can be attributed to the relatively small number of cases in these groups. Children who attended LEA nursery schools, hall playgroups or home playgroups consistently achieved higher test scores than non-attenders. The higher level of statistical significance achieved by children who attended hall playgroups is attributable to the large numbers in this category, since the adjusted mean scores of these children differed little from those who attended LEA nursery schools.

Figure 10.11 shows the effects on mean reading scores for the preschool groups as a result of the statistical adjustment for the five intervening variables in the analysis of variance in Figure 10.8, and the 17 intervening variables in the multiple regression analysis.

The effect on preschool group mean scores resulting from their adjustment in the analysis of variance was that the relatively high unadjusted mean scores were reduced after adjustment for the five main variables whereas low initial scores were increased. It can be seen that although the overall difference was much reduced (i.e. from 11.81 to 4.21 points), the ranking, with some exceptions indicated by crossing lines, was much the same after adjustment for the intervening variables. The regression analysis contained twelve additional independent variables over and above those in the analysis just described yet the shift in mean scores shown in Figure 10.11 was negligible and the strength of the preschool association with reading score was just as great. A similar picture was obtained for all the other test outcomes.

The reason why the additional intervening variables made so little difference to the results was (a) their association with type of preschool experience or test outcome was relatively weak, or (b) the variance explained by these additional variables had already been accounted for by the initial set of independent factors in the analysis of variance. This is because many of these social and family variables overlap each other so that by adjusting for one factor one is already indirectly taking some account of others. **Thus the crux of our argument is that only by finding a factor that is totally**

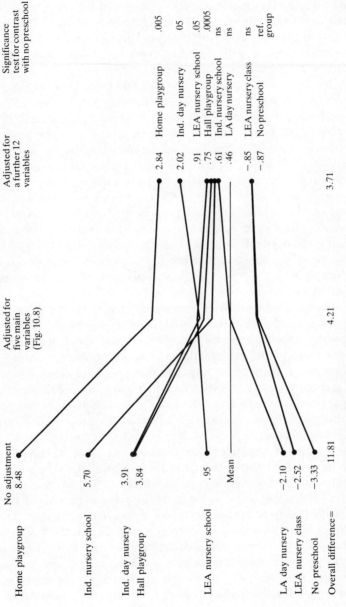

Deviation from mean ten-year reading score

	No adjustment	Adjusted for five main variables (Fig. 10.8)	Adjusted for a further 12 variables		Significance test for contrast with no preschool
Home playgroup	8.48		2.84	Home playgroup	.005
Ind. nursery school	5.70		2.02	Ind. day nursery	.05
Ind. day nursery	3.91		.91	LEA nursery school	.05
Hall playgroup	3.84		.75	Hall playgroup	.0005
			.61	Ind. nursery school	ns
LEA nursery school	.95		.46	LA day nursery	ns
	Mean				
			−.85	LEA nursery class	ns
			−.87	No preschool	ref. group
LA day nursery	−2.10				
LEA nursery class	−2.52				
No preschool	−3.33				
Overall difference =	11.81	4.21	3.71		

FIG. 10.11. Preschool experience and reading analysis

independent of all those already in the analysis, and which varies according to the type of preschool placement the child had, and is also associated with test performance, is it at all likely that these mean scores associated with preschool groups can be affected.

Explanations for the preschool education effect on children's ability based on the argument that parents that do not make use of preschool facilities are less motivated and less stimulating in their relationship with their children, are not supported by results from the National Survey of Health and Development (Wadsworth, 1981, 1986). This shows only small differences in parents' attitudes toward the value of preschool education according to the type of facility used, and concludes that maternal education is a more powerful intervening factor in the association between preschool experience and verbal ability at 8 years than are parenting methods. It is unlikely, therefore, that parents who obtained a preschool place for their child were of such exceptional motivation, independent of class, education, family configuration, maternal depression and the other factors we have taken into account, that this created a spurious association between preschool experience and subsequent attainment.

If it is argued that all the intervening variables in the analysis do not adequately measure the (unknown) factor which is the real reason for the apparent preschool effects, why should it be that the preschool variable itself should measure this factor so effectively? It is far more plausible to conclude that preschool education itself produces the effect—probably by increasing the child's ability to adapt to and benefit from infant and junior school experience with subsequent cumulative benefits in a transactional process (Clarke, 1984(a) and (b)).

A potential methodological concern was that certain of the groups in our sample, especially those who attended home playgroups, independent nursery schools and LA day nurseries, were so small and highly selected that normal regression procedures might not adequately adjust for the effects of intervening variables (Lord, 1967). Since this was not a problem affecting children who had attended LEA nursery schools and classes and hall playgroups, analyses of variance and regressions were carried out for these children plus those with no preschool experience. The results from these analyses differed hardly at all from those already reported for these four groups. Attendance at LEA nursery schools or hall playgroups was associated with increased test scores, but LEA nursery class attenders achieved similar results to those with no preschool education for the majority of the tests. This contrast between the educational progress of children who attended LEA nursery schools and those who went to LEA nursery classes is particularly significant in view of the very similar socio-economic and family background of these two groups and those who had no preschool education. The similarity between these three groups in their social circumstances also means that less dependence needs to be placed on the efficiency of the statistical manipulation and that, hence, the findings for the positive effects of LEA nursery school experience can be accepted with even greater confidence.

As a final check on the robustness of the results, regression analyses were carried out to test the associations between children's main preschool placement and each of the ten-year outcomes (BAS, PLT, reading, mathematics and communication) after adjustment for eleven independent variables from the *ten-year* data set. Our main analytical approach has been to select five-year independent variables that were likely to have been important in determining the type of preschool education the child received. Ten-year variables, however, were more strongly associated with ten-year test scores, thereby reducing the probability that the longitudinal effects of preschool experience could be sustained. The ten-year variables selected were those known to have a strong independent effect on children's ability at ten years and included: Social Index score, number of children in the family, mother's age, maternal depression, parental interest in the child's education, type of junior school attended, type of family (one or two parents), country of residence, child's gender, height and any disability. Some of these factors were included in our earlier analyses and others correlated with their five-year counterparts, nevertheless these regressions drew far more on the ten-year situation. This alternative approach did not substantially alter the main effects of preschool experience on the ten-year test outcomes; if anything, the preschool education effects were slightly stronger.

We can conclude from these three checks on the robustness of the findings that the higher average level of achievement in cognitive and educational tests attributed to attendance at preschool institutions was unlikely to be the spurious result of other unmeasured factors, or a consequence of our particular methodological approach. Even if the high scores of children who attended home playgroups are disregarded on the assumption that they were a highly selected group, the positive results associated with LEA nursery school or hall playgroup attendance persist through all the rigorous tests we have applied.

Effectiveness of preschool education for different social groups

Generally speaking we found that children from all types of social background benefited from attending a preschool education facility. However, socially disadvantaged children were found to gain slightly more from their preschool experience than were socially advantaged children. This was discovered by carrying out a series of analyses of variance related to the seven test outcomes for the 30% most disadvantaged children (according to the Social Index) and separate analyses for the 30% most advantaged children. Attendance at LEA nursery schools or hall playgroups was associated with significantly increased mean scores compared with non-attenders in five out of the seven tests for the disadvantaged group, but there were no significant differences for the advantaged group with respect to their preschool experience.

Analyses focussing on the most severely disadvantaged 10% of the sample, reported in Chapter 4, found significant gains in only two of the seven tests for children who had attended LEA nursery schools or hall playgroups, although the general trend across all the tests was for children who attended these types of preschool institution to achieve higher mean scores than the non-attenders.

From this evidence we conclude that the advantages of nursery education were marginally greater for socially disadvantaged children than for their more advantaged peers, but this difference was quite small in comparison with the general benefit of preschool education for all children.

Pattern of attendance

Children's preschool experience has been described hitherto simply in terms of the type of preschool institution they attended just before starting infant school, but the actual situation was inevitably far more complex than can be represented in a single classification. Some children started their schooling earlier in life than others, some attended more than one institution concurrently. There were those who attended full-time (10 sessions per week), whilst others attended half-time, and of those who joined playgroups many were there only 1 or 2 sessions per week. The majority of institutions operated during normal school hours, 9.00 a.m. to 3.30 p.m. during school terms. Day nurseries, however, were open for more hours during the day and for fifty weeks a year.

We anticipated that this variation in the duration and frequency of children's attendance at preschool institutions would modify the general picture that was emerging of the association between different types of preschool experience and children's cognitive and educational development. To check for the effect of such factors analyses were carried out to examine how the five- and ten-year test scores and the behavioural assessments at age 5 were affected by the ages at which the child first started his preschool education and when he entered the infant reception class, and the number of preschool sessions attended.

We were surprised to discover that these factors had little independent effect on test results, although there was a tendency for differences in mean test scores between preschool groups to reduce slightly after adjustment for pattern of attendance. Thus the observed differences in attainment between children who attended different types of institution are partly attributable to the particular patterns of attendance which characterise them. We found no differences in achievement between children with long experience of preschool education and those who attended for a relatively short time, and children who attended ten sessions a week achieved the same scores as those who attended five, three or only two sessions weekly. These results held using several different analytical approaches.

This suggests that the advantages of long as against short, and frequent as against occasional periods of attendance at a preschool institution depend on the individual child's readiness for preschool education at a particular age and the number of sessions with which he can cope. These are matters requiring judgement on the part of the mother, teacher or playgroup supervisor and, as Margaret Bone's (1977) survey revealed, children who are unhappy in their preschool placement are likely to leave and return later when they are more confident. This process of fitting the pattern of attendance to suit the needs of the individual child will inevitably result in reducing variation in cognitive development between children due to differences in duration and frequency of attendance at preschool institutions.

Social composition of the institutions

We have shown that maintained preschool institutions accommodated a higher proportion of socially disadvantaged children than did those in the independent sector. This simple fact generated the hypothesis that it may be more difficult to sustain a successful teaching programme in institutions attended by many children from disadvantaged families than in facilities with only a few such children. This is because there is a strong likelihood that children from deprived homes would have reached a lower level of cognitive development and present more behaviour problems than their better-off peers of the same age.

By this reasoning one child from our sample attending a preschool facility which included many socially disadvantaged children may have made less progress than another child of comparable ability and similar home background whose preschool institution had only a few deprived children. This contrast is intended to emphasise the effect of the social composition of the institution rather than the child's own social background, and to test this hypothesis we made a number of comparisons between LEA nursery schools and hall playgroups.

The mean test scores of children who attended either LEA nursery schools or hall playgroups did not differ significantly after statistical adjustment had been made for the home circumstances of the study children themselves. When the social composition of the preschool institution was added to the model, differences in mean test scores between children who attended these two types of institution remained non-significant. As a further test we compared the mean test scores of children who attended LEA nursery schools and hall playgroups that accepted similar proportions of socially disadvantaged children, and still no significant differences were found after adjustment for the study children's own home circumstances.

These findings support those shown in the tables in Figures 10.4 to 10.10, namely that attendance at LEA nursery schools and hall playgroups resulted in similar cognitive and educational gains, and contrary to our expectations, taking account of the social composition of the institution made no appreciable difference to this finding. One explanation for this unexpected result is that there was a strong correlation between the social composition of the institution and study children's personal home circumstances. Thus statistical adjustment for the powerful home background effect would also indirectly take account of differences attributable to the social composition of the institution. In short, since socially disadvantaged children were likely to attend institutions accommodating many others from similar backgrounds, it is impossible to separate out the institutional and home background effects on their cognitive and educational progress.

Parental involvement

The involvement of parents is a key feature of preschool playgroups which make a point of parents helping directly with the children in the sessions and assuming various management responsibilities. In the maintained sector parents support nursery schools in various ways, such as helping with outings or fund-raising events, but are less frequently involved in the actual sessions with the children. The Nursery/Playgroup survey showed that more than two-thirds of the hall playgroups had some parental involvement, compared with less than a quarter of LEA nursery schools. Reports from the parents in the CHES cohort study, however, indicated that fewer than half of the mothers had been involved in the hall playgroups attended by their children, and only 13% of those whose children went to LEA nursery schools or classes had helped in any way.

Two questions were investigated concerning the possible effect of parental involvement on children's cognitive development. These were: what were the implications for child development (1) if the child attended an institution which used parent helpers, and (2) if the child's *own* mother was involved in the institution?

We found that parental involvement made no significant difference to the child's cognitive or educational attainment unless the child's own mother was involved. Children whose mothers helped in some way at the preschool institution had better vocabulary at ages 5 and 10, were better at reading and mathematics at 10 and were assessed by their teachers as having better communication skills when compared with children whose mothers did not help.

These results were independent of the type of preschool institution attended, the child's own social and family circumstances, and parental interest in the child's education. Parental involvement was also found to be a contributory factor in the higher test scores of children who attended hall playgroups which were the type of institution in which such involvement was most often found. These findings clearly support the principle of parental involvement in preschool institutions.

Preschool experience and behaviour

Our behavioural assessments were based on two scales of behaviour in the home completed by the mother when the child was 5, and seven scales of behaviour at school at age 10 completed by the child's class teacher. In addition the children completed two self-concept scales. Thus the following behavioural dimensions were constructed:

Five-year (mother's assessment): antisocial behaviour, neurotic behaviour.

Ten-year (teacher's assessment): conduct disorder, hyperactivity, application (to school tasks), extroversion, peer relations, anxiety, clumsiness.

Ten-year (pupil self-concept): locus of control, self-esteem.

Exactly the same methods of analysis were used with these behavioural outcomes as for the cognitive tests in that we tried to explain away any associations found between preschool experience and later behaviour by statistically adjusting for the effects of a number of intervening variables identified at the preliminary stages of our analysis as described in Chapters 4 to 8.

Figures 10.12 to 10.15 show the results of the analyses of variance for the only behavioural measures for which there was a statistically significant association with preschool experience, the relevant intervening variables having been taken into account. The types of behaviour that seem to be influenced by preschool experience were mainly those concerned with level of activity and aggression—conduct disorder, hyperactivity and extroversion—although there was also an association with five-year neurotic behaviour. Preschool experience did not foster the children's ability to get on well with peers in school—a surprising fact bearing in

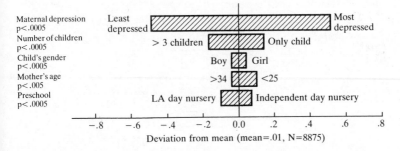

Preschool groups and five-year neurotic behaviour score

Main preschool placement	N	Deviation from mean
Independent day nursery	147	.07
Hall playgroup	3,104	.06
LEA nursery school	628	.04
Independent nursery school	39	.00
Home playgroup	177	−.01
LEA nursery class	1,080	−.03
No preschool	3,594	−.05
LA day nursery	106	−.10
OVERALL MEAN		.01
TOTAL N	8,875	

FIG. 10.12. Preschool experience and five-year neurotic behaviour score

mind the emphasis on social behaviour and interaction in preschool education. Self-concept was unaffected by attendance at nurseries or playgroups, and there was no increase in the ability of the preschool group to apply themselves effectively to their work in the junior school.

Referring to Figures 10.12 to 10.15 we find several general points emerging. The preschool effect on five-year neuroticism achieved statistical significance only after maternal depression was added to the analyses. This can be explained by the fact that neuroticism was strongly correlated with maternal depression and mothers of children who attended LA day nurseries were at high risk of depression; thus adjustment for maternal depression in Figure 10.12 reduced the mean score of children who attended LA day nurseries. The results of this analysis suggest that children who attended

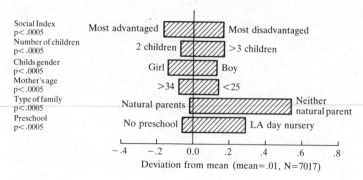

Preschool groups and ten-year conduct disorder score

Main preschool placement	N	Deviation from mean
LA day nursery	75	.29
Independent nursery school	31	.21
Independent day nursery	122	.20
LEA nursery class	862	.09
Home playgroup	135	.05
Hall playgroup	2,489	.01
LEA nursery school	500	−.01
No preschool	2,803	−.06
OVERALL MEAN		−.01
TOTAL N	7,017	

Fig. 10.13. Preschool experience and ten-year conduct disorder score

independent day nurseries, hall playgroups or LEA nursery schools were, according to their mothers, most at risk of being worried, miserable or fearful. As Figure 10.12 shows, however, this was a small effect in comparison with that of maternal depression.

Children who attended LA day nurseries were the most deviant group in terms of ten-year conduct disorder, hyperactivity and extroversion, and non-attenders were the least deviant. It is possible that long hours and full-time attendance at LA day nurseries or the fact that some children attended them from an early age contributed to the increased risk of later deviance in this group. This finding makes even more interesting the higher educational attainment of day nursery children in view of the negative correlation between educational achievement and behavioural deviance.

As with the cognitive and educational outcomes discussed earlier in this chapter, the robustness of these behavioural findings was checked by comparing them with the results of multiple regression analyses involving a set of 17 independent variables (these variables are specified in Tables 4.3, 6.1 to 6.4 and 9.5). This procedure demonstrated that the mean behaviour scores for the numerically small groups (LA day nurseries, independent nursery schools and day nurseries, home playgroups) varied depending on the particular

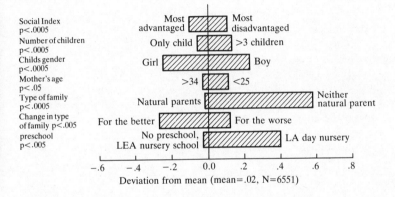

Preschool groups and ten-year hyperactivity score

Main preschool placement	N	Deviation from mean
LA day nursery	69	.40
Independent day nursery	113	.12
LEA nursery class	800	.10
Independent nursery school	29	.05
Home playgroup	128	.02
Hall playgroup	2,354	−.01
LEA nursery school	462	−.03
No preschool	2,596	−.03
OVERALL MEAN		−.02
TOTAL N	6,551	

FIG. 10.14. Preschool experience and ten-year hyperactivity score

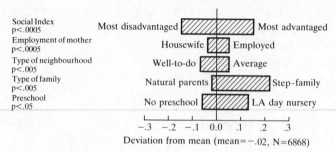

Preschool groups and ten-year extroversion score

Main preschool placement	N	Deviation from mean
LA day nursery	78	.13
LEA nursery school	498	.08
LEA nursery class	848	.06
Hall playgroup	2,426	.03
Independent nursery school	30	.03
Independent day nursery	120	.03
Home playgroup	131	.00
No preschool	2,737	−.06
OVERALL MEAN		−.02
TOTAL N	6,868	

FIG. 10.15. Preschool experience and ten-year extroversion score

set of independent variables entered into the analysis. However, the mean scores for the large preschool groups (LEA nursery schools and classes, hall playgroups and those with no preschool experience) were relatively stable. Figures 10.16 and 10.17 show the results for two of the behaviour scales—conduct disorder and hyperactivity at 10 years.

These diagrams show the non-adjusted mean scores for the preschool groups at the left of the diagram, the mean scores after adjustment for the main intervening variables in analysis of variance (Figures 10.13 and 10.14) at the centre, and the scores after adjustment for a total of 17 independent variables in the multiple regression at the right of the diagram. It can be seen that considerable changes occurred in preschool group mean scores as a result of adjusting for the specially selected main variables. However,

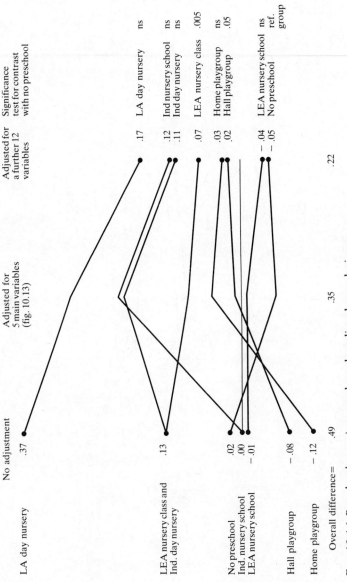

FIG. 10.16. Preschool experience and conduct disorder analysis

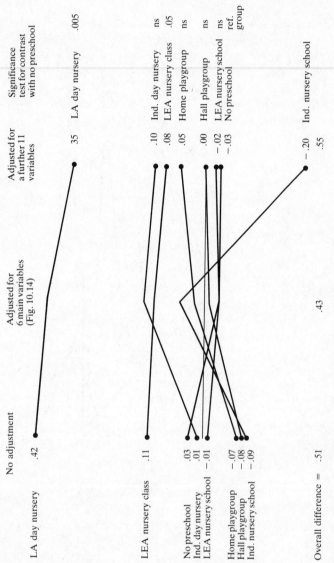

Fig. 10.17. Preschool experience and hyperactivity analysis

further changes resulted with the addition of more intervening variables. Our main conclusions from these analyses of the four behavioural scales are as follows:

1. Attendance at LA day nurseries was associated with the lowest mean neuroticism score and the highest mean score on the other three scales. However, the difference in score compared with non-attenders retained statistical significance only for hyperactivity ($p < .005$) and extroversion ($p < .05$).

2. Children who attended LEA nursery classes were at increased risk of conduct disorder ($p < .005$) and hyperactivity ($p < .05$) at 10 years of age and were also more likely to be extrovert ($p < .05$) compared with non-attenders.

3. Hall playgroup children were likely to be described as neurotic at 5 years of age ($p < .005$) by their mothers, but at age 10 their teachers' responses to the behavioural scales suggested a small increased risk of conduct disorder ($p < .05$).

4. Attendance at LEA nursery schools was associated with increased neuroticism at 5 compared with non-attenders ($p < .05$) but there were no long-term behavioural effects.

These results are less convincing than were those found for the cognitive and educational criteria described earlier. Only 4 of the 11 different behavioural assessments were found to be significantly associated with children's preschool experience, and levels of statistical significance and proportion of variance explained were generally low. There was no overall consistency in the pattern of results with the possible exception of increased risk of conduct disorder, hyperactivity and extrovert behaviour in children who had attended LA day nurseries or LEA nursery classes in infant schools. The evidence, therefore, does not support the hypothesis that preschool education reduces the risk of behaviour problems or improves a child's self-image in the long term.

Conclusions

This study was designed to investigate one question: can preschool education have a beneficial effect on the subsequent cognitive development, educational achievement and behaviour of the children concerned? The simple answer is, indubitably, yes. Of the 7 different types of preschool institution which the children in our study had attended, LEA nursery schools, hall-based playgroups and home-based playgroups increased children's achievement in 7 different tests embracing cognitive ability, verbal skills and mathematics. The results for LA day nurseries, independent day nurseries and independent nursery schools were less conclusive because of the smaller numbers of children involved, although in most instances attainment test scores of children who attended these institutions were increased. Children who attended LEA nursery classes in infant schools, however, had significantly increased levels of attainment in only two tests and for the other five they were indistinguishable from the non-attenders.

This study is the first to provide conclusive evidence that preschool education provided by ordinary nursery schools and playgroups in Britain can have a positive effect upon the cognitive development of the children who attend them.

The results for the behavioural outcomes were less conclusive: of the eleven assessments of behaviour and self-concept, only four retained a significant association with children's preschool experience. Three of these four were indicative of conduct disorder, hyperactivity and extrovert behaviour and suggested increased risk of deviance in children who attended LA day nurseries compared with non-attenders. However, the behavioural associations with preschool experience were weak in comparison with the educational outcomes.

These conclusions were drawn only after eliminating many other possible explanations for the associations between children's preschool experience and their subsequent test performance. In pursuing this we have examined as intervening variables socio-economic differences in the children's home backgrounds, family size, parental situation, changes in the child's home circumstances in the period between 5 and 10 years of age, the degree of parental involvement and interest in the child's formal education and the type of junior school he subsequently attended. Given such a galaxy of potential influences it is difficult to envisage any other factors that could account for the positive effects which this study associates with preschool education.

Although socio-economic position was the major determinant of children's educational attainment, we also found that other social and family factors exerted a powerful influence, and of these parental interest in the child's development was one of the most important. This was because a strong parental interest in a child's educational progress was likely to enhance that progress and also result in the parent making more effort than a less interested parent in seeking out a suitable preschool placement for the child to attend. Thus the educational benefits which in reality were due to parental interest and stimulation in the home may be spuriously attributed to the preschool institution the child attended. However, after taking account of whether or not the mother had been involved in her child's preschool placement and also parental interest in the child's education at 10 years of age, the positive associations between the child's preschool experience and subsequent attainment still held. Moreover, a child's educational achievement was enhanced still further if his own mother was involved in the preschool institution he attended.

As we have described at some length in Chapter 2, preschool provision in Britain varied a good deal in terms of organisation, staffing patterns and ratios, and premises, as well as in the social and economic backgrounds of the children attending them. Nevertheless, once differences in social and family circumstances had been taken into account, there were few statistically significant differences between the test performance of children who attended the day nurseries, LEA nursery schools, hall playgroups and home playgroups, even though they each offered quite different kinds of experience. This leads to a most important conclusion—namely that provided the child receives proper care, has interesting activities and other children to play with (which are common elements in the majority of preschool institutions) the actual type of preschool experience matters very little. The same conclusion was drawn from the American experimental preschool intervention studies which also found no long-term difference between treatment groups, the important contrast being between children with preschool experience and those with none (Lazar and Darlington, 1982; Weikart *et al.*, 1978).

However, in this connection it is worth pointing out that attendance at home playgroups was associated with the highest mean scores in four out of the seven tests and was second highest in the other three. Whilst this superiority over the other types of institution was statistically non-significant the consistency of the finding across all seven tests cannot be ignored; the small scale and homely atmosphere of home playgroups may explain this relative success.

A more detailed study contrasting home playgroups with other types of preschool institutions is needed to investigate these possibilities.

Levels of achievement of children who had attended LEA nursery classes in infant schools were a cause for concern in regard to certain attainment tests; in reading and mathematics at age 10, their test scores were no better than those of children with no preschool experience, whereas children who attended LEA nursery schools achieved markedly higher scores than non-attenders. Some LEA nursery classes may not be very much different from infant reception classes and since we found that early entry to reception classes also did not consistently result in higher test scores, this could be the explanation. In view of this, and because expansion of nursery education provision since 1975 has been almost entirely in part-time LEA nursery classes, and almost half of all the pupils under 5 in maintained schools in 1985 were in infant reception classes, there is an urgent need to check that these children are indeed receiving an educational experience appropriate to the under-five age group.

There is an important caveat to the fact that the test scores of children who went to playgroups did not differ significantly from those of children who went to LEA nursery schools; we should deprecate this fact being used as a justification for local education authorities to sponsor playgroups as a more economic alternative to maintained schools or classes. Our results indicate that facilities in the maintained sector accommodate a substantially higher proportion of socially disadvantaged children than is found in the independent sector, which leads us to surmise that the reasons for the success of LEA nursery schools may be quite different from those of the playgroups. In addition to children from economically underprivileged homes, LEA institutions accept more children with handicaps, behaviour problems and delayed development than do playgroups. These categories of children require the attention of fully-trained professional staff to help them overcome their handicaps. Children attending playgroups come in the main from secure, middle class and highly motivated homes with fewer social pressures, and are therefore better able to exploit the educational advantages of the playgroup environment.

There is another equally cogent but less obvious argument for maintaining and expanding LEA nursery provision—namely that in

1975 one child in four in our study had reached her fifth birthday without having had any organised form of preschool education and that within that 25% a large proportion of children came from families in which poor housing conditions, low income, job insecurity and other social problems combined to produce a condition of chronic social deprivation, dislocation and stress. This initial family deprivation inevitably hampers a child's development and is often a strong contributory factor to his not receiving preschool education. Parents who are preoccupied with basic problems of survival may not appreciate the value of preschool education and, in addition, stresses of living may bring on depression in mothers which saps their motivation and the ability needed to make the necessary overtures and subsequent arrangements for enrolling their children in a preschool programme (Shinman, 1981). This initial family inertia is undoubtedly compounded by the real shortage of places in preschool institutions. In either event the child suffers because the disadvantages associated with a poor and stressful family life will slow down his development and the remedial effects of preschool education which are so urgently needed are not available. As to whether severely disadvantaged children can benefit from preschool education, our findings suggest that they can; indeed there is some indication that such children are more likely to gain from such experience than are their more advantaged peers.

An abiding problem of longitudinal studies is that their early stages belong to an era that has passed by the time the follow-up data become available. In this study changes may have occurred in the preschool world which render our results out of date. However, changes in practice in the preschool institutions attended by the children in our study in 1973–75 would have been introduced in order to increase the quality of the educational experience provided, and therefore the long-term benefits that we have observed are likely to be even greater for children currently enrolling in preschool institutions. In addition it is unlikely that such changes would create differences between the *same* types of institution in 1975 and 1986 which were as great as those prevailing between *different* types of institution in 1975. This observation is very significant because our findings persistently show that despite the many and considerable differences we have found between LEA nursery schools, playgroups, day nurseries, etc., their apparent effect on children's educational progress was remarkably similar.

The main contrast in our sample was between children who *had* and children who *had not* been exposed to preschool education, and changes in preschool practice since our 1975 surveys are unlikely to affect our main conclusions substantially.

Finally, while we do not feel it should be necessary to demonstrate measurable long-term benefits in order to justify the value of preschool education, we also recognise that in a world of scarce and competitive resources the cost–benefit argument inevitably carries weight. Therefore our assertion is that adequate preschool provision can improve the quality of life of young children and their families; this conviction is given further support by the evidence we have presented in this book that preschool education will in most circumstances aid the child's development, increase his educational potential and in the long run his overall performance. Thus investment in preschool provision and the improved quality of life it bestows may pay good dividends in the shape of calculable beneficial effects on the children's educational attainments five years hence and perhaps into the longer future.

Appendix: research methods

This study of preschool education is based on data obtained in the Child Health and Education Study (CHES) which is a national, longitudinal survey of all children in Britain who were born during the week 5–11 April 1970. These children were surveyed at birth, five and ten years but for the purposes of the study reported in this book only the five- and ten-year data sets were used. The basic analytical approach has been to use the five-year data set to determine the preschool experience and social and family circumstances of each child, and to use the ten-year educational tests and behavioural assessments to evaluate the 'effects' of their preschool experience.

In addition to this cohort study, a national census of preschool educational and day care institutions was carried out in 1975 concurrent with the five-year follow-up of the cohort. This provided information on the different types of preschool facility available at the time. It was also possible to identify the particular institutions attended by the children in the cohort study thereby providing more detailed information about their preschool experience.

In this Appendix we describe the methods of data collection, the trace rates, the procedures used for linking the cohort and institutional data sets, checks for bias, social variables requiring special explanation and the tests and assessments used in the five-year and ten-year studies.

CHES five-year survey

The children were traced via the general practitioners with whom they were registered with the assistance of the National Health Service (NHS) Central Register, Family Practitioner Committees in England and Wales and Administrators of Primary Care in Scotland. The whole tracing exercise was carried out by health service personnel so that no confidential information, including the study child's current address, was disclosed to the research team until the family had agreed to take part in the survey. The Service Children's Education Authority traced 64 children of service families who had taken part in the birth survey but were resident in West Germany, Malta, Gibraltar and Singapore at the time of the CHES survey in 1975. A total of 13,135 children was traced and interviewed for the five-year survey which amounted to 81% of the expected sample (Osborn et al.,1984, pp. 260–2).

Two years later in 1977 the whole cohort was traced again through the schools they attended and a single questionnaire was completed by a further 1,917 families who had remained untraced for the five-year survey. The main purpose of this special seven-year survey was to check for possible sources of bias due to non-response in the main survey. It was found that certain groups of children were slightly under-represented in the five-year survey. These were children who lived in the South East region of England, children whose fathers were in a non-manual occupation, children not living with both natural parents, ethnic minority children, geographically mobile children, and children who had been in care (op. cit. pp. 266–8). The relatively low ascertainment rate of middle class families was probably due to the difficulty of tracing children in the densely populated South East region of England where there were higher than average proportions of such occupational groups. Most of the tracing problems in the preschool period were due to families having moved away from the neighbourhood of the NHS doctor with whom they were registered. However, as the five-year sample was large relative to the untraced group, this introduced little bias in our analyses. Also statistical adjustment for such factors in analysis of variance minimised the effect of any bias due to certain groups being under-represented in the survey. In Table A.1 we compare utilisation of preschool educational and day care services by the 1975 and 1977 samples. Different methods of obtaining these data were used in the two surveys because of the necessity to obtain the information retrospectively in the 1977 follow-up; this has caused some of the observed

Table A.1   *Distribution of 1975 and 1977 samples by main preschool placement*

Main preschool placement	1975 sample		1977 sample		All	
	N	%	N	%	N	%
No preschool education or care	3,681	28.4	602	32.2	4,283	28.9
Maintained	2,652	20.5	416	22.2	3,068	20.7
Independent or voluntary	6,612	51.1	854	45.6	7,466	50.4
ALL	12,945	100.0	1,872	100.0	14,826	100.0
No information	190		45		235	
TOTAL	13,135		1,917		15,052	

Note: Chi square = 19.9 (2df) p< .0005. 47 cases in the 1975 sample who attended special institutions for handicapped children were added to the group with no preschool experience in this table.

differences between the classifications. We have grouped together maintained institutions (LEA nursery schools and classes and LA day nurseries), and independent institutions (private nursery schools, day nurseries and voluntary playgroups) because we found the mother's report unreliable for the detailed classification, but reliable in distinguishing between institutions in the maintained and independent sectors.

The results suggest that children with no preschool experience or who had attended maintained institutions were slightly under-represented in the five-year survey. However, it is important to note that the addition of the 1977 data to the 1975 main preschool placement distribution hardly affects the proportions because, as we have indicated, the 1975 sample was very large compared with the 1977 sample. This is shown in Table A.1 where the distribution for the combined sample barely differs from that for the 1975 survey. Thus findings based only on the 1975 data set are unlikely to introduce serious errors.

The fieldwork for the 1975 survey was carried out by health visitors with the agreement of the (then) Area Health Authorities. Four research questionnaires published in Osborn *et al.* (1984) were used:

Home Interview Questionnaire (HIQ)
Maternal Self Completion Questionnaire (MSCQ)
Developmental History Schedule (DHS)
Test Booklet (TB)

The HIQ was administered by health visitors who carried out the interviews in the children's own homes. This was the primary source of information concerning the child's preschool education and day care experience. The HIQ also enquired about family circumstances, housing conditions and the child's medical history.

The MSCQ was usually left with the mother to complete in her own time unless she specifically asked the health visitor to help. This form included the Rutter child behavioural scale (described later in this Appendix), maternal depression (op. cit. pp. 284–5), and an attitudinal scale concerned mainly with child-rearing methods.

The DHS was completed by the health visitor from child health records and provided a record of the child's contact with the health visiting service and child health clinic attendances. These data are not used in the present study.

The Test Booklet contained a number of developmental tests which could feasibly be carried out within the survey methodology. Health visitors conducted the tests with the five-year-olds in their own homes. Only two of the tests, Copying Designs test and English Picture Vocabulary Test, have been used in the present study and they are described later in this Appendix.

CHES ten-year survey

Tracing was considerably simplified for the ten-year survey because almost all of the children were attending school thus enabling education authorities to arrange for primary school teachers to scan their class registers for children born during the week 5–11 April, 1970. Separate tracing exercises were carried out in independent schools and in special schools for handicapped children. A total of 14,906 children were successfully traced which was more than 90% of the total expected sample. Complete data were not available on all these children, however, because there was a total of six different questionnaires plus the tests and not all these questionnaires or tests were completed for every child. A further complication was that the administration of the survey was carried out by two separate authorities; the social and health questionnaires were administered by District Health Authorities, and the educational questionnaires and tests by Local Education Authorities. Inevitably there were children for whom social/health questionnaires had been completed but no educational questionnaires and vice versa. However, information from both health *and* education authorities was available for a total of 11,838 children (Table A.2).

Longitudinal analysis between the five-year and ten-year surveys resulted in a further reduction in the available sample as data from both the 1975 and 1980 surveys were not available for all the cases identified in 1975, even though there were more cases in the ten-year than the five-year survey. This was because some cases in the five-year survey had not taken part in the ten-year survey, usually because they were untraced. Also, difficulties

Table A.2 *Numbers of cases for whom different sections of ten-year data were available*

Sections of data available	Number of children
Both social/health and educational sections	11,838
Social/health section only	1,944
Educational section only	1,067
Insufficient data available from either section	57
Total cases in ten-year survey	14,906

Note: A child was considered to have social/health data if the Parental Interview was completed. A child was considered to have educational data if the Educational Questionnaire or the Educational Score Form or the BAS, reading test or mathematics test was completed. If none of these questionnaires or tests was completed the child had insufficient information for further analysis. These children would have had only one or more of the following: Maternal Self-completion Form, Medical Examination Form, Pupil Questionnaire or Special Educational Test Pack (for children of very low ability).

Table A.3 *Number of children in longitudinal sample*

	N	% of five-year sample	% of ten-year sample
Children in both five- and ten-year surveys (matched cases)	12,051	91.7	81.2
Children in five-year survey but not matched with ten-year data	1,084	8.3	—
Children in ten-year survey but not matched with five-year data	2,798	—	18.8

occurred when children's names changed as a result of their mother remarrying or because of adoption, thereby making a reliable match between five-year and ten-year data sets uncertain.

The maximum number of children in the longitudinal sample was 12,051 which amounted to 92% of the five-year sample and 81% of the ten-year sample (Table A.3). However, the longitudinal analyses described in this report always contain fewer cases than this (a) because of incomplete social, health or educational data as described in Table A.2, (b) because of small proportions of non-response to individual questions, and (c) because of the exclusion of cases whose preschool placement could not be confirmed from the survey of preschool institutions; this is explained in more detail later in the Appendix.

The most important information from the ten-year survey for the purposes of the present study was the set of educational and cognitive tests and behavioural assessments, which were used as criteria for the evaluation of children's preschool experience. However, a small number of ten-year social and educational variables was selected to explore the effect of children's subsequent social and educational experience on the associations between their preschool experience and ten-year test scores. Apart from this, most of the analysis was based on the five-year data. Further details of the range of information obtained in the six questionnaires used in the ten-year follow-up are provided elsewhere (Butler *et al.*, Reports to DES and DHSS, 1982) but descriptions of the tests and assessments used in this study are given later in this Appendix.

The Nursery/Playgroup survey

This survey was based on a single questionnaire which was sent to every LEA nursery school and class, LA day nursery, and independent nursery school, day nursery or playgroup that could be traced in England, Scotland and Wales. This was achieved with the cooperation of Local Education Authorities and Social Services Departments throughout Britain as well as that of voluntary organisations such as the Preschool Playgroups Association and Save the Children Fund. A total of 18,209 institutions took part in the study and a comparison with official statistics showed that the survey reached 93% of LEA nursery schools, 64% of nursery classes and 88% of LA day nurseries in the maintained sector (Table A.4). Although the actual number of playgroups in Britain was difficult to determine, we estimated that 83% of all playgroups completed a questionnaire. Thus the coverage throughout Britain was very good.

Table A.4 *Estimated proportion of preschool institutions taking part in the Nursery/Playgroup survey*

	Number in survey	Number officially recorded in 1975	Proportion in survey (%)
Maintained			
LEA nursery schools	713	765	93.2
LEA nursery classes	1,932	3,011	64.2
LA day nurseries	544	616	88.3
Independent			
Nursery schools	195	nk	—
Day nurseries	712	917	77.6
Playgroups	12,852	14,916–15,975	83.2
Other types of institutions	1,261	nk	—
TOTAL in survey	18,209		

The Nursery/Playgroup questionnaire was carefully designed so that the same document could be completed by all types of preschool institution. Although this posed problems when designing questions to obtain information about staffing, parental involvement, patterns of attendance and similar factors, which vary so much between types of institution, this approach was necessary in order to avoid prejudging the characteristics of different types of institution. It was important for our study that we classify the institutions according to criteria that we decided on, rather than have different questionnaires for different types of institution and expect those within the local authorities who distributed the questionnaires to decide which questionnaire to send to which institution. The actual procedure adopted for classifying the institution was complex and involved numbers of assumptions; it is necessary, therefore, to describe this in detail.

The classification of preschool institutions

Respondents to the Nursery/Playgroup survey—most of whom were in charge of their institution—were invited to describe their provision by name (see Table A.6). Specifically, they were asked: 'Which one of the following best describes your institution?' and they were then offered the following choice: 'nursery school, nursery class, reception class, day nursery, playgroup, or "other" '. If they specified 'other', they were then invited to elaborate on the nature of their provision.

In the event, these broad categories of institution were considerably changed and refined for the purposes of this study. Why was it that we were not able simply to accept the responses given, and thereby create our classification according to the list which we ourselves offered to the respondents? There were a number of reasons. The independent sector offered a wide variety of descriptions which created doubt about their precise nature. Was an institution called a 'kindergarten', a 'school' or a 'play centre' really a playgroup, a nursery school or a day nursery? Simply to create new categories for such descriptions would have posed considerable problems of comparison. Moreover, it was an important consideration that if we were to be able to make genuine comparisons between groups, then the characteristics of those groups should be internally consistent, or homogeneous, and not simply labels for widely differing forms of provision.

Given the need for a limited number of relatively disparate categories of institution, we were nevertheless inhibited from specifying precisely what the characteristics of these groups should be. That, after all, was the main thrust of the actual research enquiry. On the other hand, we could not simply allow the categories to arise without imposing some guiding constraints. So the principles we adopted to ensure that we ended with groups which were genuinely discrete and independent were threefold:

1. to respect, as far as possible, the description given to them by those responding to the questionnaire,
2. to be parsimonious, involving as few variables as possible,
3. to ensure a 'cutting' property, partitioning one set from another and producing relatively homogeneous sub-sets.

Two initial groupings were made at the coding stage. Institutions which indicated that they had a special involvement with handicapped children, or children in hospital, or which called themselves 'special schools' or 'opportunity groups' or in any other way suggested that they played a specific role in providing specialised medical care and facilities for children, were assigned to a special group. Secondly, all provision specifically falling under the control of branches of the armed services—a total of 246 cases—was coded as such.

The next decision was to accept two major descriptive forms—'playgroup' and 'day nursery'—and to use these as the basis for decisions about other types of provision. Consequently, 12,852 institutions calling themselves 'playgroups' were hived off to form one major category, and a further 1,000 cases were subdivided into maintained or independent day nurseries.

The judgement as to whether or not a day nursery fell into the maintained sector was based on three criteria: it had to call itself a 'day nursery'; it had to be registered with a Social Service department, and it had to declare itself a fully maintained institution. Day nurseries which did not meet this constellation of criteria were then 'tested' to see whether they called themselves 'independent' rather than 'maintained' but met the two other requirements. If they did, they became candidates for the category labelled 'independent day nurseries'. If they failed this test, they were left to be sorted by some other criteria later on in the procedure.

Following these initial decisions, we now had five major groups: special institutions, armed forces provision, playgroups, and two types of day nursery. Three more categories were identified by using a cluster of only three variables: whether they were called 'nursery schools', 'nursery classes' or 'reception classes'; whether they were registered as such with their local education authority or the Department of Education and Science or Scottish Education Department; and whether they were fully maintained. Using these criteria, we identified 713 maintained nursery schools, 1,932 nursery classes and 415 reception classes. Again, institutions which called themselves nursery schools, nursery classes or reception classes and were registered with the appropriate authority, were tested to see if they considered themselves to be 'independent'. If so, they were placed in a new category of 'independent nursery schools and classes'. Again, if they failed these tests, they were retained in the unclassified sector.

With these classifications achieved, it was then possible to move to a new stage of the procedure and to examine those institutions which had already been consigned to a specific group, to search for common features within each group which would establish what came to be known as 'strong variables'. We could then use these to consign other, as yet unclassified, institutions to specific groups. For example, among the 12,000 playgroups which had been identified as such, it was found that 97.3% did not provide dinners; that 98% were not open before 9 a.m. and that 94% described themselves as 'independent'. We were therefore able to produce a 'profile test' involving some or all of these variables, and to consign unclassified institutions which had these characteristics but which did not describe themselves specifically as 'playgroups', to this category.

In the case of maintained day nurseries, it was found that, among the 492 identified cases, 98% had one child or more under the age of 2 years on its register; that 97% were open at, or before, 8.30 a.m.; that 97% were open 10 sessions a week. Again, we were able, as a result of these analyses, to produce a cluster of variables which, taken together, provided a specific test for this category on the hitherto unclassified institutions remaining in our sample.

For maintained nursery schools, the 'strong variables' were different again. Almost all of those already identified said they had no children under 2 years of age; 98% reported that they were open ten sessions a week, and 96% said that they were open for 36–42 weeks in the year. So, here again, the 'test' became a specific cluster of variables relating to maintained nursery schools.

The 'strong variables' for maintained nursery classes were the same as for 'nursery schools', but in addition 95% of those already identified as nursery classes reported that they occupied premises that were a separate or integral part of an infant school building.

For independent day nurseries, the variables were again different. It was seen that 98% of those identified charged fees, that they were all registered with Social Service departments and called themselves 'independent', and that 95% operated for 40–52 weeks in the year. These therefore became the test items for this particular group.

At this point it is worth stressing that only variables which enjoyed almost universal agreement within groups already sorted were used as criteria for classification purposes. Secondly, these variables arose from large samples of the data—more than 12,000 in the case of playgroups but even some 500 in the case of LA day nurseries. The point about these issues is to refute any suggestion that homogeneity was 'created' by this process of testing; rather, the tests were designed to fit a relatively small group of unsorted institutions by the use of templates which had already created themselves. One further group was formed by separating out from the large playgroup category those being run in private houses as distinct from community or church halls which were the venues for the majority of playgroups.

Following this selection procedure, and the distribution of many of the previously unsorted responses to existing categories, a remaining clutch of some 700 institutions was sorted by hand and, given the existence of the newly established groups, assigned on a variety of criteria to one or another. The only restriction on this hand-sorting process was that no institution should be 'pigeon-holed' simply in order to find it a home; it must have a *bona fide* case for being thus assigned. Despite this condition, the remarkable fact emerged that in the end only 51 of the 18,209 institutions were not consigned to a specific group. This 'unclassified' group included playbuses, joint nursery centres, family units and even such an oddity as a 'horticultural crèche run in a cricket pavilion'—obviously designed to defeat even the most exhaustive sorting procedure! For the purposes of the study reported in this book, however, only the seven major groups of preschool institutions were retained for analysis, and the distribution of institutions between these groups is given in Chapter 2, Table 2.1.

Linking the child-based and Nursery/Playgroup survey data

One of the main reasons for carrying out the Nursery/Playgroup survey was to obtain information from the particular preschool institutions that had been attended by the children in the cohort study. This entailed identifying the institutions from among the 18,209 questionnaires in the Nursery/Playgroup survey that had been attended by 9,415 of the children in the cohort study. This was a difficult task which was feasible only because information had been obtained in both surveys to assist in this matching procedure. These details are given in Tables A.5 and A.6 for the child-based and Nursery/Playgroup surveys respectively.

Table A.5 *Questions in child-based five-year survey to aid matching with Nursery/Playgroup study*

D.1 A. Ring in the first column **A** any school, playgroup, or nursery placements N attends at the present (or attended last term if at present on holiday).

B. Ring in the second column, **B** all other placements attended previously for three months or longer, that he/she has since stopped attending. *Ring all that apply in both columns*

	A Present placement(s)	B Previous placement(s)
Nursery school—		
Local Education Authority (free)	1	1
Private (fee charged)	2	2
Nursery class attached to infant/primary school—		
Local Education Authority (free)	3	3
Private (fee charged)	4	4
Normal school, full or part-time—		
Infant/primary school (L.E.A.)	5	5
Independent/private	6	6
Playgroup	7	7
Special day school, nursery or unit for physically or mentally handicapped children	8	8
Day nursery—		
Local Authority	9	9
Private	10	10
Creche, kindergarten	11	11
Mother and toddler club	12	12
Sunday school	13	13
Other placement, please specify	14	14
....		
Attends/attended none of these	15	15
Not known	0	0

If child has attended none of the above in the past or at the present proceed to D.10.

If child is attending, or has attended any of the above, *please complete D.2 onwards.*
Do not give further details of "mother and toddler club" or Sunday school.

D.2 Present placement – **A**

Name and address in full of the place N attends at present or, if on holiday, attended last term. (If child currently attends more than one place, please give details of the main one).

Designation of main place N attends now, i.e. as specified in D.1 A. ....

Name of place N attends now ....

Full postal address ....

....

Name of head teacher, supervisor, etc. ....

D.3 Previous placement – **B**

Name and address in full of place N has attended previously that he/she has since stopped attending. (If the child has attended more than one place previously for three months or longer give details of the one he/she left most recently).

Designation of previous place N attended, i.e. as specified in D.1 B ....

Name of previous place N attended ....

Full postal address ....

....

Name of head teacher, supervisor, etc. ....

The following questions D.4 to D.8 refer to: **A** – *the present placement and* **B** – *the previous placement as identified above.*

D.4 Type of premises N attended for present and previous placements

	A Present placement	**B** Previous placement
Normal school or nursery premises	1	1
Village or community hall	2	2
Church hall	3	3
Private house	4	4
Nursery in factory/industrial premises	5	5
Other kind of premises, please specify	6	6
....		
Not known	0	0

The information in the child-based study was usually obtained from the child's mother during an interview with a health visitor. Questions D.1, D.2 and D.3 (see Table A.5) provided the basic information for the classification of the child's main preschool placement. Since the children were just 5 years old at the time of the survey, the majority, though not all, had already started infant school. It was necessary, therefore, to enquire about the child's current or present placement and the one attended before the current one, if any. As a few children were currently attending more than one educational or day care placement, or had attended more than one in the past, mothers were asked to say which was the *main* present placement (question D.2) and *most recent* previous placement (question

Table A.6 *Questions in Nursery/Playgroup survey to aid matching with child-based study*

PLEASE ANSWER EVERY QUESTION   CONFIDENTIAL

Name of *institution* ....

Full postal address ....

....

SECTION A   DESCRIPTION OF PREMISES AND LOCALITY

A.1   With which of the following is your *institution* registered?

Local Authority Dept. of Social Services/Social Work ....☐

Local Authority Dept. of Education. ....☐

Dept. of Education and Science/Scottish Education Dept. ....☐

Other answer, give details. ....☐

....

A.2   Which one of the following best describes your *institution*?

Nursery school..☐

Nursery class(es). ....☐

Reception class(es). ....☐

Day nursery. ....☐

Playgroup. ....☐

Other, please describe. ....☐

....

A.3   Is your *institution* maintained (i.e. by local authority) or independent (i.e. private)?

Fully maintained by local authority...☐

Independent...☐

Other, please describe. ....☐

....

A.4   Is your *institution* set up by the place where the parents of the children work, e.g. factory, shop, university, hospital, business concern, etc.?

No. ....☐

Yes, specify type of work place..☐

....

A.5   Approximately how long has your *institution*, i.e. nursery school/class, day nursery, playgroup, etc. been operating?   *If less than one year, put UNDER1*

Enter number of years .... ☐

A.6 **Which one of the following best describes your *institution's* premises?**

Church, village, community or other hall .... ☐

Nursery premises standing on their own .... ☐

Part of a larger building but self-contained as completely separate unit, e.g. with own exit(s), toilet facilities, etc. .... ☐

Part of a larger building but occupying room(s) or space not completely separate from rest of building, e.g. shares corridors, main exit(s), toilet(s) or other facilities .... ☐

If premises part of larger building, is this a

School building? .... ☐
Private house? .... ☐
Other place, please describe ☐

Other type of premises, please ☐
describe ....
....

D.3). From this information it was possible to create the classification used in Chapter 3 which specifies the child's most recent preschool placement. The other details in questions D.2 and D.3 and question D.4 were included in order to facilitate the linking process with the Nursery/Playgroup study for which comparable data were obtained (see Table A.6).

Two methods were used to reduce to manageable proportions the daunting clerical exercise to match children with institutions. The first made use of Ordnance Survey map references that had been coded into the two data sets related to the children's home addresses and the locations of the preschool institutions. A computer program was written which listed the fifty institutions that were closest to a child's home address. In urban areas this identified institutions that were relatively short distances away from the child's home, whilst in rural areas the distances could be quite considerable. The listing included coded details of each institution that enabled clerical assistants to pick out those that offered a good chance of being a match with the institutions described in the child's questionnaire. The questionnaires for the selected institutions were then consulted to find the one institution which most closely matched with the description given by the child's mother. The most important pieces of information for establishing that a match was correct were the institution's address and type of premises. This procedure resulted in 58% of the children who had attended a preschool placement being matched with an institution in the Nursery/Playgroup study.

To increase the matching rate, a completely new approach to the problem was developed. This entailed creating a computer file of the names, addresses and designations of all maintained institutions from the Nursery/Playgroup survey. The Oxford Concordance Program (OCP) was then

Table A.7 *Matching rates by main preschool placement (mother's report)*

Main preschool placement (mother's report)	Matching with Nursery/Playgroup data						Total children
	Exact match	Explicable match	Inexplicable match	Not matchable	Not matched		
Maintained							
LEA nursery school	536	224	28	19	242		1,049
LEA nursery class	827	102	14	23	463		1,429
LA day nursery	103	0	34	3	34		174
Independent							
Nursery school	24	66	221	27	386		724
Nursery class	0	11	20	4	90		125
Day nursery	38	0	17	9	62		126
Playgroup	3,079	0	86	168	2,237		5,570
Crèche	0	0	0	0	10		10
Special institution for handicapped	5	6	0	1	37		49
Other	1	0	1	3	7		12
Started at LEA infant school before 4 years 4 months	0	32	0	0	115		147
ALL	4,613	441	421	257	3,683		9,415

Note: 36 cases in this table matched with a reception class in the Nursery/Playgroup survey were subsequently analysed as part of the 'no preschool' group.

used to generate an alphabetical list of keywords from all the names and addresses given, together with the serial numbers of questionnaires in which each keyword occurred. The keywords list provided a means of linking additional children who had attended LEA nursery schools or classes to the correct institution in the Nursery/Playgroup data set. This procedure resulted in the successful matching of a further 320 children who had attended LEA nursery schools or classes or LA day nurseries. The expense entailed in keying in the institutional identification data ruled out the possibility of repeating this exercise for institutions in the independent sector.

Table A.7 shows the matching rates achieved for children who had attended different types of institution based on their mothers' reports. Of all the 9,415 children who were reported as having attended some type of preschool institution, fewer than half (4,613) were matched with an institution of a type which agreed exactly with the description provided by the mother. A further 441 (5%) were matched with institutions of a very similar type; for example the mother might have reported that her child attended a LEA nursery school, but this was matched with an institution we had classified as a LEA nursery class. The mother's and institution's descriptions were contradictory for 421 (5%) of the children; each of these was carefully checked and found to be a correct match according to all our criteria. The 257 (3%) cases who are described in the table as unmatchable had either provided no institutional address, or the child had attended two institutions simultaneously thereby making a link with either institution spurious. This left 3,683 (39%) children who could not be matched with an institution because the preschool institutions they attended were absent from the Nursery/Playgroup survey, or because the family had moved away from the vicinity of the institution the child had attended.

The matching rate was higher for children who attended local authority institutions than for those in the private sector. The extra matching exercise contributed to this, but in addition, local authority institutions were more readily identifiable both by the mothers and within the Nursery/Playgroup study than were the independent or voluntary institutions. In the maintained sector between 66% and 79% of the children were matched with a Nursery/Playgroup questionnaire. In the independent sector the proportion matched varied from 57% of those who went to playgroups, to little more than 40% of those who attended private nursery schools or day nurseries.

Implications of matching for analysis

There were two main reasons for linking the Nursery/Playgroup and child-based data sets. Firstly, the Nursery/Playgroup data provided additional

Table A.8 Comparison of mother's and Nursery/Playgroup study classification of main preschool placement

Main preschool placement (mother's report)	Type of institution (Nursery/Playgroup classification)										All
	Maintained			Independent							
	LEA nursery school	LEA nursery class	LA day nursery	Nursery school	Day nursery	Hall play-group	Home play-group	Special insti-tution	Other nec	LEA reception class	
Maintained											
LEA nursery school	536	215	3	2	2	17	2	1	2	8	788
LEA nursery class	77	827	3	1	1	6	1	0	2	25	943
LA day nursery	18	9	103	0	4	2	0	0	1	0	137
Independent											
Nursery school	2	3	0	24	66	172	39	0	5	0	311
Nursery class	1	3	0	7	4	12	3	1	0	0	31
Day nursery	0	0	2	0	38	14	1	0	0	0	55
Playgroup	12	13	7	6	37	2,945	134	0	8	3	3,165
Special institution for handicapped	0	3	1	0	1	1	0	5	0	0	11
Other nec	0	0	0	1	0	0	0	0	1	0	2
Started at LEA infant school before 4 years 4 months	0	32	0	0	0	0	0	0	0	0	32
ALL	646	1,105	119	41	153	3,169	180	7	19	36	5,475

Note: nec = not elsewhere classified in this table.

information about the institution the child attended; since this was available only for those children whose nursery or playgroup had been identified, analyses relating to the type of preschool environment, i.e. staffing, curriculum, etc., to the child's test scores could be carried out only for the matched subsample. Secondly, matching with the Nursery/Playgroup data enabled us to check the validity of the mothers' descriptions of the children's main preschool placements. If there had been a high degree of concurrence between the mothers' and institutions' preschool classifications for the matched subsample, we could have inferred that the classification for the unmatched subsample was also valid and hence be able to include *all* the children in any analysis not involving the Nursery/Playgroup data.

These possibilities were investigated using the detailed breakdown in Table A.8 which compares the mothers' and institutions' descriptions of the children's main preschool placements for all those who were successfully matched with a preschool institution in the Nursery/Playgroup survey.

This revealed a number of important discrepancies between the classification of children's main preschool placement based on the mothers' and institutions' reports. 27% of children whose mothers reported that they attended LEA nursery schools were linked with LEA nursery classes, and one in five of those who were reported as attending LA day nurseries had actually attended a LEA nursery school or class. Playgroups were the most reliably identified; 97% of children who, according to their mothers, attended playgroups were linked to an institution classified as such. The worst discrepancy affected children whose mothers reported that they went to private nursery schools. Only 8% of the matched cases in this group were actually linked to a private nursery school whereas 68% were linked with playgroups. A better rate of agreement was achieved between the mother's report and the Nursery/Playgroup classification for children who attended private day nurseries (69%), although 27% were linked to playgroups. Despite these discrepancies in definitions, mothers rarely confused institutions in the maintained and independent sectors. Only 92 (1.7%) of the whole matched subsample of children were attending maintained institutions which their mothers had described as independent institutions or vice versa.

These results suggested, therefore, that analysis based on the detailed classification of main preschool placement should be limited to the matched subsample of children. Analysis at the very general level of maintained versus independent provision, however, could include the whole child sample, although for many purposes this would be of limited interest.

Check for bias in matched subsample

Comparisons were made between the matched and unmatched subsamples of children in terms of the five-year factors summarised in Table A.9. The results suggest that socially disadvantaged children were slightly over-represented in the matched sample and children in rural neighbourhoods slightly under-represented. Although some of the factors achieved a high degree of statistical significance due to the large numbers involved, the observed differences in percentages were very small and were unlikely to adversely affect analysis based on the matched subsample. Comparisons between the matched and unmatched samples in terms of five-year and ten-year test scores did not reveal any important differences between the two subsamples.

We concluded from this that our analysis should be limited to the matched cases only. This was because of the inconsistencies between the mother's reported description of the type of preschool placement attended by her child and that obtained from the Nursery/Playgroup survey. Also, no substantial bias could be detected in the matched subsample when

Table A.9   *Comparison of matched and unmatched subsamples in terms of home background factors*

	Chi square test statistical significance	Matched (%)	Unmatched (%)
Child's gender	ns		
Male		50.2	52.0
Social class	p< .001 (5df)		
Nonmanual		38.7	43.5
Neighbourhood	p< .001 (3df)		
Well-to-do		26.8	29.1
Rural		17.6	21.7
Mother's qualifications	p< .01 (7df)		
None		49.3	46.3
Number of children in family	ns		
≥ 3		36.5	34.5
Age of mother	ns		
< 30		44.3	43.6
Number of household moves	p< .001 (4df)		
None		44.8	41.3
Standard Region	p< .001 (9df)		
West Midlands		9.1	12.3
Wales		4.4	5.9

compared with the unmatched subsample which was likely to affect the validity of the results obtained.

Time-lag between child-based survey and Nursery/Playgroup survey

Although the two surveys were carried out concurrently in 1975, many of the children in the study had already started school having left their preschool placement. Thus information about the institutions the children had attended may have been obtained some time after they had left. To check for the extent to which this might be a problem, we calculated the period between the time the child left his main preschool placement and the date of completion of the Nursery/Playgroup questionnaire for that institution.

As many as 87% of the Nursery/Playgroup questionnaires for the matched subsample were completed within a year of the date the child had left. This proportion increased to more than 90% of those who attended LEA nursery schools or classes or independent nursery schools and was lowest (76%) amongst those who went to LA day nurseries.

This time-lag was not important for the analyses based only on data from the children's survey, but where Nursery/Playgroup data were involved, any changes in the institutions that may have occurred since the child left could have introduced additional random variation into the data and thereby reduced the likelihood of obtaining significant results.

Variables which require definition

The majority of variables used in this report are self-explanatory. However, certain variables have been specifically devised for this study and the derivation of such variables is described below (see also Osborn *et al.*, 1984, pp. 270–8).

Type of family (Table A.10). A six-category classification was devised which described the child's parental situation:

1. Both natural parents. Included all children living with both natural parents at the time of the survey whether or not the parents were married to each other.

2. Stepfamilies. Included children living with one natural parent and another person who was described as a parent figure but who was not the child's grandparent or elder sibling.

3. Adoptive families. Included children who were legally adopted by both parents. Because of tracing difficulties this group was under-represented in the five-year follow-up. Children living with one natural parent and one adoptive parent were included in the stepfamily category.

Table A.10   *Classification of types of family*

	Five-year		Ten-year	
	N	%	N	%
Two-parent families				
both natural parents	11,851	90.2	11,244	82.6
step-family	357	2.7	975	7.2
adoptive family	96	0.7	177	1.3
One-parent families				
supported	250	1.9	283	2.1
lone	505	3.8	844	6.2
Other families	62	0.5	95	0.7
TOTAL	13,121	100.0	13,618	100.0

Note: Children living in residential institutions were excluded from this classification.

4. Supported one-parent families. Children who had only one parent figure were divided into two groups depending on whether or not there were other adult members of the household, for example grandparents or a cohabitee not described as a parent figure. If there were other adults in the household the child was deemed to be in a supported one-parent family. The term 'supported one-parent family' is meant to suggest that the other adult members of the household were at least available to help the single parent in various ways such as looking after the child whilst he or she was at work. Economic support might also have been forthcoming through the provision of a home or in financial emergencies.

5. Lone one-parent families. These children were living with one natural parent in households where there were no other resident adults. These lone one-parent families were more isolated emotionally and socially with the single parent carrying the full burden of maintaining a separate home.

6. Other families. These children were living with neither natural parent and were with foster-parents, grandparents or other relatives.

Children living in residential institutions were excluded from this classification.

Type of neighbourhood (Table A.11). The subjective rating of the type of neighbourhood in which the child lived was made by the health visitor who conducted the interview in the child's home. A validity and reliability study of this simple scale produced an inter-rater reliability coefficient of .70 (Kendall's Tau B, $p < .001$, N = 322). A strong association was also found between this subjective rating and a classification of the neighbourhoods in which the children lived based on social indicators from the 1971 census small area statistics (Osborn and Carpenter, 1980).

Table A.11 *Type of neighbourhood*

	N	%
Poor		
In this district houses are closely packed together and many are in poor state of repair. Multi-occupation is a common feature, and most families have low incomes	1,037	8.2
Average		
This district consists largely of council houses and flats or less expensive privately owned houses, for example, older terrace houses. Multi-occupation is unusual and families have average incomes. Include 'new towns' here	6,317	49.7
Well-to-do		
In this district houses are well spaced and the majority are well maintained. Multi-occupation is rare and most families have higher than average incomes	2,954	23.2
Rural		
This district is part of a small market town, rural community or village. Some families may lack basic amenities but others may be fairly well-to-do. It is mainly characterised by the fact that well-to-do and poorer families live fairly close together in the community	2,403	18.9
ALL	12,711	100.0
Insufficient information	424	
TOTAL	13,135	

Ethnic origin (Table A.12). The classification by ethnic origin was developed for a special study undertaken for the Commission for Racial Equality (Osborn and Butler, 1985). This classification was based on the ethnic origin of the parents rather than the child because a significant number of children born to ethnic minority group parents were recorded on the questionnaire as European (UK) because they were born in the UK and were British citizens. Although it was technically possible for a child in the

Table A.12 *Ethnic origin of child's parents (five-year)*

Ethnic origin of parents	N	%
Both European		
Britain	11,907	90.8
Northern Ireland	29	0.2
Eire	168	1.3
Other and mixed European countries of origin	414	3.2
Both Non-European		
Afro-Caribbean	187	1.4
Indian/Pakistani	241	1.8
Other and mixed non-European countries of origin	40	0.3
One parent European, other parent:		
Afro-Caribbean	32	0.2
Indian/Pakistani	22	0.2
Other non-European	77	0.6
ALL	13,117	100.0
Insufficient information	18	
TOTAL	13,135	

study not to have the same ethnic origin as his parents, for example when fostered or adopted, this was unlikely to occur frequently and for most purposes it was the cultural and socio-economic milieu of the home that was of importance rather than skin colour or genetic factors.

For analyses in this report involving the child's ethnic origin the four European categories were grouped together and categories other than Afro-Caribbean and Indian/Pakistani were excluded as these were small and heterogeneous groups.

Social Index (Table A.13). A composite index of socio-economic inequality was developed for this study which comprises 7 social indicators of parents' occupational and educational status, and housing conditions. The Social Index is used in place of the more conventional indicator of social class based on the occupation of the head of the household, over which it has five main advantages:

1. It provides an index of social position for households where an appropriate occupation is not available—for example one-parent families (6.5% of the five-year sample had no occupational data).

2. An index based on several social indicators provides a more reliable measure, as any inaccuracies in one of the indicators will be compensated for by the others.

Table A.13   *Five-year Social Index items*

Description of item	N	%	weight
Classification of father's occupation (OPCS Social Class)			
I	843	6.4	+5
II	2,405	18.3	+3
III (non-manual)	1,069	8.1	+1
III (manual)	5,726	43.6	−1
IV	1,620	12.3	−3
V	605	4.6	−5
No information	212	1.6	0
No father	655	5.0	0
TOTAL	13,135	100.0	
Highest educational qualification of either parent			
No qualifications	5,166	39.3	−2
Vocational qualifications, e.g. trade apprenticeships	1,888	14.4	−1
GCE 'O' level or equivalent	2,703	20.6	0
GCE 'A' level or equivalent	990	7.5	+1
State Registered Nurse	228	1.7	+2
Teacher's Certificate of Education	216	1.6	+4
Degree or equivalent or higher qualification	1,739	13.2	+5
No information	205	1.6	0
TOTAL	13,135	100.0	
Housing tenure			
Owner occupation	7,386	56.2	+2
Local Authority rented	4,231	32.2	−3
Privately rented:			
unfurnished	689	5.2	−1
furnished	126	1.0	−5
No information	703	5.4	0
TOTAL	13,135	100.0	
Type of accommodation			
House or bungalow:			
detached	2,488	18.9	+3
semi-detached	5,350	40.7	+1
terrace	3,660	27.9	−2
Flat or maisonette	1,342	10.2	−4
Rooms	117	0.9	−6
No information	178	1.4	0
TOTAL	13,135	100.0	

Table A.13 *continued*

Description of item	N	%	weight
Persons per room ratio			
< .50	275	2.1	+4
≥ .50 ≤ .75	4,089	31.1	+2
> .75 ≤1.00	6,256	47.6	0
>1.00 ≤1.50	1,869	14.2	−3
>1.50 ≤2.00	367	2.8	−5
>2.00	87	0.7	−8
No information	192	1.5	0
TOTAL	13,135	100.0	
Car ownership			
Has car	9,201	70.0	+1
Does not have car	3,904	29.8	−3
No information	30	0.2	0
TOTAL	13,135	100.0	
Telephone availability			
Has telephone	7,520	57.3	+2
Does not have telephone	5,585	42.5	−2
No information	30	0.2	0
TOTAL	13,135	100.0	

3. It provides a more finely graded scale than occupational class which has only six categories and 'social class III (manual)' contains 47% of the five-year sample.

4. The Index is scored in such a way that it approximates to a normal distribution and therefore can be used as a covariate in multivariate analysis. The advantage of this is that it allows more independent variables to be added to an analysis of variance designed to 'explain away' the association between preschool education and test scores and thereby provides a more rigorous test of these associations.

5. It provides a useful means of measuring social mobility in this longitudinal survey.

A more detailed account of the rationale and evaluation of the Social Index is given in Osborn (1987) and Osborn and Morris (1979).

The Social Index items are given in Table A.13 together with item frequency distributions and the weights assigned to each category. Cronbach's alpha, as a measure of internal reliability, was .78 (N = 11,231). A measure of the robustness of the scale if information on any one item was not available is demonstrated by the fact that Cronbach's alpha for any combination of 6 Social Index items did not fall below .73. Also the full scale score had a Pearson's correlation coefficient of .98 with a score which excluded the weight for father's occupation. Thus the Index can be used reliably for cases which lack occupational data.

The Social Index score is obtained by totalling the weights for the 7 items and adding this sum to a base of 50. To increase still further the accuracy of Social Index scores for cases with information missing on one item, an adjustment for any missing data was made using regression equations based on the score from the 6 items that were available.

The resulting score has a mean of 50.0 and standard deviation of 10.2 (N = 12,950 cases with information on 6 or all items). In this report cases with data missing on more than one item and 14 children in residential care at the age of 5 (total N = 185 cases) were excluded from the Social Index classification.

For tabular analyses, the Social Index score was grouped into five categories as in Table A.14. The particular grouping chosen was intended to identify, as closely as the distribution of scores would allow, the 10% most advantaged and the 10% most disadvantaged children, and for the intermediate groups to approximate a normal distribution.

Table A.14   *Social Index groups*

Score	Group	N	%
19–36	Most disadvantaged	1,183	9.1
37–43	Disadvantaged	2,636	20.4
44–55	Average	5,070	39.2
56–63	Advantaged	2,606	20.1
64–73	Most advantaged	1,455	11.2
	ALL	12,950	100.0
Insufficient information		171	
In residential care		14	
TOTAL SAMPLE		13,135	

The same 7 items given in Table A.13 were used to create a ten-year Social Index having a mean of 51.8 and standard deviation of 8.7 (N = 13,289). The arithmetic difference between the five- and ten-year Indices was then used as a measure of social mobility between the two stages of the study (see Chapter 6).

Educational and cognitive tests

Two five-year tests were used in the present study—Copying Designs and English Picture Vocabulary Test (EPVT). Both these tests are described in detail in Osborn *et al.* (1984).

Copying Designs test. Children in our sample were asked to make two copies of each of the 8 designs shown in Figure A.1. Not all children completed two drawings of each design, therefore a score of one was given if at least one good copy was made of a given design. The total score was the sum of the scores obtained on each design, thus giving a range of 0 to 8. Zero score was obtained when a child attempted to copy at least one design but all attempts were judged to be poor copies. The distribution obtained was transformed to give a mean of zero and standard deviation of one.

English Picture Vocabulary Test. The English Picture Vocabulary Test (EPVT) is an adaptation by Brimer and Dunn (1962) of the American Peabody Picture Vocabulary Test. It consists of a series of 56 sets of four different pictures with a particular word associated with each set of four pictures. The child is asked to point out the one picture which corresponds to the given word, and the test proceeds with words of increasing difficulty until he makes five mistakes in a run of eight consecutive items. The final item achieved is designated the ceiling item. The EPVT raw score is the total number of correct items occurring before the ceiling item. The resulting distribution of raw EPVT scores was transformed to give a mean of zero and standard deviation of one.

Four tests and one teacher's assessment were chosen from the ten-year study which were representative of a broad range of cognitive and educational skills.

British Ability Scales (BAS). These scales were developed in the University of Sheffield (Elliott *et al.*, 1979) and, with the advice of one of the designers of the test, two verbal and two non-verbal scales were selected for use in the ten-year CHES follow-up. The verbal subscale included word definitions (37 items) and similarities (42 items). The non-verbal subscale included recall of digits (34 items) and matrices (28 items). For the purposes of the present study the total BAS score was used based on all 141 items and the raw score was transformed to give a mean of 100 and standard deviation of 15.

Picture Language Test (PLT). This test was created specially for the ten-year follow-up and was based on the same principles as the English Picture Vocabulary Test used at 5. The child was asked to identify the one picture from a set of four which corresponded to a spoken word. The test proceeded with words of increasing difficulty for up to 71 items but testing stopped when the child made five mistakes in eight consecutive items. The raw PLT score was the total number of correct responses before reaching

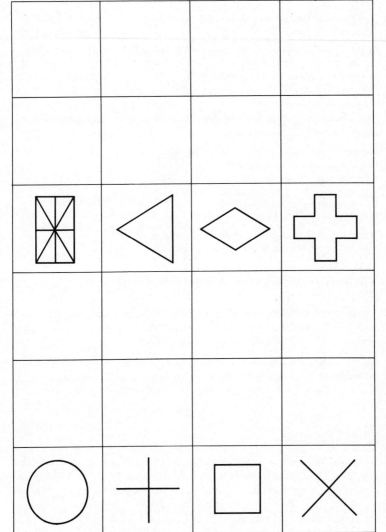

FIG. A.1. Copying Designs test

Table A.15 *Items comprising ten-year communication scale and results of principal components analysis*

Item	Component loading
Language structures used by the child are very simple	−.87
When describing his or her own experience to the teacher the ideas do not come out coherently in a sequence which makes sense for the listener. In other words the child's thoughts are poorly organised	−.87
When describing his or her own experiences the child's vocabulary is very simple	−.86
Given that most children's spoken language understandably reflects the importance of regional accents and dialect, the child, in the appropriate situation, can speak in such a way that he or she is clearly understood within the language context of 'standard English'	.81
When the class is given new work and concepts, the child readily assimilates and uses the new vocabulary	.80
In ordinary conversation the child's words tend to be well finished	.79
The articulation of the child's speech is slurred	−.77
When talking to the teacher, the child does not make syntactical mistakes which make it difficult to understand him or her	.76

Note: Variance explained = 66.9%. High score indicates good communication.

the ceiling item. This score was transformed to give a mean of 100 and standard deviation of 15.

Reading test. This was a shortened version of the Edinburgh Reading Test (Godfrey Thompson Unit for Educational Research, 1977, 1980) from which items were specially selected to give a wide ability range. The test contains a total of 67 items examining vocabulary, syntax, comprehension and retention. A total reading score was computed and was transformed to give a mean of 100 and standard deviation of 15.

Mathematics Test. The non-availability of a suitable mathematics test for 10-year-olds necessitated a test being designed specifically for the ten-year follow-up. This consisted of 72 muiltiple choice questions covering the four rules of arithmetic (addition, subtraction, multiplication and division), number concepts, measure, algebra, geometry and statistics. The total raw score was transformed to give a mean of 100 and standard deviation of 15.

Communication. A measure of expressive language or communication skill was obtained from assessments made by the children's class teachers using semantic differential analogue scales. The communication scale consisted of 8 items that were analysed and scored by means of principal components analysis giving a mean of zero and standard deviation of one. These items are given in Table A.15 together with their component loadings which indicates the strength of their association with the hypothesised underlying dimension. High scores on this scale indicate children with good communication skills, expressive language and articulation.

Further details of all the ten-year educational tests and assessments are given in an unpublished report to the DES (Butler *et al.*, 1982).

Behavioural assessments

In the five-year survey, mothers answered a self-completion questionnaire which included an assessment of the child's behaviour at home (Rutter *et*

Table A.16 *Items comprising five-year antisocial behaviour scale and results of principal components analysis*

Item	Component loading
Is often disobedient	.67
Often destroys own or others' belongings	.60
Frequently fights with other children	.60
Irritable. Is quick to 'fly off the handle'	.60
Very restless. Often running up and down. Hardly ever still	.58
Has temper tantrums (that is, complete loss of temper with shouting, angry movements, etc.)	.58
Cannot settle to anything for more than a few moments	.56
Often tells lies	.54
Is squirmy or fidgety	.54
Bullies other children	.53
Sometimes takes things belonging to others	.49

Note: Variance explained = 33.0%. High score indicates antisocial/aggressive behaviour.

al., 1970, pp. 412–21). Principal components analysis was used to define an 11-item antisocial behaviour scale and a 9-item neuroticism scale (Osborn *et al.*, 1984, pp. 282–4). The items comprising these scales are given in Tables A.16 and A.17 with the component loadings which indicate the strength of association between the items and the hypothesised underlying dimension.

Behavioural scales were completed by the child's mother and class teacher in the ten-year survey but for the purposes of the present study only the information on behaviour at school has been used. Behavioural items were selected from two published scales (Connors, 1969; Rutter, 1967) and analogue scales rather than discrete category response scales were used (Butler *et al.*, 1982, DES Report pp. 21–3). Items were subjected to principal components analysis which resulted in the identification of seven behavioural dimensions: conduct disorder, hyperactivity, application to school work, extroversion, peer relations, anxiety and clumsiness (Tables A.18 to A.24). Each set of items was subjected to separate principal components analysis which generated scores with a mean of zero and standard deviation of one.

Measures of self-esteem and locus of control were obtained in a Pupil Questionnaire completed by the 10-year-olds themselves. It was hypothesised that preschool education might have raised self-esteem and the child's sense of inner-directedness thereby enhancing motivation in school tasks leading in turn to increased levels of achievement. The instruments

Table A.17   *Items comprising five-year neurotic behaviour scale and results of principal components analysis*

Item	Component loading
Often worried, worries about many things	.66
Often appears miserable, unhappy, tearful or distressed	.56
Tends to be fearful or afraid of new things or new situations	.54
Is fussy or over-particular	.50
Complains of stomach ache or has vomited	.42
Complains of headaches	.40
Does child have any eating or appetite problems?	.40
Tends to do things on his own—rather solitary	.39
Does your child have any sleeping difficulty?	.34

Note: Variance explained = 22.9%. High score indicates neurotic behaviour.

described in Tables A.25 and A.26 were devised by Denis Lawrence (1973, 1978) and Philip Gammage (1975) respectively. The children responded 'Yes', 'No', or 'Don't Know' to all the items in each scale. Items marked 'd' are distractors and do not contribute to the score.

Table A.18 *Items comprising ten-year conduct disorder scale and results of principal components analysis*

Item	Component loading
Quarrels with other children	.84
Displays outbursts of temper, explosive or unpredictable behaviour	.82
Teases other children to excess	.81
Interferes with the activities of other children	.81
Bullies other children	.80
Changes mood quickly and drastically	.79
Complains about things	.72
Destroys own or other children's belongings	.72
Request must be satisfied immediately—is easily frustrated	.70

Note: Variance explained = 60.5%. High score indicates antisocial/aggressive behaviour.

Table A.19 *Items comprising ten-year hyperactivity scale and results of principal components analysis*

Item	Component loading
Shows restless or over-active behaviour	.85
Squirmy and fidgety	.84
Hums or makes other odd vocal noises at inappropriate times	.77
Given to rhythmic tapping or rhythmic kicking during class	.77
Is excitable, impulsive	.75
Has twitches, mannerisms or tics of the face or body	.54

Note: Variance explained = 57.6%. High score indicates hyperactive behaviour.

Table A.20   *Items comprising ten-year application scale and results of principal components analysis*

Item	Component loading
Lacks concentration on educational tasks, in comparison with the average-10 year-old	.87
Shows perseverance in the face of difficult tasks	−.85
Is easily distracted	.85
Shows perseverance; persists with difficult or routine work	−.81
Pays attention to what is being explained in class	−.81
Becomes bored during class	.79
Is forgetful when given a complex task	.79
Fails to finish things he starts	.79
Completes tasks which are started	−.78
Becomes confused or hesitant when given a complex task	.72
Is given to daydreaming	.68
Cannot concentrate on any particular task, even though the child may return to it frequently	.68
Works independently	−.67
Accepts the goals of the school curriculum	−.62
Shows lethargic and listless behaviour	.62

Note: Variance explained = 57.8%. High score indicates poor concentration/application to school work.

Table A.21   *Items comprising ten-year extroversion scale and results of principal components analysis*

Item	Component loading
When talking to friends is very talkative (compared to the rest of the class)	.84
When talking to teacher is very talkative (compared to the rest of the class)	.82
An extrovert, lively, likes company	.78
When something important has happened does not endeavour to tell his or her friends about it.	−.77
When something important has happened does not endeavour to tell his or her teacher about it.	−.71

Note: Variance explained = 59.8%. High score indicates extrovert behaviour/talkative.

Table A.22   *Items comprising ten-year peer relations scale and results of principal components analysis*

Item	Component loading
Is highly popular with his peers	.91
Has no friends	−.91
Very co-operative with peers	.78
Tends to do things on his or her own, is rather solitary	−.68

Note: Variance explained = 68.6%. High score indicates child is popular with peers.

Table A.23   *Items comprising ten-year anxiety scale and results of principal components analysis*

Item	Component loading
Is worried and anxious about many things	.83
Behaves 'nervously'	.79
Is an anxious child	.77
In relations with others appears to be miserable, unhappy, tearful or distressed	.70
Is fearful or afraid of new things or situations	.69
Becomes obsessional about unimportant tasks	.64
Is fussy or over-particular	.62
Cries for little cause	.61
Fearful in movements, requires much encouragement to move faster	.57

Note: Variance explained = 48.7%. High score indicates anxious/nervous behaviour.

Table A.24   *Items comprising ten-year clumsiness scale and results of principal components analysis*

Item	Component loading
Shows difficulty when picking up small objects	.75
Is noticeably clumsy in formal or informal games	.73
Drops things which are being carried	.72
Can use scissors and similar manipulative equipment competently	−.71
Trips or falls easily or bumps into objects or other children	.66

Table A.24 *continued*

Shows inadequate control when handling a pencil or paint brush	.66
Manipulates small objects easily with his or her hands	−.62
Finds it difficult to kick a ball forward	.61
Holds writing and drawing instruments appropriately	−.60
Works deftly with his or her hands	−.58
Experiences classroom or playground accidents	.55
Dresses and undresses competently (e.g. for PE)	−.43

Note: Variance explained = 40.9%. High score indicates clumsy behaviour.

Table A.25 *The LAWSEQ Pupil Questionnaire (self-esteem)*

1. Do you think that your parents usually like to hear about your ideas?	
2. Do you often feel lonely at school?	
3. Do other children often break friends or fall out with you?	
4. Do you like team games?	d
5. Do you think that other children often say nasty things about you?	
6. When you have to say things in front of teachers, do you usually feel shy?	
7. Do you like writing stories or doing other creative writing?	d
8. Do you often feel sad because you have nobody to play with at school?	
9. Are you good at mathematics?	d
10. Are there lots of things about yourself you would like to change?	
11. When you have to say things in front of other children, do you usually feel foolish?	
12. Do you find it difficult to do things like woodwork or knitting?	d
13. When you want to tell a teacher something, do you usually feel foolish?	
14. Do you often have to find new friends because your old friends are playing with somebody else?	
15. Do you usually feel foolish when you talk to your parents?	
16. Do other people often think that you tell lies?	

Note: Items marked 'd' are distractors. High score indicates positive self-esteem.

Table A.26 *The CAROLOC Pupil Questionnaire (locus of control)*

---

1. Do you feel that most of the time it's not worth trying hard because things never turn out right anyway?
2. Do you feel that wishing can make good things happen?
3. Are people good to you no matter how you act towards them?
4. Do you like taking part in plays or concerts?   d
5. Do you usually feel that it's almost useless to try in school because most children are cleverer than you?
6. Is a high mark just a matter of 'luck' for you?
7. Are you good at spelling?   d
8. Are tests just a lot of guess work for you?
9. Are you often blamed for things which just aren't your fault?
10. Are you the kind of person who believes that planning ahead makes things turn out better?
11. Do you find it easy to get up in the morning?   d
12. When bad things happen to you, is it usually someone else's fault?
13. When someone is very angry with you, is it impossible to make him your friend again?
14. When nice things happen to you is it only good luck?
15. Do you feel sad when it's time to leave school each day?   d
16. When you get into an argument is it usually the other person's fault?
17. Are you surprised when your teacher says you've done well?
18. Do you usually get low marks, even when you study hard?
19. Do you like to read books?   d
20. Do you think studying for tests is a waste of time?

Note: Items marked 'd' are distractors. High score indicates inner-directed locus of control.

Table A.27 *Correlations between five-year tests and assessments*

Test or assessment	Neurotic behaviour	Antisocial behaviour	EPVT
Copying Designs	−.01 12,972	−.19 12,965	.34 12,214
English Picture Vocabulary Test	−.04 12,184	−.18 12,177	
Antisocial behaviour	.31 13,059		

Note: All correlations significant at p< .0005 except Copying Designs by Neurotic behaviour (ns).

In the LAWSEQ (self-esteem) scale a point was scored by each 'No' response except item 1 for which a 'Yes' response scored a point. The raw scores ranged from 0 to 12. In the CAROLOC (locus of control) scale a point was scored by each 'No' response except item 10 for which a 'Yes' response scored a point. The raw scores ranged from 0 to 15. The raw scores from each scale were transformed to give a mean of 100 and a standard deviation of 15.

The correlations in Tables A.27 to A.29 show a strong tendency for children who performed well in one test also to do well in other tests. This was particularly evident in Table A.28 showing the associations between the ten-year cognitive and educational tests where the correlations between British Ability Scales, reading and mathematics were .74 and .75.

Certain behavioural characteristics were also found to correlate; notably conduct disorder and hyperactivity (Table A.29, r = .75). Children who were popular with their peers (peer relations) were also more likely to apply themselves well to their school work (application, r = −.50), to be non-aggressive (conduct disorder, r = −.44) and to show extrovert behaviour (extroversion, r = .43). Curiously, anxious children (anxiety) were also likely to show conduct disorders (r = .40), but a similar association was found between antisocial and neurotic behaviour at 5 (r = .31). Anxious children also tended to be clumsy (r = .52) and to have poor concentration (application, r = .48). The application scale was associated with a number of other behavioural traits also: hyperactivity (r = .59), conduct disorder (r = .56) and clumsiness (r = .55).

No causal inferences can be made about these associations and the correlations were not so high that different scales were in effect measuring the same pattern of behaviour. Such scales are, however, constructs which define the patterns of behaviour in different ways. It should also be noted

Table A.28   *Correlations between ten-year educational tests*

Educational test	Communi-cation	Mathematics test	Reading test	Picture Language Test
British Ability Scales	.58 12,328	.74 12,420	.74 12,468	.57 12,431
Picture Language Test	.42 12,610	.49 12,649	.53 12,686	
Reading test	.62 12,589	.75 12,700		
Mathematics test	.56 12,584			

Note: All correlations significant at p< .0005.

Table A.29 *Correlations between ten-year behavioural assessments*

Behavioural assessment	Locus of control	Self-esteem	Clumsiness	Anxiety	Peer relations	Extroversion	Application	Hyper-activity
Conduct disorder	-.12 12,332	-.15 12,404	.42 12,708	.40 12,708	-.44 12,706	.19 12,708	.56 12,708	.75 12,708
Hyperactivity	-.11 12,332	-.11 12,404	.49 12,708	.39 12,708	-.30 12,706	.22 12,708	.59 12,708	
Application	-.31 12,336	-.20 12,408	.55 12,709	.48 12,708	-.50 12,706	-.11 12,712		
Extroversion	.11 12,336	.05 12,409	-.15 12,708	-.33 12,708	.43 12,706			
Peer relations	.20 12,330	.20 12,402	-.45 12,706	-.55 12,706				
Anxiety	-.19 12,332	-.18 12,404	.52 12,708					
Clumsiness	-.18 12,333	-.14 12,405						
Self-esteem	.44 12,322							

Note: All correlations significant at $p < .0005$.

that these ten-year behaviour scales were based on teachers' observations of the children at school; their behaviour in other settings might be quite different, and another person's observations, e.g. those of a child's mother or of a peer, could result in different constructs.

An example of this can be seen in the correlations between the children's self-assessments of self-esteem and locus of control and the assessments made by class teachers. These correlations were generally lower than the ones between the scales derived from the teacher's observations, and yet, the correlation between self-esteem and locus of control was relatively high (r = .44). The consistently high correlation between the communication scale and the behavioural assessments compared with the other educational assessments shown in Table A.30 can, again, be put down to the fact that communication and the behavioural scales were based on teacher assessments and therefore involve a degree of subjectivity. It is important, therefore, to recognise the subjective element in these scales which contributes to the associations between them.

Table A.30   *Correlations between ten-year educational tests and behavioural assessments*

| Behavioural assessments | Educational tests | | | | |
	British Ability Scales	Picture Language Test	Reading test	Mathematics test	Communication
Conduct disorder	−.20 12,344	−.12 12,627	−.23 12,607	−.20 12,566	−.31 12,684
Hyper-activity	−.19 12,344	−.10 12,627	−.24 12,607	−.20 12,566	−.35 12,684
Application	−.47 12,349	−.29 12,632	−.54 12,612	−.51 12,571	−.68 12,689
Extroversion	.13 12,349	.11 12,632	.12 12,612	.12 12,571	.28 12,690
Peer relations	.22 12,342	.15 12,625	.25 12,605	.25 12,564	.41 12,682
Anxiety	−.23 12,344	−.15 12,627	−.24 12,607	−.25 12,566	−.38 12,684
Clumsiness	−.25 12,345	−.15 12,628	−.30 12,608	−.28 12,567	−.46 12,685
Self-esteem	.20 12,211	.15 12,465	.19 12,448	.21 12,409	.18 12,386
Locus of control	.42 12,146	.30 12,395	.41 12,379	.41 12,340	.36 12,314

Note: All correlations significant at $p < .0005$.

Finally, Table A.30 shows the associations between the behavioural assessments and test scores at age 10. The highest correlations were found between application and locus of control in relation to the four ten-year educational tests and the communication scale. Such associations need not imply a causal relationship although a teacher's assessment and a child's self-image are enhanced by success in school work as well as vice versa. Thus, it is essential to acknowledge the transactional process within the school which results in these associations between behaviour and test performance.

References

Atkins, E., Cherry, N. M., Douglas, J. W. B., Kiernan, K. E. and Wadsworth, M. E. J., 1980, The 1946 British Birth Survey: An account of the origins, progress and results of the National Survey of Health and Development, in Mednick, S. A. and Baest, A. E. (eds.), *An Empirical Basis for Primary Prevention: Prospective Longitudinal Research in Europe*, Oxford: Oxford University Press.

Barron, A. P. and Earls, F., 1984, The relation of temperament and social factors to behaviour problems in three-year-old children, *Journal of Child Psychology and Psychiatry*, 25, 23–33.

Bereiter, C. and Engelmann, S., 1966, *Teaching Disadvantaged Children in the Preschool*, New Jersey: Prentice-Hall, Inc.

Bernstein, B., 1961, Social class and linguistic development: a theory of social learning, in Halsey, A. H., Floud, J. and Anderson, C. A. (eds.), *Education, Economy and Society*, New York: The Free Press.

Bissell, J. S., 1973, Planned variation in Head Start and Follow Through, in Stanley, J. C. (ed.), *Compensatory Education for Children, Ages Two to Eight*, Baltimore, Md.: Johns Hopkins.

Blackstone, T. A. V., 1971, *A Fair Start: The Provision of Pre-School Education*, London: Penguin Press.

Bloom, B. S., 1964, *Stability and Change in Human Characteristics*, New York: Wiley and Sons.

Board of Education, 1905, *Reports on Children Under Five Years of Age in Public Elementary Schools by Women Inspectors*, London: HMSO.

Bone, M., 1977, *Preschool Children and the Need for Day Care*, OPCS Social Survey, London: HMSO.

Bowlby, J., 1951, *Maternal Care and Mental Health*, Geneva: World Health Organization.

Bradley, M., 1982, *Coordination of Services for Children Under Five*, Windsor: NFER-Nelson.

Brimer, M. A. and Dunn, L. M., 1962, *English Picture Vocabulary Test*, Bristol: Education Evaluation Enterprises.

Brodman, K., Erdmann, A. J., Lorge, I., Gershenson, C. P., Wolff, H. G. and Broadbent, T. H., 1952, The Cornell Medical Health Questionnaire IV: The recognition of emotional disturbances in a general hospital, *Journal of Clinical Psychology*, 8, 289–93.

Bronfenbrenner, U., 1974, *A Report on Longitudinal Programs*, Vol. 2: *Is Early Intervention Effective?* Washington DC: Department of Health, Education and Welfare.

Brown, B. (ed.), 1978, *Found: Long-term Gains from Early Intervention*, American Association for the Advancement of Science, Boulder Colo.: Westview Press.

Brown, G. and Harris, T., 1978, *Social Origins of Depression*, London: Tavistock Publications.

Brown, M. and Madge, N., 1982, *Despite the Welfare State*, London: Heinemann Educational.

Butler, N. R., Haslum, M. N., Barker, W. and Morris, A. C., 1982, *Child Health and Education Study: First Report to the Department of Education and Science on the 10-year Follow-up*, University of Bristol, Department of Child Health.

Butler, N. R., Haslum, M. N., Stewart-Brown, S., Howlett, B. C., Prosser, H. and Brewer, R., 1982, *Child Health and Education Study: First Report to the Department of Health and Social Security on the 10-year Follow-up*, University of Bristol, Department of Child Health.

Centre for Educational Research and Innovation, 1977, *Early Childhood Care and Education: Objectives and Issues*, Paris: OECD.

Chamberlain, G., Philipp, E., Howlett, B. and Masters, K., 1978, *British Births 1970*, Vol. 2: *Obstetric Care*, London: W. M. Heinemann.

Chamberlain, R., Chamberlain, G., Howlett, B. and Claireaux, A., 1975, *British Births 1970*, Vol. 1: *The First Week of Life*, London: W. M. Heinemann.

Chazan, M., Laing, A. and Jackson, S., 1971, *Just Before School*, Schools Council Research and Development Project in Compensatory Education, Oxford: Basil Blackwell.

Chazan, M., Laing, A. F., Jones, J., Harper, G. C. and Bolton, J., 1983, *Helping Young Children with Behavioural Difficulties: A Handbook*, London: Croom Helm.

Clarke, A. D. B. and Clarke, A. M., 1981, 'Sleeper effects' in development: fact or artifact? *Developmental Review*, 1, 344–60.

Clarke, A. M., 1984(a), Early experience and cognitive development, in Gordon, E. W. (ed.), *Review of Research in Education*, 11, 125–57, Washington DC: AERA.

Clarke, A. M., 1984(b), Heritability, social disadvantage and psychosocial intervention, *Educational Psychology*, 4, 5–19.

Clarke, A. M. and Clarke, A. D. B. (eds.), 1976, *Early Experience: Myth and Evidence*, London: Open Books.

Clement, J., Schweinhart, L. J., Barnett, W. S., Epstein, A. S. and Weikart, D., 1984, *Changed Lives: The Effects of the Perry Preschool Program on Youths through 19*, Ypsilanti, Michigan: High/Scope Press.

Community Relations Commission, 1976, *Between Two Cultures: A Study of Relationships between Generations in the Asian Community in Britain*, London: Community Relations Commission.

Connors, C. K., 1969, A teacher rating scale for use in drug studies with children, *American Journal of Psychiatry*, **126**: 6, 884–8.

Curtis, A., 1985, *A Curriculum for the Preschool Child*, Windsor: NFER-Nelson.

Curtis, A. and Blatchford, P., 1981, Meeting the needs of socially handicapped children: an account of the project Social Handicap and Cognitive Functioning in Pre-school Children: curriculum development phase, *Educational Research*, 24, 31–42.

David, M. E., 1982, Day care policies and parenting, *Journal of Social Policy*, 11, 81–92.

Davie, R., Butler, N. R. and Goldstein, H., 1972, *From Birth to Seven*, a report of the National Child Development Study, London: Longman.

Department of Education and Science, 1963, *Higher Education*, Report of the Committee on Higher Education (Robbins Report), London: HMSO.

Department of Education and Science, 1972, *Education: A Framework for Expansion*, London: HMSO.

Department of Health and Social Security and Department of Education and Science, 1976, *Low Cost Day Provision for the Under-fives*, Papers from a conference held at the Civil Service College, Sunningdale Park, 9–10 January 1976.

Department of Health and Social Security and Department of Education and Science, 1978, *Joint Circular: Coordination of Services for Children Under Five*.

Douglas, J. W. B., 1964, *The Home and the School*, London: MacGibbon and Kee.

Douglas, J. W. B. and Blomfield, J. M., 1958, *Children Under Five*, London: Allen and Unwin.

Douglas, J. W. B. and Ross, J. M., 1965, The later educational progress and emotional adjustment of children who went to nursery schools or classes, *Educational Research*, 7: 2, 73–80.

Elliott, C. D., Murray, D. J. and Pearson, L. S., 1979, *British Ability Scales*, Manual 3: *Directions for Administration and Scoring*, Windsor: NFER.

Elliott, C. D., Murray, D. J. and Pearson, L. S., 1979, *British Ability Scales*, Manual 4: *Tables of Abilities and Norms*, Windsor: NFER.

Equal Opportunities Commission, 1986, *Response to the DHSS Consultative Paper on Revision of the Nurseries and Childminders Regulation Act 1948*, Manchester: EOC.

Evans, E. D., 1985, Longitudinal follow-up assessment of differential preschool experience for low income minority group children, *Journal of Educational Research*, 78, 197–202.

van der Eyken, W., 1977, *The Preschool Years* (4th edition), Harmondsworth: Penguin.

van der Eyken, W., 1981, *Education of 3- to 8-year-olds in Europe in the 1980s*, Standing Conference of European Ministers of Education, Lisbon, 3–4 June 1981, Strasbourg: Council of Europe.

van der Eyken, W., 1984, *Day Nurseries in Action: A National Study of Local Authority Day Nurseries in England, 1975–1983*, Report to the Department of Health and Social Security, University of Bristol, Department of Child Health.

van der Eyken, W., Osborn, A. F. and Butler, N. R., 1984, Preschooling in Britain: A national study of institutional provision for under-fives in England, Scotland and Wales, *Early Child Development and Care*, 17: 2, 79–122.

Ferri, E., Birchall, D., Gingell, V. and Gipps, C., 1981, *Combined Nursery Centres*, A New Approach to Education and Day Care, London: Macmillan Press Ltd.

Fogelman, K. R. and Goldstein, H., 1976, Social factors associated with changes in educational attainments between 7 and 11 years of age, *Educational Studies*, 2: 2, 95–109.

Gammage, P., 1975, *Socialisation, Schooling and Locus of Control*, Bristol University: unpublished PhD thesis.

Garber, H. L., 1979, Bridging the gap from preschool to school for the disadvantaged child, *School Psychology Digest*, 8: 3, 303–10.

Godfrey Thompson Unit for Educational Research, 1977, *Manual of Instructions for the Edinburgh Reading Test Stage 4*, Sevenoaks: Hodder and Stoughton Educational.

Godfrey Thompson Unit for Educational Research, 1980, *Manual of Instructions for the Edinburgh Reading Test Stage 2* (2nd edition), Sevenoaks: Hodder and Stoughton Educational.

Halsey, A. H., 1972, *Educational Priority*, Vol. 1: *EPA Problem and Policies*, London: HMSO.

Halsey, A. H., 1980, Education can compensate, *New Society*, 24 Jan. 1980, 172–3.

Harmon, C. and Hanley, E. J., 1979, Administrative aspects of the Head Start program, in Zigler, E. and Valentine, J. (eds.) *Project Head Start: A Legacy of the War on Poverty*, 379–96, New York: The Free Press.

Hewison, J. and Tizard, J., 1980, Parental involvement and reading attainment, *British Journal of Educational Psychology*, 50, 209–15.

Hohman, M., Banet, B. and Weikart, D., 1979, *Young Children in Action: A Manual for Preschool Educators, the Cognitively Orientated Preschool Curriculum*, Ypsilanti, Mich.: High/Scope Press.

Hughes, M., Mayall, B., Moss, P., Perry, J., Petrie, P. and Pinkerton, G., 1980, *Nurseries Now*, Harmondsworth: Penguin Books.

Jencks, C., 1972, *Inequality: A Reassessment of the Effect of Family and Schooling in America*, New York: Basic Books.

Jensen, A. R., 1969, How much can we boost IQ and scholastic achievement? *Harvard Educational Review*, 39, 1–123.

Jowett, S. and Sylva, K., 1986, Does kind of preschool matter? *Educational Research*, 28: 1, 21–31.

Kagan, J. and Moss, H. A., 1962, *Birth to Maturity: A Study of Psychological Development*, New York: Wiley.

Labov, W., 1969, *The Logic of Non-standard English*, Georgetown Monographs on Language and Linguistics, 22.

Lawrence, D., 1973, *Improved Reading Through Counselling*, London: Ward Lock.

Lawrence, D., 1978, *Counselling Students with Reading Difficulties: A Handbook for Tutors and Organizers*, London: Good Reading.

Lazar, I., 1985, On bending twigs and planting acorns: some implications of recent research, *Association for Child Psychology and Psychiatry Newsletter*, 7: 1, 28–32.

Lazar, I. and Darlington, R., 1982, *Lasting Effects of Early Education: A Report from the Consortium for Longitudinal Studies*, Monographs of the Society for Research in Child Development, Serial No. 195, 47.

Lefcourt, H. M., 1972, in Maher, B. A. (ed.), *Progress in Experimental Personality Research*, Vol. 6, New York: Academic Books.

Lewis, D. G. and Garvey, J., 1980, Evidence of long-term effects from unsupplemented nursery education, *Educational Review*, 32: 1, 87–94.

Lord, F. M., 1967, Elementary models for measuring change, in Harris, C. W. (ed.), *Problems in Measuring Change*, 21–38, Madison: University of Wisconsin Press.

Mayall, B. and Petrie, P., 1983, *Childminding and Day Nurseries: What Kind of Care?* Studies in Education, 13, London: Heinemann Educational Books.

Moore, S. G., 1979, Past research and current perspectives on Head Start and Follow Through, *Viewpoints in Teaching and Learning*, 55: 3, 75–82.

Moray House College of Education, 1980, *Manual of Instructions for the Edinburgh Reading Test Stage 3* (2nd edition), Sevenoaks: Hodder and Stoughton Educational.

Morsbach, G., Kernahan, P. and Emerson, P., 1981, Attitudes to nursery school, *Educational Research*, 23: 3, 222–3.

Mortimore, P., Davies, J., West, A. and Varlaam, A., 1983, *Behaviour Problems in Schools: An Evaluation of Support Centres*, London: Croom Helm.

Moss, P., 1978, *Alternative Models of Group Child-Care for Pre-School Children with Working Parents*, Manchester: Equal Opportunities Commission.

Mosteller, F. and Bush, R. R., 1954, Selected quantitative techniques, in Lindzey, G. (ed.), *Handbook of Social Psychology*, Vol. 1, Reading, Mass.: Addison-Wesley.

Mottershead, P., 1978, *A Survey of Child Care for Pre-School Children with Working Parents: Costs and Organization*, Manchester: Equal Opportunities Commission.

Office of Population Censuses and Surveys, 1980, *Birth Statistics 1978*, London: HMSO.

Organisation for Economic Cooperation and Development, 1979, *Equal Opportunities for Women*, Paris: OECD.

Osborn, A. F., 1981, Under-fives in school in England and Wales, 1971–9, *Educational Research*, 23: 2, 96–103.

Osborn, A. F., 1987, Assessing the socio-economic status of families, *Sociology*, in press.

Osborn, A. F. and Butler, N. R., 1985, *Ethnic Minority Children: A Comparative Study from Birth to Five Years*, Report of the Child Health and Education Study (1970 Birth Cohort), London: Commission for Racial Equality.

Osborn, A. F., Butler, N. R. and Morris, A. C., 1984, *The Social Life of Britain's Five-Year-Olds*, A report of the Child Health and Education Study, London: Routledge and Kegan Paul.

Osborn, A. F. and Carpenter, A. P., 1980, A rating of neighbourhood types, *Clearing House for Local Authority Social Services Research*, 3 1–37, Birmingham: University of Birmingham.

Osborn, A. F. and Morris, T. C., 1979, The rationale for a composite index of social class and its evaluation, *British Journal of Sociology*, 30: 1, 39–60.

Palmer, F. H. and Anderson, L. W., 1979, Long-term gains from early intervention: findings from longitudinal studies, in Zigler, E. and Valentine, J. (eds.), *Project Head Start: A Legacy of the War on Poverty*, New York: The Free Press.

Palmer, R., 1971, *Starting School*, London: University of London Press.

Parry, M. and Archer, H., 1974, *Preschool Education*, London: Macmillan.

Penn, H., 1984, Tokenism on Under-fives, *Where, Number 194*, 6 Jan. 1984.

Pilling, D. and Pringle, M. K., 1978, *Controversial Issues in Child Development*, London: Paul Elek.

Plowden, (Lady) B., 1982, Speech at PPA annual conference, Apr. 1982.

Plowden Report, 1967, *Children and their Primary Schools*, Central Advisory Council for Education (England), Vols. 1 and 2, London: HMSO.

Preschool Playgroups Association, 1985, *Facts and Figures*, London: PPA.

Pringle, M. Kellmer, 1976, A policy for young children, in *Low Cost Day Care Provision for the Under-fives*, Papers from a Conference held at the Civil Service College, Sunningdale Park, 9–10 January, 1976, Department of Health and Social Security and Department of Education and Science.

Pringle, M. Kellmer, 1980(a), *The Needs of Children: A Personal Perspective* (2nd edition), London: Hutchinson.

Pringle, M. Kellmer (ed.), 1980(b), *A Fairer Future for Children*, London: Macmillan.

Raven, M., 1981, Review of Oxford Preschool Research Group, *Educational Research*, **23**, 153–5.

Reader, L., 1984, Preschool intervention programmes, *Child: Care, Health and Development*, **10**, 237–51.

Royce, J. M., Lazar, I. and Darlington, R. B., 1983, Minority families, early education and later life chances, *American Journal of Orthopsychiatry*, **53**, 706–20.

Rutter, M., 1967, A children's behaviour questionnaire for completion by teachers: preliminary findings, *Journal of Child Psychology and Psychiatry*, **8**, 1–11.

Rutter, M., 1972, *Maternal Deprivation Reassessed*, Harmondsworth: Penguin.

Rutter, M., Tizard, J. and Whitmore, K., 1970, *Education, Health and Behaviour*, London: Longman.

Schultz, E. W. and Heuchert, C. M., 1983, *Childhood Stress and the School Experience*, New York: Human Sciences Press.

Schweinhart, L. J. and Weikart, D., 1980, *Young Children Grow Up: The Effects of the Perry Preschool Program on Youths through Age 15*, Ypsilanti, Michigan: High/Scope Press.

Shinman, S., 1981, *A Chance for Every Child? Access and Response to Preschool Provision*, London: Tavistock Publications.

Smith, G. and James, T., 1977, The effect of preschool education: some American and British evidence, in Halsey, A. H. (ed.), *Heredity and Environment*, London: Methuen.

Stevenson, J. and Ellis, C., 1975, Which three-year olds attend preschool facilities? *Child: Care, Health and Development*, **1**, 397–411.

Study Commission on the Family, 1980, *Values and the Family: A Review of Some United Kingdom Surveys*, London: Study Commission on the Family.

Sylva, K., Roy, C. and Painter, M., 1980, *Childwatching at Playgroup and Nursery School*, London: Grant McIntyre.

Tizard, B., 1975, *Early Childhood Education: a Review and Discussion of Current Research in Britain*, Windsor: National Foundation for Educational Research.

Tizard, B. and Hughes, M., 1984, *Young Children Learning: Talking and Thinking at Home and at School*, London: Fontana.

Tizard, B., 1986, *The Care of Young Children*, London: Thomas Coram Research Unit.

Tizard, B., Mortimore, J. and Burchell, B., 1981, *Involving Parents in Nursery and Infant Schools: A Source Book for Teachers*, London: Grant McIntyre.

Tizard, J., 1976, Effects of day care on young children, in Fonda, N. and Moss, P. (eds.), *Mothers in Employment*, Papers from a conference held at Brunel University, 24–5 May 1976, Uxbridge: Brunel University.

Tizard, J., Moss, P. and Perry, J., 1976, *All Our Children: Pre-school Services in a Changing Society*, London: Temple Smith.

Turner, I., 1977, *Pre-school Playgroups Research and Evaluation Project*, Report submitted to Government of Northern Ireland Department of Health and Social Services, Queen's University of Belfast.

Wadsworth, M. E. J., 1981, Social class and generation differences in pre-school education, *British Journal of Sociology*, 32: 4, 560–82.

Wadsworth, M. E. J., 1985, Intergeneration differences in child health, in *Measuring Sociodemographic Change*, London: Office of Population Censuses and Surveys.

Wadsworth, M. E. J., 1986, Effects of parenting style and preschool experience on children's verbal attainment: results of a British longitudinal study, *Early Childhood Research Quarterly*, 1.

Weber, C. V., Foster, P. W. and Weikart, D. P., 1978, *An Economic Analysis of the Ypsilanti Perry Preschool Project*, Monographs of the High/Scope Educational Research Foundation, No. 5, Michigan.

Wedge, P., Alberman, E. and Goldstein, H., 1970, Health and height in children, *New Society*, 10 Dec. 1970, 1044–5.

Weikart, D. P., Bond, J. T. and McNeil, J. T., 1978, *The Ypsilanti Perry Preschool Project: Preschool Years and Longitudinal Results through Fourth Grade*, Ypsilanti, Michigan: High/Scope Educational Research Foundation.

Weikart, D. P., Epstein, A. S., Schweinhart, L. and Bond, J. T., 1978, *The Ypsilanti Preschool Curriculum Demonstration Project: Preschool Years and Longitudinal Results*, Ypsilanti, Michigan: High/Scope Educational Research Foundation.

Wellman, B. L., 1945, IQ changes of preschool and non-preschool groups during the preschool years: a summary of the literature, *The Journal of Psychology*, 20, 347–68.

Wells, C. G., 1984, *Language Development in the Preschool Years*, Cambridge: Cambridge University Press.

Westinghouse Learning Corporation, 1969, *The Impact of Head Start: An Evaluation of the Effects of Head Start on Children's Cognitive and Affective Development*, Executive Summary, Ohio University Report to the Office of Economic Opportunity. Washington DC: Clearing House for Federal Scientific and Technical Information.

Woodhead, M. (ed.), 1976, *An Experiment in Nursery Education*, Windsor: NFER.

Woodhead, M., 1979, *Preschool Education in Western Europe*, Report of the Council of Europe's project on Preschool education, London: Longman.

Woodhead, M., 1985, Preschool education has long-term effects — but can they be generalized? *Oxford Review of Education*, 11, 133–55.

Zigler, E. and Anderson, K., 1979, An idea whose time had come: the intellectual and political climate for Head Start, in Zigler, E. and Valentine, J. (eds.), *Project Head Start: A Legacy of the War on Poverty*, New York: The Free Press.

Zigler, E. and Valentine, J. (eds.), 1979, *Project Head Start: A Legacy of the War on Poverty*, New York: The Free Press.

Index